PENGUIN BOOKS

THE CHINESE

David Bonavia is Peking correspondent of *The Times* and the *Far Eastern Economic Review*. Fluent in Russian as well as in Chinese, Mr Bonavia was posted to Moscow by *The Times* in 1969, after serving for two years as their Saigon correspondent. Expelled three years later by the Soviets for contacting dissidents, he became *The Times*'s first correspondent in Communist Peking and travelled extensively in China, covering major political and social developments there.

The Chinese (Allen Lane, 1981) has been substantially updated and revised for this paperback edition.

DAVID BONAVIA

THE 中國人 CHINESE

PENGUIN BOOKS

Penguin Books Ltd, Harmondsworth, Middlesex, England
Viking Penguin Inc., 40 West 23rd Street, New York, New York 10010, U.S.A.
Penguin Books Australia Ltd, Ringwood, Victoria, Australia
Penguin Books Canada Limited, 2801 John Street, Markham, Ontario, Canada L3R 1B4
Penguin Books (N.Z.) Ltd, 182–190 Wairau Road, Auckland 10, New Zealand

First published in the United States of America by Lippincott & Crowell, Publishers, 1980
First published in Canada by Fitzhenry & Whiteside Limited 1980
First published in Great Britain by Allen Lane 1981
Published in Pelican Books in the United States of America and Canada by
arrangement with Harper & Row, Publishers, Inc.
Revised edition published in Pelican Books 1982
Reprinted 1984, 1985
Reprinted in Penguin Books 1987

Filmset in Monophoto Ehrhardt by Northumberland Press Ltd,
Gateshead, Tyne and Wear
Printed and bound in Great Britain by
Cox & Wyman Ltd, Reading

Map drawn by Phillip Hall

To Phyllis and Frank

Contents

8   CONTENTS

Preface

The aim of this book is to present a realistic picture of life today in the People's Republic of China. Reference has been made to Chinese communities in other places – Hong Kong, Taiwan, South-east Asia. But to describe their lives in detail would take one or several more books, so they are discussed only insofar as they make possible a better understanding of the life of Chinese people in the PRC. Similarly, no attempt has been made to give a detailed description of the lives of ethnic minorities in China, who are discussed only in the context of national policy as a whole.

Certain terms used commonly in this book need to be defined from the outset. The phrase 'the Eleven Years' denotes the period from 1966 through 1976, when left-wing Maoist ideas about society and government were generally dominant in the PRC. The term has been used quite frequently in the Chinese media, and it is the only one which neatly covers the period of the Cultural Revolution and its aftermath up till the purge of the 'Gang of Four'.

The term 'Euro-American' has been chosen in preference to the misleading and racially charged word 'Caucasian', to refer to various common concepts and attitudes found in West European and North American culture.

The Maoist political line has been called 'left-radical', while the 'pragmatic' approach to policy matters (typical of Vice-Chairman Deng Xiaoping) has been called 'right-moderate'. Some scholars of Chinese affairs dispute the ability of such a simple antithesis to portray the country's politics, but it is the one which makes the most sense in surveying the events of recent years and corresponds closely to the model used by the Chinese themselves.

On the whole, the modern pinyin system of romanizing Chinese words and places has been adhered to. But in the case of exceptionally well-known place names – such as Peking, Tientsin, and Canton – the traditional versions have been used. Names commonly spelled in dialect pronunciations – such as Chiang Kai-shek – have been left in those forms, and the older Wade-Giles system of romanization has been kept for Taipei and the Kuomintang (Nationalist Party – Guomindang in pinyin). Hong Kong, Kowloon, and Macau have also been left in their familiar spellings.

The information in the book is drawn from many sources – first and foremost from my own experience of living in China and working as a newsman there, in addition to several years spent following Chinese affairs in Hong Kong. I have also made extensive use of published materials, especially the press and broadcasting services of the PRC, both in the original and in the expertly prepared abstracts of the United States Foreign Broadcast Information Service. I have learned much from the Chinese-language daily and periodical press in Hong Kong, where in recent years there has been a steadily increasing flow of useful information about conditions in the PRC. Chinese friends and people who have recently worked or lived in China have helped me greatly with their observations and reminiscences. I am grateful also for the help and guidance of numerous friends in the academic, diplomatic, and business communities, foreign students and specialists working in China, and casual visitors.

The greatest help has been provided by my wife, Judy, whose own Chinese-language studies and enthusiasm for the project have been invaluable.

I am grateful to Derek Davies, Editor, and the Directors of the *Far Eastern Economic Review* for agreeing to an arrangement whereby I could find time to write the book, and to the Editors of *The Times*, who posted me to Peking in the first place.

DAVID BONAVIA

Peking
January 1982

The Chinese

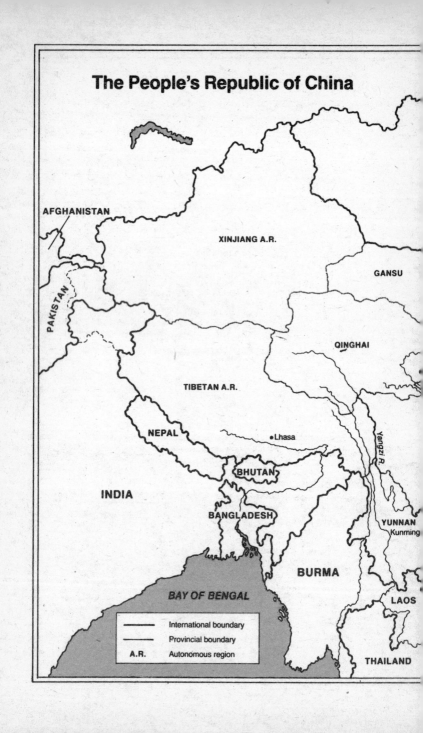

The People's Republic of China

AFGHANISTAN

XINJIANG A.R.

GANSU

PAKISTAN

QINGHAI

TIBETAN A.R.

NEPAL

•Lhasa

Yangzi R.

BHUTAN

INDIA

BANGLADESH

YUNNAN
Kunming

BURMA

BAY OF BENGAL

LAOS

International boundary
Provincial boundary
A.R.   Autonomous region

THAILAND

Prologue

Between roughly the same latitudes as the United States, the East Asian land mass bulges pendulously into the shallow seas which mark the westernmost extension of the Pacific. Within this bulge, and in adjoining parts of Central and North-east Asia, live close on a billion people – by far the largest nation and arguably the most coherent civilization our planet has ever known.

Their numbers are increasing annually by about twelve million, a figure equivalent to the entire population of Australia. They are already more numerous than the peoples of the United States, the Soviet Union, and all of Europe put together – but their gross national product is less than that of France.

Scholars differ over the origin of these people, but no solid evidence shows that they came from anywhere more than a few hundred miles distant from the historic heartland of their modern state. A half-day bus excursion can bring inhabitants of their capital city to view the site where, several thousand centuries ago, a manlike creature lit fires and hunted the now long-extinct animals which roamed the surrounding plain. This creature's teeth show a remarkable resemblance to the dental structure of the people who now inhabit the region – and who share a striking homogeneity of hair colour, eye colour, blood group, and other physiological characteristics.

Paleontologists may argue about ancient origins. Wherever these people came from, the civilization they built is the last survivor of the great agrarian states of ancient times, those of Mesopotamia, Egypt, and Central America. Like the ancient Egyptians and Mayans, they write their language with complex pictographic and ideographic symbols which are still in everyday use in half a dozen countries and territories of the East Asian region. Their astronomy and irrigation techniques match those of the other old agrarian states. But unlike their ancient contemporaries, they have preserved their culture up to the present day in the shape of literature, living customs, historical records, and art objects still well understood and appreciated by people of reasonably good education. Their recognizable cultural roots go back well over three thousand years.

They are the most paradoxical of nations. Masters of agriculture, they have to import grain. Possessed of the most refined musical tradition, they write the worst modern music in the world. Their ancient political theorists rivalled the Greeks and made possible a stable society which survived invasion, famine, and civil war for more than two millennia, yet their modern political theory is crude and derivative – little more than a set of rationales for what they find it expedient to do. With a *per capita* national income less than that of many countries generally accounted poor, they have launched earth satellites and developed nuclear weapons and ICBMs. Possessing the most voluminous literary tradition of any country, they have produced barely a dozen works worth reading in the past two decades. They have some of the most beautiful women in the world, but until very recently had deliberately set out to make them the ugliest. Child-loving to a fault, they have made it virtually a crime for a couple to have more than two children. Derisive of religion, they turned a man into a god for ten years and then discarded his memory without regret. Always mindful of personal comfort and good food, they can endure hardships beyond the breaking point of most other people.

They are admirable, infuriating, humorous, priggish, modest, over-weaning, mendacious, loyal, mercenary, ethereal, sadistic, and tender. They are quite unlike anybody else. They are the Chinese.

1.   *The City Scene*

Like the tidal flow in some vast river delta, China's city dwellers surge
out of their alleyways and apartment blocks around daybreak. Com-
muters swirl around the bus stops, waiting for the big trolley buses
to nudge their way out of the main channel and rest at the curb for
a moment while seemingly impossible numbers of people squeeze
aboard. Hundreds of thousands of cyclists, moving at a stately and
near-uniform pace, flow down the main boulevards past frantically
gesticulating traffic police. Trucks and cars and small three-wheelers
skirt the edge of the flow with much beeping and honking, answered
by the jingle of the bicycle bells. As the commuter flood ebbs, motor
vehicles reclaim their dominance of the highways, lurching from lane
to lane as they speed down spacious roads built for some future age
of mass motoring. Pedestrians chance their lives, stepping off pavements without a glance behind or to the side. Workers cycling home
after late shifts wobble uncertainly down the highway to the raucous
displeasure of the motor horns.

'These people really need some road-drill training,' I suggested one
day to a Chinese driver.

'Huh!' he replied. 'That's progress. They've seen so many cars
they're not scared of them any more.'

His comment had a logic of its own, which tells much about city
life in modern China. The 200 million-odd city dwellers – by comparison with the 800 million peasants – are the country's elite,
enjoying fairly stable food supplies, modern health care, superior
schools, and housing which may be cramped but where at least the
roof will not leak if there is a storm. They have known material

sufficiency – though not prosperity – for long enough to be no longer frightened by the spectre of poverty. But the political and social upheavals of the past three decades have prevented many necessary improvements in standards of living, and the ruling authorities have a heavy task ahead of them in rationalizing the way the country is run and meeting the rising expectations of the people.

There are not many cities in modern China where a person would choose to live on account of their mystique, beauty, or historical interest. Peking still has its splendid imperial sites, Suzhou its canals and gardens, Guilin its fantastic rock formations and majestic river landscapes. But after decades of war, revolution, and stopgap construction programmes aimed at providing the bare minimum of housing for the most needy, China's cities have all but lost the quaintness and exuberance of decor for which they were once so admired. City walls, gates, memorial arches, temples, and pagodas have either been demolished or closed or turned to practical purposes. Ancient carvings and tombs were vandalized by the Red Guards in the late 1960s, some beyond repair. The post-Mao regime is mounting a programme to restore and reopen historic buildings and sites, and a vigorous excavation effort is in progress, yearly turning up fantastic archaeological finds from the vast museum which is the Chinese earth.

The cities have mostly lost their obvious Chineseness – without acquiring any other especially admirable features apart from drainage. Whole districts have been destroyed, in order to throw up red-brick factory buildings and vehicle depots. Oil-slicked canals, heavy with industrial waste, intersect the urban areas where dilapidated old houses accommodate many more people than they were ever meant to. One could swear that paint and whitewash had long been unobtainable. Telephone cables and power lines swing drunkenly from the eaves, piles of soft coal almost block the narrow alleyways, and a sulphurous haze pollutes the air.

The big boulevards which were sliced through the hearts of many Chinese cities in the 1950s boast some tall buildings in the 'wedding-cake' style of Soviet architecture of the period. Western merchants and missionaries of bygone ages have left their stone memorials – a bombastic bank building here, a cathedral there – converted after the foreigners' departure to warehouses, hostels, or Party headquarters.

The fascination of most of China's cities today lies not so much in their relics as in the life of the people, a unique experiment in the rapid modernization of a society which a mere century ago consisted of a medieval aristocracy and gentry living off the labour of a peasantry of almost neolithic backwardness.

A secure factory job is the highest goal most Chinese city dwellers aspire to. To take an administrative job – clerking, filing, running a store – will not mean higher wages or bestow any particular social status. Only a tiny handful of people can qualify for the extra-high salaries and fringe benefits bestowed on top scientists and physicians and senior Party officials. A factory job is the best insurance anyone can have, for it does not usually carry the risk of political entanglement for which several million Chinese intellectuals and administrators paid with bitter humiliation and maltreatment in the years 1966–76. A blue collar is the cachet of social respectability, the membership card of a massive mutual-benefit society which looks after its own, provided they toe the line and do their jobs.

Just about all Chinese people know that life in a city, preferably a really big city like Shanghai or Peking, will be immeasurably more pleasant and comfortable than it can be on a muddy commune somewhere. Unfortunately, there are barely enough urban jobs to provide employment for the present population of the cities, let alone throw them open to peasants who want to leave the land and seek higher earnings and an easier life in industrial work.

Building on the industries which the imperialist powers set up in China – to make use of her natural resources and endless supply of cheap labour – the modern state has expanded its industrial inventory to take in just about everything that could have been manufactured in Europe or America in the 1950s. This is no mean achievement. Overmanned and underproductive though they are, China's industries today can make aircraft, ships, television sets, tanks, textiles, space satellites, nuclear weapons, petrochemicals, trucks – and need to import only the most advanced plant and technology, certain scarce raw materials, and some food grains for the workers. They can export goods to the tune of over US$30 billion annually and have industrial construction teams so skilled they are being offered for hire to Middle Eastern countries. At the same time, to supplement China's shortage of capital and experienced engineers and designers, foreign and overseas Chinese businessmen are being invited to set up factories and service industries and speed the country's modernization.

Modernization is the catchword of the decade – more specifically, the 'Four Modernizations', meaning the rapid improvement of China's agriculture, industry, science and technology, and defence. Seemingly essential for any modern nation, these goals were bitterly challenged by the group around Mao Zedong – the so-called 'Gang of Four' who were arrested in October 1976, less than a month after the Chairman's death.

The result of that crucial confrontation between Mao's followers and those of his old rival – the tough, short-statured veteran from the independent-minded province of Sichuan, Vice-Chairman and former Party Secretary General Deng Xiaoping – promises a new life for China's run-down cities. Though Deng specifically favours increasing peasant incomes as a top national priority, he is also eager to boost light industrial output of consumer goods, most of which is centred in the towns and cities. And amazingly – for the leader of any socialist country – he has ridiculed the importance previously ascribed to steel production and excoriated the steel industry and other heavy industries as wasteful of resources and funds. The prospects for China's cities seem to be a steady development of plant and labour force for textiles and household necessities, while the steelworkers and other former 'heroes of socialist labour' will have to take a lower place in the scale of working-class honour.

The life of industrial workers, key link in the economic chain which is to pull the Four Modernizations together, is secure but monotonous. The normal working day is eight hours, excluding a short break for lunch and often a nap in the middle of the day. The pace of work is slow, with much standing around and cigarette smoking. Workshops are roomy but untidy, the floors slippery with oil spillings and sharp with metal shavings. The noise level is extremely high, especially in the textile mills, where women in their white caps flit from machine to machine, making adjustments. Factory courtyards are decorated with blackboards and wall posters urging the workers to greater efforts and honouring those who have overfulfilled their planned quotas. Canteens serve plain but wholesome meals of rice, dumplings, bread, vegetables, and a little fish or meat. Worried-looking officials bustle in and out of their offices with bundles of production statistics in their hands.

On some evenings there are political meetings, but fewer than there used to be and concentrating more on work enthusiasm than on the factional hair-splitting which during the Eleven Years resulted in stoppages, strikes, and fights at industrial premises. Usually 5 p.m. is the time to get on one's bicycle or board a bus to head towards home.

First, though, there is shopping to be done. The worker's spouse may also be employed and unable to do the marketing. Queues, containing, by Western standards, a high proportion of men, form in the markets and department stores. But by 5.30 p.m. the best and freshest food has usually been sold. Harassed parents, unable to devote much time to cooking, can buy ready-made meals of chopped-up meat and vegetables which just have to be thrown into the stir-fryer with some vegetable oil and served with boiled rice or dumpling-shaped rolls of steamed bread.

Many people live on or near the premises where they work. A factory apartment is one of the great benefits of a steady industrial job. Large plants can afford to run generous medical insurance schemes for their workers and dependants, as well as providing sports and recreational facilities, kindergartens, and schools. Far from resenting the impersonal atmosphere of a big industrial plant, employees count themselves lucky to share its prosperity and security. Jobs in industry are so highly prized that meritorious workers are sometimes allowed to pass them on to their offspring when they retire.

The trade unions, which were disbanded between 1966 and 1973 and only began functioning properly again in 1977, are not champions of labour's interests in conflicts with management. The unions are arms of management and channels whereby the Communist Party exercises control. Unions organize workers to take part in technical and political study, look into the problems of idle or obstreperous persons, supervise welfare facilities, and discuss bonus allocations. Members pay 0.5 per cent of their monthly wage as union dues, while the management contributes a further two per cent of the wage bill from profits. Forty per cent of total union income is used for administrative costs at the local or provincial level. The remainder is spent organizing special courses, lectures, reading materials, and spare-time schools for adults, paying the costs of entertainment groups, and helping out members in financial difficulties.

The right to strike is specified in the State Constitution, but it has been laid down that strikes can only be held if they do not disrupt production – an odd sort of protest.

The organizational form of the unions – which are managed mainly on a factory-to-factory basis – is copied from that of the Soviet trade unions, even down to the provision of sanatoriums and rest cures for convalescent workers.

Industrial wages vary from about 35 yuan monthly for an apprentice to about 112 yuan for a veteran worker with a good political record – about US$19 to $62, at an exchange rate of 1.8 yuan to the dollar. Wages are arranged on a scale of eight grades, up which a worker used to climb slowly through the course of his or her working life. The payment of bonuses for productivity – an innovation – will blur the eight grades, and wages paid to individual workers are likely to become matters of controversy from time to time.

Chinese wives are encouraged to work, either as full-time labourers in textile mills or other industrial plants or as teachers, shop assistants, nurses, or bus drivers. An increasing number are qualifying as doctors and other professionals. In many (but by no means all) places it is possible to leave the children in a day nursery or kindergarten run by the mother or father's place of employment, whether full-time or only during the day. But large numbers of women prefer to stay closer to their children during the working day and, after handing the infant over to a grandparent, will go instead to neighbourhood workshops, turning out flashlights, garments, or almost any other form of light industrial manufacture.

These neighbourhood workshops have provided the model for the most important measure being taken now to solve the serious problem of youth unemployment in Chinese cities – estimated at between ten and twenty million in the 1980s. This measure is in the creation of thousands of urban 'collectives' as opposed to 'enterprises under the ownership of the whole people'. In the past, collectives existed mostly in rural areas in the form of small factories and workshops supplying the needs of the peasants and earning some extra cash by making such things as paper, machine parts, nails, and farm implements. Instead of paying their profits to the State – as in the case of 'enterprises owned by the whole people' – collectives could split them up among the workers and the other peasants. They have been a bone of contention politically, because they often draw able-bodied peasants away from grain production, which Mao considered the most vital of all economic activities.

The urban collectives being set up to absorb the labour of jobless young people will bring about a significant change in the socio-economic life of the cities and in economic planning. Collectives are easy to set up because they are small and need not be accounted for in the State Plan, though they account for an increasing share of the country's total production and are especially useful for meeting the incidental needs of their city district or neighbourhood. School graduates and youths returning from the countryside are being encouraged to get together in collectives making furniture, paper goods, leather shoes, electric fans, clothing, embroidery, canned foods, fur goods, bamboo and palm and straw products, ceramics, zip fasteners, hairpins ... the list is endless. They are also taking over such simple but important service trades as running teahouses and transport centres, repairing shoes, sharpening knives and scissors, recycling waste materials, and setting up training classes for accountants, drivers, waiters, and those in other professions. Some of the collectives are able to farm out the services of their members on a contract basis to large industrial enterprises needing temporary extra labour.

The importance of the role played by collectives in providing jobs is highlighted by figures from the big southern city of Changsha, where in 1979 11,000 out of 23,000 school graduates were reported to have entered them. Instead of finding young people jobs by liaison between the schools and the State employment bureau, the authorities are now letting neighbourhood organizations steer them into gainful work. The only restriction is that such jobs are supposed to be open only to those under the age of thirty-five – which should cover most of the young people who were assigned to rural areas during the Eleven Years and have now returned to the cities.

The authorities are being careful to emphasize that employment in a collective will not spoil a young man or woman's chance of getting a job in a fully State-owned enterprise, when one becomes available, or count them out for university entrance or recruitment into the Army. In skilled trades, they will be able to qualify after shorter apprenticeships than normal.

The members of each collective determine their own wage rates, bonuses, and fringe benefits. The State only collects taxes on their profits (the rate of tax has not been disclosed). After paying management expenses, putting funds aside for new equipment, and financing welfare schemes, the young workers distribute the profits of their collective among themselves, so that everyone has a stake in its efficiency.

The effect of a growing collective sector in the cities will be to transform the Chinese economy into a joint State–private system, in which heavy industry, major transport facilities, and key agricultural products will be under the supervision or management of the government ministries but consumer goods and services will be increasingly provided on a supply-and-demand basis without State intervention.

Another effect of the growth of collectives – which a Peking municipality report said were 'springing up like mushrooms' – is to increase the responsibilities of the neighbourhood organizations and bring more unmarried people into the scope of their day-to-day work. At present, the neighbourhood organizations are run mainly by women, though some retired men also take part and the most vigorous or ambitious male workers may also devote some spare time to them. Their function is to propagate national plans for social development and deal with such routine problems as delinquency, bad hygiene, illicit sex, and wife-beating. Neighbourhood committees number between 100 and 600 families each, subdivided into street committees of between 15 and 40 households, all of whom are pretty familiar with each other's private affairs. In the larger cities, they report to city district offices, which report to high State and Party organs; in towns and small cities, they report directly to Party committees, Public Security (police) bureaux, and other organs of power.

In times of highly charged political activity or nationwide campaigns, the neighbourhood committees may be turned into organs of petty harassment against any person or family not thought to be going along enthusiastically enough. This is socialism at its worst: the violation of privacy and the leverage applied to people with social problems, in order to enforce 100 per cent assent to some dimly understood policy handed down from remote and awesome authorities. But socialism at its best can also work through such organizations, helping out families in financial difficulties, caring for old people with no families, pulling up teenagers who are 'going bad', and spreading information and technical aids to improve birth control.

Until only a few years ago, family life in Chinese cities was under threat of disruption through politics. Young people were specifically encouraged to 'draw a line' between themselves and their parents if the latter were thought to be taking a wrong political or social attitude. Husbands and wives often split up over disagreements about the current political line. Now, however, such practices have been largely dropped.

School attendance is pretty near universal in the urban areas among children aged seven and over, though there are inevitably some truants and dropouts. For the children, school is the focus of their social and ethical upbringing. Schoolteachers are skilled at interpreting the meaning of whatever political line is being broadcast, whereas ordinary workers might find it difficult to understand, let alone communicate to their children. But even teachers will be at a loss to present convincing explanations as to why – for the sake of argument – Deng Xiaoping is being fulsomely praised one year, when only the year before he was held up to hatred and ridicule. Fortunately for the children, their minds seem flexible enough to accept such changes of line in the political education they get at school.

In the intervals between classes, schoolchildren turn out to play basketball on small courts sandwiched between the buildings. There is rarely enough room to play soccer without danger of broken windows, a minor disaster in a country where glass is expensive and in short supply. However, many young Chinese are soccer fans; they turn out in their tens of thousands to watch local and regional matches at the big stadiums, and there is sometimes a spot of hooliganism in the crowds. The department stores have fairly good supplies of inexpensive sports goods. The government is encouraging sports that emphasize arduous training and do not involve a lot of body contact or risk of injury. Swimming, diving, table tennis, traditional martial arts, gymnastics, running, and athletics are favoured, and ice-hockey teams are being trained – perhaps in the hope that one day China will succeed in defeating the USSR.

To pursue hobbies other than sport, Chinese children may have to join clubs or associations – for instance, to get the materials needed to build model aircraft or make elaborate kites. In the big cities there are 'children's palaces' where youngsters can learn to play musical instruments, paint, dance, and make models. Boys with a day off from school may take a bus out to the suburbs and prowl around with airguns, shooting at birds. Or they catch crickets, with long sticky-tipped poles, or fish for minnows in ponds and canals. It is no longer thought 'bourgeois' to keep pets, though feeding them may be too expensive for the average family, except in the case of gold-fish and tiny songbirds. Cats are kept in the house (the widow of a famous Peking Opera star is reported to have nine white Persians). Dogs are found mostly in rural areas.

The scope and variety of stage entertainment both for children and adults has increased enormously since 1977. The Peking Opera – banished from the theatres by Mao's wife, Jiang Qing, to make room for her highly political 'revolutionary operas' – is back in vogue, and Peking has its own weekly newspaper of opera news. Comedians, con-jurers, acrobats and circus acts can be seen. And the conventional theatre has made a big comeback with an expanding repertoire of Chinese plays and works by foreign playwrights – Shakespeare and Molière being among the favourites, with Chinese actresses sporting long blonde wigs. Black make-up was used in a performance of *Guess Who's Coming to Dinner?* Chinese-style and Western-style orchestras give numerous concerts, and internationally known per-forming artists are again being invited to China to play, including the once-exiled pianist Fou Tsong.

Cinemas – which during the Eleven Years showed little except film versions of Jiang Qing's favourite revolutionary operas, trite war films, and films of novels by the far-left novelist Hao Ran – are now showing some of the many good films made before 1966 as well as foreign movies; *The Hunchback of Notre Dame* and *The Mark of Zorro* are among the favourites.

The spirit of liberalization has begun transforming the visual arts, too. It is now acceptable to paint non-political themes, such as flowers and goldfish, or landscapes without the disfiguring little red flag or factory chimney which was considered indispensable in the art of the Eleven Years. The first full-frontal nude has appeared, in a mural at the new Peking Airport terminal, scandalizing the older generation before it was covered up and then removed. Legendary immortals, gods, dragons, and demons figure in the revived full-length cartoon of the Monkey legend, one of the most entertaining stories in traditional Chinese fiction.

Portraits of Mao – which used to be *de rigueur* in all public places – have mostly come down, and the big red billboards carrying inscriptions or poems by him have begun to fade. Many have been replaced – by posters promoting traffic safety, for example.

Social customs and festivals are coming alive again with colour and spluttering firecrackers. Brides can hire long white wedding gowns, and bridegrooms are again putting on suits and ties (though austere weddings, sometimes of many couples at a time, are still officially recommended). Honeymoon couples are being encouraged again in cities and resorts, where previously bride and groom would have had to sleep in segregated hostels. Old customs associated with such traditional festivals as the Chinese New Year, the Moon Festival, and the Lantern Festival are being revived, with their special food recipes and delicacies rooted in ancient religious beliefs.

Food is one thing which has not had to change in the new liberal atmosphere of China's cities. Even during the stern days of the Cultural Revolution, skilled cooks went on preparing the exquisite cuisine which puts China on a gastronomic par with France. Just about all Chinese people attach great importance to the proper enjoyment of food. Ancient medical traditions ascribe extraordinary properties to different foodstuffs, usually on the lines of 'the rarer the better', and make an inseparable link between nutrition and health care. People put great faith in the enjoyment of special dishes at different seasons of the year: snake soup in the winter, crabs with ginger tea in the autumn. The restaurants of China's big cities cater to many tastes: porkless dishes for the Muslim minority people called Hui; shishkebabs for the Turkic races of Central Asia; seafood and salty soups from east China; blistering-hot chilli dishes from the provinces of Hunan and Sichuan. Chefs prepare elaborate cold appetizers decorated with chrysanthemum petals, and thin strips of mutton are scalded in boiling water in the manner of the northern nomads. Wines come in all strengths, colours, and flavours, made from bamboo leaves, cassia flowers, and ginseng, on a base of grain liquor – which can be drunk on its own to slice through the fattiness of certain dishes. Beer is brewed in many parts of the country, and most half-big shopping streets have one or two little pubs where men sit chatting over a pint – or a teapot of warm rice wine.

Foreigners are welcome in these small taverns – and indeed in most places, for the natural curiosity of the Chinese is now spiced with the knowledge that people from other countries are of great value in the modernization drive, whether they come as free-spending tourists or as industrial and technical specialists, businessmen, reporters, or language teachers. The surly aggressiveness which marked the

Chinese approach to strangers in the years 1967–70, and again to a lesser extent in 1974, has gone – with luck, for good. The Polaroid camera is a big draw, capable of making instant friends for visitors to restaurants and local places of interest.

The craze for foreign languages, and especially English, which swept the country in the wake of the diplomatic breakthrough with the United States in 1971, has risen to unheard-of heights, with science students and hotel attendants mumbling over textbooks in their free moments and many people simply coming up to foreigners in the streets to test what they have learned, falling into a bashful silence when their vocabulary runs out. English-language periodicals brought into the country are eagerly snapped up, where previously they would have been ostentatiously returned if left lying around. Newspapers and magazines are running long feature articles describing foreign countries, and more people are travelling abroad than ever before – though still only a tiny percentage of the population. Crowds cluster around television sets showing foreign places and people, and Western TV news companies supply regular clips on matters of topical interest.

Next to languages, the great craze is for technical studies – nowadays the best way for an intelligent young man or woman to get on in life. Too much book study used to be thought politically decadent, and textbooks are lacking in many subjects. But a new drive in paper production is boosting the publishing industry.

The centring of most big colleges and universities in the cities means a shortage of technically qualified people in the rural areas and remote borderlands being brought under cultivation. Inevitably, there has to be an export of qualified and skilled people from the cities. Most accept their assignments cheerfully enough, knowing that this is a good way to further their careers. Only if they are sent to live in the rural areas for a long time or indefinitely do they become dispirited and surly and seek ways to return to the city.

The constant traffic of people going about their professional and personal business makes the railway station the focal point of many Chinese cities. Crowds of people, with multiple layers of clothing and innumerable lumpy bundles in lieu of suitcases, line up for tickets to places which – in their old-style spelling – have a magical ring to the Western ear: Lhasa, Foochow, Amoy, Harbin, Hankow, Chungking,

Chengtu, Kunming, Nanking, and Soochow. In the 'hard class' of the long-distance trains ('soft class' is reserved for foreigners, overseas Chinese, and senior officials or army officers) the travellers sprawl on hard bunks and eat simple hot meals from metal boxes brought around by the attendants. Intercity airline passengers sip orange juice or watery tea – strictly no alcohol on internal flights – and help themselves to paper fans, bags of sweets and chewing gum distributed by stewardesses in neat pantsuits.

Nothing is usually done without an announcement on the public-address system – 'Passengers with firearms, ammunition, radioactive materials, or other dangerous substances should hand them to the attendant, who will return them safely at the end of the journey ... We are now approaching Wuhan, a big industrial city of central China ... It is forbidden to take photographs from the aircraft window ... passengers wishing to alight here should do so' – and there is endless music. Formerly it was all revolutionary songs. Now there is traditional Chinese music, interspersed with 'Jingle Bells', 'Beautiful Dreamer', 'Auld Lang Syne', and selections from *The Sound of Music*.

Noise is the essential accompaniment to almost any activity in China. People have a tendency to shout at each other, especially on the telephone, and noise-prevention devices in industry and construction are barely used. Where there is no habitual noise of talk or machinery, it may be supplied over loudspeakers – most maddeningly, in parks and once-quiet woodlands open for the recreation of the public. As the blaring of one loudspeaker fades behind the stroller, another one looms within hearing distance. Teenagers shamble past, laughing and playing transistor radios. Grown-ups precede their frequent spitting spasms with raucous hawking in the back of the throat.

Noise means company, and company means security. Most Chinese people are happiest in a crowd, feeling cheerful and safe in the anonymous throng. Favourite occasions are the national holidays of 1 May and 1 October, when the city parks used to blossom with amusement stands, dance stages, ice-cream carts, and huge signboards for championships in Chinese chess. Heavily rouged schoolgirls performed 'folk dances' while schoolboys dressed in sailor suits and performed routines in honour of the Navy. Infants took aim at 'enemy' tanks on simulated firing ranges. These festivities have been dropped now for reasons of economy.

The parks are always favourite places for old people. The shortage of jobs means that fit and healthy men have to retire at sixty – women workers at fifty, women doing non-manual work at fifty-five – when many could still give another good ten years' service. A retiring worker is given a big send-off with red drums and cymbals on the back of a truck or three-wheeler. But the festive mood inevitably gives way to a feeling of anticlimax and fear of boredom in retirement. Some workers may be able to put in a few hours at their former place of employment, as advisors or instructors. But massive pressure from the younger generation is forcing more and more people to retire promptly – and the State is so anxious to relieve the strain on municipal amenities and housing that it offers retired people a lump sum of 150 yuan (US$ 83) to settle outside the city limits and 300 yuan (US$ 166) if they will consent to live in the rural areas. The old-age pension (paid only to urban workers) varies between 60 and 90 per cent of salary, though a retired person with no children may be awarded 100 per cent.

Those who stay on with their families in the city will render valuable service by looking after the children and doing the chores and marketing. The neighbourhood or street committee may be able to assign old people some useful tasks. But at the end of the day they still have a lot of time on their hands, so many of them loiter by newspaper boards, reading methodically, or gather in the parks with their friends to have a smoke or play chess.

Chinese medical care is aimed primarily at keeping the work force fit and strong. A terminally ill patient will not usually be kept in hospital – there are not enough beds – and will be expected to go home to die.

Funeral ceremonies are brief and simple, except for eminent people. The favoured method of disposing of the body is by cremation, though Chinese tradition opposes it and many peasants still insist on burial. The cremation is quick and businesslike, with mourning families present when the remains are pushed into the oven. Some of the older people will burn a few incense sticks and mumble a prayer. Who knows? Perhaps the ancestors survive in some shadowy form, as people have believed for millennia. Even Mao talked about 'going to see Marx'.

'If there is life after death,' a Chinese friend of mine once reflected aloud, 'I'd like to know whether the leaders will still be arguing about politics.'

2.   *The Returning Tide*

In the late 1970s, after Mao's death, a swelling tide of young men and women converged on the large cities of China, hunting desperately for jobs, ration coupons, and residence permits.

They staged riots and sit-ins, hung around teashops and cinemas, and formed street gangs which posed mounting problems of public order. Alarmed at this turn of events, the authorities in the cities – with the go-ahead from the government in Peking – undertook crash programmes to settle them in any kind of job that could be found and bring them back into the orderly pattern of society.

These young people were the so-called 'down-to-the-countryside' contingents: graduates of secondary schools who from the mid 1960s on were shunted off to remote communes and wild frontier areas to be 're-educated' by the peasants and help pioneer new tracts of farmland to grow more food. At a rough estimate, they numbered about fifteen million, and they came preponderantly from the big self-governing cities of Peking, Shanghai, and Tientsin; youths in other cities were normally allowed to settle on communes in their home provinces, sometimes a mere bicycle ride from their families. The youth contingents from the three main cities, by contrast, tasted the full agony of long separation from their families, crude and harsh living conditions, and frequently an end to their hopes of higher education and satisfying careers.

In 1977–8 the word got out that the 'down-to-the-countryside' movement was being wound down, and young people all over China began inventing excuses and clambering on to trains to get back to their homes. The Chinese New Year in 1979 gave them a specially good pretext, for it had been accepted practice to let the young people visit their families at that time of year. Previously, the end of the visit and the impending journey back to the endless round of commune drudgery were moments of grief and pathos.

This time a lot of the young people just refused to go back to the communes. Bereft of ration coupons, and in some cases without even a roof over their heads, they were a big headache for the city police forces. Many of them having been Red Guards, thoroughly conversant with the tactics of harassing the bureaucracy, they forced their way into public buildings to demand assistance, stormed trains, and sometimes resorted to robbery and picking pockets to stay alive. Shanghai – which had sent over a million young people to the countryside – was among the cities worst affected by the returning tide. Tientsin took the initiative in soaking up the sudden flood of surplus labour; unable to force the truants to return to their distant exile, the city authorities found jobs for them by dismissing thousands of peasants who had been employed in temporary jobs such as construction projects. The peasants – doubtless to their indignation and disgust – were packed off home, and the Tientsin-born youths took their jobs.

Such temporary jobs in Chinese industry and construction do not carry the security and privileges of regular industrial jobs, which provide free or highly subsidized medical treatment, pensions, and often housing. Temporary workers get their pay, perhaps a bed in a dormitory, ration coupons – and nothing else. But for the young people returning from the countryside, anything in the city was better than the backbreaking chores and coarse, meagre rations on the communes.

New jobs were also created by setting up extra service facilities in residential districts, and the young people did such things as repairs, hairdressing, and laundry. The city authorities, aware that this had the appearance of a mere stopgap measure, argued that the extra services were badly needed in any case.

The 'down-to-the-countryside' programme, which used to be held up as a shining example of the new China's social policies, in fact made some sense when Mao put it into effect. Many city youths did despise manual labour and looked down on the peasants. There was certainly some scope for employing them on big irrigation projects or terracing of fields to make more arable land. In theory, the programme was an excellent way of evening out the gap between the living standards and educational levels of people in the cities and on the communes. Some of the young people were genuinely dedicated to Mao's ideal, and they worked hard, cultivating warm relations with the peasants who became their hosts. But the system had one totally unacceptable trait, from the young people's point of view: they were supposed to be prepared to settle down on the commune where they were sent, marry there, and literally become peasants. This was something that most of them just could not countenance. A few years among the peasants? Well, all right. Become a peasant? Not on your life!

The 'down-to-the-countryside' policy was partly rooted in Mao's insistence that youth be composed of three categories: peasants, soldiers, and workers. Only these categories were to be admitted to universities when they reopened in 1971. This had the bizarre effect of forcing educated young people from the bureaucratic class, or from families of the intelligentsia, to 'qualify' as peasants by living a while on a commune, to join the armed forces, or to do a stint in a factory, and thus become workers – then off to university, to rejoin the ranks of the intelligentsia. String-pulling by parents in influential positions inevitably meant that a high proportion of the 'peasants' entering university were simply city kids with relatively well-off families.

But while this odd system made it possible for some bright young people – peasants in name alone – to get away from the communes where they were assigned, genuine peasant youths continued to have considerable difficulty in qualifying for university entrance and finding places. It also killed the hopes of many city-born youths for higher education, for in the countryside they would have neither the facilities nor the leisure to keep up their studies.

The Party is greatly concerned at the cynical, sceptical attitude which many young people now take towards politics and ideology. Having seen the official line shift so often and so wildly, they profess to 'see through' everything and have decided just to look out for themselves.

Disillusionment is only natural on the part of young people who were once fired with ardour to take part in the building of socialism, but who stubbed their toes on the lethargy of the bureaucracy and the misinformation fed them by the official press. The highest ambi-

tion of such people now is to have nice clothes, a decently furnished home, and plenty to eat and drink (ideals which would hardly
be considered decadent in the West, but which in China still smack of
'bourgeois' self-indulgence). Some young people consider that they
have been used as guinea pigs and sacrificial victims of the Cultural
Revolution.

One cause of disillusionment among certain types of young people
is the new materialism which is sweeping Chinese society in the
wake of the post-Mao leadership's emphasis on raising living standards and incomes. A Peking author who published a story about a
young girl still under the influence of Maoist ideas received the following letter from one of his readers, describing her own dead
sister:

All the year round she would only wear black, white, grey, and
blue. She berated me for getting a special hairdo. She only read
the *People's Daily* and the *Red Flag* [the Party's theoretical journal].
She thought everything else was decadent or pornographic or
reactionary, feudal, capitalist, or revisionist. After the Gang of Four
was overthrown she still persisted in her attitude. She worked in a
factory and came home angry, saying the other workers were all
reactionary; the younger ones would only talk about clothes,
while the older ones would only talk about housekeeping and shopping for food. Why didn't they want to talk about global and
national affairs? When it was payday, she didn't want to take any,
saying, 'What do I want with stinking money?' She was living off
her father, but couldn't even grasp what that meant. When bonuses
began to be paid, she called it revisionist restorationism. She said
people were trying to corrupt her with money. She kept a diary,
but it was just full of Mao quotes. She had a few friends she had
met during the Red Guard period, and she wrote to them. Their
letters were always the same: first a bit about the 'excellent
situation prevailing', then something on the latest slogans in the
press, like 'plant the country with green trees'; then she would
criticize a few people who were backward, and not revolutionary,
and say, 'We are the only revolutionaries, we have the friendship
of comrades in struggle' – and end up with some revolutionary
salute. She wanted to go to university, but wasn't good at her
courses because she didn't think it important to study culture. But

she wanted to be a teacher, feeling this was 'noble and lofty' – not thinking that teachers have to accept wages too. She was madly revising for the exam, when Father offered her some water-melon and advised her to go to bed. She said, 'You want to corrupt me with melon, but I won't eat it.' Father said, 'You've lived this long, and you still don't understand a thing.' Then she ran into her room, took poison, and hanged herself.

This real-life tragedy – though an extreme case – reflects the disturbed mental state of some young people in China who, like adherents of fanatical religious sects, have been incurably indoctrinated and live in terror of corruption and damnation, unable ever to adjust to the real world.

The Party has shown mounting signs of anxiety at the incidence of juvenile delinquency in China. Reports of gang fighting, pocket-picking, loose sexual morals, and vandalism have become noticeably more frequent since the 'down-to-the-countryside' movement gave way. Laws are applied with added rigour to teenage criminals, who in the case of serious offences may not enjoy the protection normally extended to them on grounds of age. One of the main problems is the protection given delinquent children by influential parents. The authorities in the central China city of Wuhan took to task a man and his wife, both of whom held fairly senior positions, for not preventing their son's antisocial behaviour. They were said to be trying to protect him by behind-the-scenes string-pulling after he was allegedly expelled from a drama troupe for bad behaviour and violence, cheated people, instigated gang fights, seduced or raped eleven girls – including some army recruits – by pretending he could find them jobs, went on illicit vacation trips with girls, escaped from labour camp, and beat people up. His father, asked about his whereabouts, hinted that he had high-level political contacts which protected him.

Most Chinese people are conservative about social mores, believing firmly in the usefulness of old virtues such as propriety, moderation, good manners, public-spiritedness, and self-respect. Many middle-aged and elderly people in British-ruled Hong Kong, while proud of being Chinese and pleased by China's achievements in the post-war period, are distressed by the unruliness of some young people on the adjacent mainland, who have broken out of the docility and submissiveness expected from them as children. Quite apart from the horrors of the Cultural Revolution – when the country's youth seemed to be taking revenge for 3,000 years of subjugation to their elders – the influx of peasants to the big cities during the industrialization drive of the 1950s and 1960s has coarsened people's manners. Returning to Hong Kong after a visit to the twice-yearly Canton Trade Fair, a Cantonese businesswoman told me she was horrified by the bad language of the waiters in the hotel – the young girls included.

Paradoxically, conservative-minded Chinese people living in Hong Kong are often shocked and disgusted by the admiration for Hong Kong things among young people in Guangdong province. 'They think only things made here are any good,' a Chinese journalist in Hong Kong said. 'But we are the ones who are to blame. We like to show off by wearing expensive clothes and taking TV sets to relatives in China. It's not surprising if the young people began to think Hong Kong's streets are paved with gold and make illegal border crossings at the risk of their lives.'

However the Chinese middle class of Hong Kong might feel about the state of Chinese youth across the border, there is no mistaking the compelling sense of futility and grievance in a youth protest song which has reportedly enjoyed a vogue in Canton. I reproduce it here – in a translation which takes minimum poetic liberties with the original – because it seems to strike a poignantly familiar note in the context of youth protest the whole world over.

> If they de-ration pork tomorrow,
> I'll eat two stone, no sweat.
> If the price goes up tomorrow,
> For the kids I'll give up meat.
>
> If prices rise tomorrow,
> I'll buy the town, no fear.
> If they plan to change our wages,
> I'll treat my rivals to a beer.
>
> If I get a twelve-foot room tomorrow,
> I'll build a kitchen too.
> But if I get the chairman's flat –
> Furnish it? – On my pay? No can do.

If I get a call from outer space,
I'll think it over for a while.
Then on a UFO I'll take a place ...
But if they let us go abroad, quite free –
Perhaps it isn't quite the thing for me.

If the neighbours fight tomorrow,
I'll go and egg them on.
If war's declared –
Air-raid shelter, here I come!

If the boss and I change place,
I'll throw so much in his face.
But if I get demoted – why,
I'll suck up to the other guy!

If I were just a drop of Coca-Cola,
I'd let myself be drunk by someone new.
If I were a fat chicken from Macau,
I'd fly out from the high-ups' banquet stew!

But

If tomorrow nothing happens,
If it's just the same as today,
Breakfast at six,
Congee for a cent,
A steamed bun for two,
On the job at seven,
With my cracked rice bowl
In the crowded trolley –
If tonight my burning anger
And my feeble terror
Could be swept away –
I'd pour my hope into my curses
And hope they'd make me mad the quicker!

3. The Hungry Earth

Water and pig manure are as essential to China as petrol and fuel oil are to America and Europe: the chief sources of energy, movement, and growth.

It takes the labour of four or five Chinese peasants to produce food for themselves plus enough surplus to sell to the State to feed one city dweller – and even so, grain has to be imported to the tune of several million tons a year. This is partly because most of China has capricious patterns of rain and snowfall, which to a large extent govern the size of the harvest.

Cold dry air from Mongolia and Central Asia meets warm humid air from the Pacific over northern China, producing sudden heavy rainfalls which can cause flooding and heavy soil erosion, aggravated by centuries of wanton deforestation of the hillsides. At other times, there are prolonged droughts.

The coastal provinces of the south and east have more regular rainfall, and they have to guard against waterlogging. They are also exposed to the typhoons which spring up over the western Pacific in summer and often expend their force over coastal China, causing great damage to crops and buildings.

The valleys of the Changjiang or Yangzi and the Yellow River (Huanghe) receive the melting snows of remote Qinghai province, bordering Tibet. (Tibet itself discharges its snowmelt into India and South-east Asia, along the basins of the Brahmaputra, the Mekong and the Salween.) The early summer floods of the Yellow River also bring down abundant silt, thirty times more concentrated than that of the Nile. The big San Men Gorges dam on the Yellow River, one of the

Soviet Union's biggest aid projects in the 1950s, has been made almost useless for power generation by silting. Down in the plains of Henan province, the historic heartland of China, the river can stand up as much as five metres – more than sixteen feet – above the surrounding fields between huge embankments, a product of millennia-long silting and dyke-building. A huge flood on the Yangzi in 1981 drowned thousands of people in Sichuan province.

Lacking adequate water supplies in many parts of the country, and having to control the flow and guard against flooding in others, the Chinese are compulsive irrigators. Their most ancient legends deal with river control as the true test of kingship. In northern China, the main problem is to raise water supplies to the level of the fields, from rivers or from wells – a tremendous drain on human, animal, and mechanical energy. In the south, the more common problem is to guide the gravitational flow of water so that it irrigates the right fields at the right time.

Improvements in water supply were the most important and enduring achievements of Mao Zedong's twenty-seven-year-long domination of national farm policies. Dams, canals, reservoirs, aqueducts, small channels, ditches and pumping systems were constructed in such numbers that most parts of the country can now survive a prolonged drought without emergency aid.

Mao also attached great importance to the pig, which he called 'a walking fertilizer factory'. (It is sometimes nicknamed 'the farmer's bank'.) Because chemical fertilizer supplies are inadequate, manure is so highly prized in China that even the word *fen*, meaning shit, has only a faintly derogatory context in everyday speech and crops up in the oratory of leaders and in articles in the Party press. The manure of domestic animals other than pigs – mostly water buffaloes, donkeys and ponies, and camels in the west and north-west – must be collected where it falls. The pig, making its home among the hens in the peasant's backyard or in the collectively owned stye, obligingly deposits its fertilizer output by the doorstep, where it can be most conveniently collected.

The contribution of human faeces – 'nightsoil' – is also important. Village latrines are just huts, in which slit trenches give directly on to a collection area at the back. Nobody worries about defecating side by side with a neighbour, without benefit of a partition. Compared to the filth and disorder of villages in some other poor countries, where human manure is just left to gather flies in the sun, this treatment of it is scientific and purposive. Marsh-gas pits – which have begun to make a significant contribution to the problem of rural fuel supplies – are regarded also as an efficient means of fermenting various manures and other waste products for the hungry fields. But pig manure still reigns supreme.

Pigs are bred both privately, by individual families, and collectively. They can nourish themselves on a more mixed diet than any other scavenging animal: grain, husks, leaves, food scraps, water plants, even the excrement of dogs. Owning a pig gives the peasant a chance to earn some cash by selling it to a state butchery, while collectively bred pigs can be sold to buy better fertilizers or farming equipment, or to build a schoolhouse.

The peasants themselves rarely eat pork – which Chinese people rate as the finest of all readily available meats, using the word *rou* (meat) to designate pork unless otherwise specified. In the better-off cities, people may be able to buy up to 250 g of pork per person per month – about half a pound. But peasants rarely eat such expensive food; they might consume about 100 g (3 oz) a month, and that mainly at festivals and weddings. The rest of the time they eat rice; flour products such as noodles, ravioli and hard buns made of coarsely milled corn (a staple in times of food shortage); vegetables, sweet potatoes and bean curd; and small quantities of egg, chicken, fish, shellfish, fruit and nuts. Other adjuncts to the peasant diet are sugar cane, and some vegetable oil for cooking. In addition, the production brigades and teams – sub-units of the rural communes – provide cooking straw and distribute 15 to 17 feet of cotton cloth per person per annum.

The Chinese village – home for some 800 million people – is still the basic unit of the rural economy. It typically consists of a few dozen families, sometimes with only one surname, more often with several. Their houses are built of wattle covered with dried mud, or stone, fired brick or concrete blocks, according to the prosperity of the locality and the individual family. Two or three generations normally live under one roof. The commonest form of floor is of pressed earth, though the better-off may have concrete.

The village streets are narrow and mostly unpaved, with open drains. Where there are many animals, a layer of straw is put down to gather the manure and urine as fertilizer. The communal latrines are dry. Water for all purposes is from wells or streams, sometimes from a standpipe in the street, rarely from indoor taps – and carrying water is a major chore. Lighting in each home is by a bare light bulb of 40 or 60 watts, except in the more remote villages not yet hooked up to the electrical system, where light for the hour or two spent out of bed after dark comes from paraffin lamps, natural pitch, or whatever other kind of oil or fat is available locally and is not too valuable to be used in this way. Glass windows are few.

In accordance with the Chinese style, beds are just wooden boards covered with some kind of plaited mat, in winter sporting thick padded quilts or coverlets. People set up their sleeping quarters in any odd corner of the house, so there is little privacy. Some sleep on a brick platform, heated – when it is very cold – by a stove underneath. Heating is mostly from twigs, straw, and a little coal or animal dung.

Like farmers anywhere, the people are up with the dawn, hoeing, transplanting, carrying water and manure, reaping, threshing, or digging ditches. After the midday meal they rest for an hour or so, then resume working until dusk. The elderly and infirm clean the house and take some products – eggs, fruit – from the family's small private plot to market, returning with such little luxuries as protein-rich bean curd, soap, soy sauce, and cheap cigarettes.

There is little entertainment except for the public-address system, which makes announcements, broadcasts national network programmes, or plays hearty music in the daylight hours. People relax by lounging around or playing a hand of cards. The more industrious weave blankets or hats out of rushes and bamboo, or sort out medicinal herbs plucked in the hills for sale at the market or the commune clinic's dispensary. With worn and patched clothes and little soap, there is an endless round of sewing, washing in cold water, and airing. Sometimes the men lend a hand with the housework, more often not.

When the mobile film projection unit visits the area, the younger people troop off to watch a show. There are political meetings on some evenings too, but not nearly as many as there were a few years ago.

Every few days the villagers gather in a barn or assembly hall in the evening to assess each other's work-points. It is usually a routine business. People are anxious to go to bed and disinclined to get into arguments about who has done what. Except in busy crop-growing and harvesting seasons, there is nothing to stop someone from taking half a day off work in the communal fields to attend some private job – but he or she will not collect work points for the hours missed.

The work-point system's dominance in the rural economy is being eroded by the piecemeal introduction – since 1979 – of the so-called 'responsibility systems'. These systems, first experimented with in the early 1960s but later condemned by Mao, involve the signing of production contracts by peasant families with the production team leadership. In return for their guarantee to produce a fixed quantity of grain and other crops in any given year, they are allotted a stretch of farmland which they can then farm as they see best. Commune officials no longer have the right to tell them what to grow as long as they fulfil their contract. Produce over and above the amount specified can be sold to the production team or on the free market, or retained for the family's own use. By 1981 the success of this system in boosting output was being widely acclaimed in the Chinese media, and it was even being taken as a model for economic reforms in industry. Material incentive had shown itself to be superior to all forms of high-level planning and political motivation in getting the most out of the peasants' labour.

The peasants' preoccupations are delimited by their fields. Great national political campaigns sweep over their heads from the cities, and sometimes an official comes from commune headquarters, or the county seat, to explain the latest policies of the leadership or investigate local problems. Reluctantly, the peasants may be persuaded to carry out some 'reform' in the way they do their work, never really convinced that outsiders can know their jobs better than they do. Sometimes a young man or woman leaves to join the Army, returning on occasional passes with an air of growing authority and a knowledge of distant places and machines far beyond the ken of the other villagers.

The peasants realize that city dwellers look down on them and laugh at their primitive customs, but they have the grim satisfaction of knowing that if all else fails they still have the fields to nourish themselves. They can more easily flout the official birth-control programme – and have three, four or more children – than can city dwellers, who incur the wrath of Party authorities if they go over one. The peasants may build on to their homes whenever they can raise enough cash to buy the materials. Their plots of private land have again been declared their inalienable property -- after two decades during which national policy changes had cast doubt over their title. Any trees they plant on the hillside will become their property too, and they can raise as many livestock as they can afford. It is a hard, simple life, and any young people who get the chance move away to the cities – but with the growing unemployment problem there are not many chances any more. The teenagers from the cities who used to arrive with their bundles on the local bus to 'temper themselves' with farm work have mostly gone home again, and they are not missed.

As a way of life it has its small triumphs and dignities – and at least the bandits and the landlords and the Japanese soldiers have gone away.

The Chinese earth today supports a population roughly six times bigger than it was two centuries ago, with horticultural techniques which in some areas have advanced little since neolithic times, when people first boiled the seeds of wild grasses in earthenware pots for food. The introduction of new crops from the Americas – especially maize, sweet potatoes and peanuts – has helped fuel a population growth which quite literally threatens to eat up every small improvement in living standards that can be achieved.

Only about 15 per cent of China's land is arable, and although Mao favoured increasing this through irrigation and the terracing of hilly ground, his successors think this policy misguided. Instead, they are examining ways of better using the country's huge tracts of grassland and semi-desert for stock-breeding, to increase the proportion of meat and dairy products in the national diet. But there are cultural impediments: most Chinese people dislike dairy products, and although they enjoy eating meat, they consider a meal is not a meal without a hearty helping of rice or flour products.

During Mao's lifetime, this national preference for food-grains was bolstered by his own policy of turning as much land as possible over to rice, wheat, millet, sorghum and other grain crops. Mao saw large grain reserves as China's security in the event of war or severe natural disasters; he called grain 'the key link' in the Chinese economy and told the nation to 'store grain everywhere'.

The importance attached to grain acquired almost the proportions of a cult, with commune officials actually ordering fruit trees cut down, fish ponds filled in, and hillsides deforested to make more cropland. I have even seen a small river roofed over with bricks and concrete so that grain could be grown on the top. When peasants disobeyed orders to grow grain and, instead, planted a more profitable crop such as water-melons, officials could and often did order the crop to be destroyed, on the grounds that it represented a 'capitalist' attitude on the part of the peasants.

Mao's fanatical belief in the importance of grain derived from his own long years as a guerrilla commander, and the periods of food shortage or famine when a mouthful of corn could make the difference between life and death. His point about grain, in essence, was that it was the most convenient means of storing, accumulating, transporting and distributing human energy – the greatest single resource at China's disposal. A few months' reserve could see a commune through a disastrously bad harvest or help the nation through the disruption of a war. With plenty of grain stored, Mao believed, China could survive anything.

But stored grain yields no interest; instead, it runs the risk of spoilage by mould or rodents. It is a relatively expensive way of purchasing basic national security, even if it is arguably the most reliable.

When Mao died, his successors reviewed and criticized his mystic attachment to grain. They saw it as uneconomic, for much farmland is more suitable for growing other major crops, such as cotton, oil seeds, hemp, jute, mulberry trees for silkworms, tea, sugar, vegetables, tobacco, fruits, and herbs for medicines. And a national diet based 95 per cent on grain requires much bigger consumption of cereals than one containing more animal protein, fruit and vegetables – so that, paradoxically, the more grain you grow, the more you have to grow.

The clearing of land for grain production also means destruction of grasslands and forests, bringing soil erosion, drought and low yields. The grassland can often be better used as pasturage for cattle and sheep, raising the amount of meat in the national diet. As long as China has to import grain to feed its big coastal cities anyway, it makes sense to divert more of the peasants' energy to growing industrial or export crops which can earn foreign exchange – with a net profit greater than the one obtained by continued emphasis on homegrown grains.

Mao's commitment to grain, and his reservations about a rapid expansion of China's foreign trade and dependence on Western technology, marked him as a traditionalist in Chinese terms. The imperial state was a bureaucratic and cultural edifice supported by the regular shipment of grain from the rich growing areas to the cities – and especially to the capital city, which in the case of Peking was located in an area where the climate was too harsh to guarantee generous harvests. China's huge river systems, and the man-made Grand Canal, gathered the energy resources of the provinces to support the magnificence of the capital and the imperial court.

But the modern State has more effective means of imposing its authority than the imperial splendour. With aircraft and telecommunications, firearms, newspapers, films and policemen, the twentieth-century State relies on technology and industry to enforce its will – and these cannot be purchased or fuelled with grain alone. The totem which the Party erected to replace the emperor is the idea of national identity, prosperity, and strength.

Mao himself was a transitional figure in this system of totems. He was the paternal 'all-wise' leader endowed with near-supernatural wisdom and goodness – or so he was portrayed in the Cultural Revolution. But he was also the symbol of a Chinese national revival through social revolution and collective effort. He was emperor and economic planner rolled into one. As emperor, he saw grain as the chief source of China's strength. As economic planner, he sometimes showed a more broad-minded approach to the problems of the economy, including foreign trade. But on the whole, as he got older, he became more and more hypnotized by the problems of grain – and by the need to push for equalization of incomes and a more determined march towards the goal of communism.

Mao wanted the peasants – however poor – to live, work, and assess their incomes together, in large units numbering thousands and even tens of thousands of inhabitants: the People's Communes which were set up all over the country from 1958 on. But this experiment did not win the peasants over to the idea of equalizing their incomes, eating in big mess halls, and putting their children into day nurseries. The most Mao could achieve was to organize what he saw as the most 'progressive' rural communities on the basis of income assessment at the next lower level of the 'production brigades', units numbering from several hundred to more than a thousand peasants.

The more than 50,000 communes which embrace China's rural

population are not in themselves considered to be state-owned. The theory behind them is that they are 'owned collectively' by the peasants themselves. They exist *vis-à-vis* the State rather than as part of it, financing their own medical and welfare schemes, running their own accounts, and trading on supposedly equal terms with the fully state-owned sectors of the economy – urban industries and services, the government, and the armed forces. They also own and operate small factories, workshops, mines, and the like, from which they derive income to finance further development and welfare projects.

The peasants pay an annual grain tax, which is not very burdensome and may be waived in times of bad harvest. Vegetables and fruit are sold to the State in accordance with preset targets, though not always for cash; sometimes chemical fertilizer is given in exchange, at a rate roughly equivalent to 2 pounds of fertilizer for every 100 pounds of fruit and vegetables.

Each commune is divided into a dozen or so brigades; the figure varies quite widely. The brigade is usually the lowest level at which officials not native to the locality hold responsible positions. It serves as a centralized point for the junior middle school, tool-making workshops, certain simple welfare facilities, cultural activities such as film shows given by mobile projection units, and the organization of the People's Militia. In some places the brigade has been the 'basic accounting unit'; now it is almost everywhere the production team – consisting of one, two, or more villages, which previously were dominated by landlords – units sometimes as few as a mere dozen families, sometimes taking in several score.

The villagers at the production-team level have little contact with the headquarters of the commune, which may be quite a few miles away from their homes. The commune is a remote entity which intrudes into their lives only occasionally, perhaps when they seek to send their children to the senior middle school or need a surgical operation in the clinic. As the commune headquarters often coincides with the old market town, it is the visible presence of the big outside world – and as such is far removed from most of the everyday concerns of the peasants in the village teams.

In areas where the 'responsibility systems' of family farming have not yet been introduced, wages on the communes are still calculated by work points. These are credited to each peasant according to the amount of time he or she has worked, or the amount of work done, multiplied by an individual assessment which takes into account such things as a person's strength, diligence, 'attitude', sex, age, and social background. A strong thirty-year-old man with a record of proven loyalty to Party policies, and a willing back, would get perhaps 11 or even 12 work-points for a single day's labour. (The amount of time spent working, and the intensity of the work, vary with the season and the state of the crops.) Another man, just strong and skilled, without any great show of political commitment, probably gets 9 or 10 work points, while a man thought to have a 'bad attitude' to work and discipline would get no more than 7 or 8, about the same as the rate paid to most women labourers. Children may expect about 4 points for a day spent watching livestock or supervising the irrigation level in the fields.

At the end of the year, the work points are added up for each family, and rations of grain and cooking oil are divided up arithmetically. Cash which the team has earned through sideline activities and grain sales is also divided, after deductions for the purchase of farm tools, welfare, medical funds, and so on. The peasants get to keep whatever cash they have earned by selling the products of their private plots or marketing handicrafts like bamboo and rattan ware, baskets, hats, and mats. They can also sell manure from the pig they may have on their private plot, and they can trade trapped wild creatures, medicinal plants, berries, and twigs or grasses for cooking fuel which they have gathered in the non-arable lands around the commune.

Each team has a standard of living different from that of others: they occupy different land, have different people farming it, and obtain different results. Families with more children under one roof – and especially more sons – will earn more. The *paterfamilias* collects the earnings of all family members and hands out cash for different individual or collective needs. 'Rich' families can spend more on superior rice, protein foodstuffs, small luxuries, wedding celebrations, and consumer durables. They can also pool their finances to buy some important item of capital equipment, such as a horse, a boat, or a pump.

Only rarely will the team give financial or food aid to poor families in the form of direct grants, but indigent old people are supposed to be fed and cared for and assured of their funeral expenses, if they have no surviving family. Especially needy families may borrow grain or other vital necessities from the team as a whole, making repayment at the next harvest.

Any group of people earning a joint income is likely to include some whose work subsidizes the others. In a family, the mature and conscientious workers subsidize the children, the old, the invalids and the incurably lazy. In China, this process is expressed in terms of the level at which work and wages are assessed in the commune. The higher the level – the highest level being the commune itself – the larger the number of people who are assessed together, and the more likely that the group's earnings will be spread relatively evenly among all the work force, which the better workers, or those with the best land, may consider unfair.

Mao's original idea in launching the communes was to turn them into vast homogeneous communities. This, as he saw it, would eliminate inefficiency and waste of time and energy on household chores. And he believed the new spirit of togetherness would make people work harder and more selflessly for the good of all. By 1961, however, the attempt to super-socialize or communize the peasants in this way had proved a failure – and not just because people preferred to go home for their meals or look after their children themselves. Much more serious was the levelling down of incomes, which penalized good workers and reduced the incentive to get the best out of the land.

In 1962, when the weaknesses of Mao's thinking were clear to all, Deng Xiaoping and Liu Shaoqi published their series of guidelines for commune administration, known as the Sixty Articles, which heavily emphasized the rights of the production team, the lowest-level unit. As a result, farm production improved steadily, until things were again thrown into chaos by the Cultural Revolution in 1966. Mao, who had lost or surrendered his position as head of state to Liu after the failure of the Great Leap Forward, fought back at the Sixty Articles by sponsoring the Dazhai concept, which emphasized the need to upgrade organization and accounting to the brigade level and made poverty and 'bitter toil' virtually ends in themselves.

Dazhai – located in the hilly terrain of the north-western province of Shanxi – was glorified almost daily in the national press from the mid 1960s until 1978, and the local brigade leader, Chen Yonggui, was promoted to Politburo membership in 1973. Hundreds of thousands of peasants and Party officials from all parts of China, and many thousands of foreign visitors, made the pilgrimage to this supposed Mecca of Maoist ideas on agriculture, where Chen and his fellow peasants terraced hillsides to boost grain yields, gave up personal privileges such as the private plot, and spread income out as evenly as possible among the families.

Within a year or two of Mao's death, the Party was putting out the word that only Dazhai's 'spirit' – and not its actual working methods – were to be emulated. In 1979, Chen was sacked from the Politburo, accused of having falsified Dazhai's successes and thus distorted production figures for the whole of Xiyang County where the brigade is located, and of having let his son run riot as a sort of rural playboy and protected him from prosecution. Dazhai was also condemned for having neglected essential farming activities such as forestry, animal husbandry and fish-breeding in the interests of turning over more quite unsuitable land to grain production.

In 1979, the dissatisfaction of the peasants with the stagnation of their living standards was such that a national movement was put under way by the Party to split production teams up into still smaller work-groups – even, in individual cases, families. The movement gathered impetus with the government's raising of purchase prices for food and other farm commodities, and in the initial stages the Party seemed alarmed by its rapid spread, which quickly eroded the authority of the commune officials at all levels down to that of production-team leader (village chief).

The upsurge in production associated with the new system of private farming of collectively owned land – finally given official blessing in 1981 – attracted considerable criticism from Maoist cadres who thought it led to rural capitalism, and from the armed forces, whose officers found it hard to accept the loss of such a cornerstone of the revolution as rural collectivism. Poor families also lost out by the reform – unless they were poor only because of their own shiftlessness – because it gave the green light to those families who had enough savings to buy private livestock, and even tractors, for their own use and for hire.

To contrast with this new wave of private enterprise in the farming areas, I recall having visited, before Mao's death, a commune at Shashiyu in Hebei province where the peasants, in a fervour of leftist collectivism, had dug a tunnel through a mountain virtually by hand, in order to bring fertile soil from the other side to the fields where it was needed. I could not help reflecting that it should have been possible to build a crude road around the mountain and hire a truck for a week or two, thus saving countless hours of human toil. But that was not the Maoist way.

Zhang Chunqiao, leading theorist for the Gang of Four, tried to push the 'transition despite poverty' theory in rural areas near Shanghai in the early 1970s. Through official decrees, teams were forced to merge. Distribution of income according to labour – the socialist principle – became 'flowers in the mirror and the moon in water', the Chinese expression for something unreal. The teams lost their control over funds, goods, manpower, and management, thus negating the idea of collective ownership. Heavy losses of livestock and farm tools were incurred, because the responsibility for them was too widely spread.

Another brigade, in Gansu province, said of its experience: 'In the past, we all worked together and messed together. This practice failed to arouse the commune members' enthusiasm for labour, and since only 120 people turned up for work each day [out of 200], we were unable to boost production.'

The Maoists claimed that closer merging of teams would increase the capital available to purchase farm machinery, and this was a strong argument in the period 1975–8, when the goal of 'basically' mechanizing all China's farms had been proclaimed as an official policy to be put into effect and completed by 1980! How such a ludicrously ambitious idea could ever have won high-level approval remains a mystery: Chairman Hua had to repudiate it publicly in 1979, to the accompaniment of a media campaign warning people not to attach too much importance to mechanization as the solution to all China's farm problems.

This about-face on agricultural policy marked a profound change in the Party's approach to the peasant problem. While instant mechanization was abandoned, the leadership announced in 1979 that peasant incomes were to be significantly increased through the raising of procurement prices for grain, to be subsidized directly by the State. Grain sold up to the official procurement quota was to be paid for at a price 20 per cent higher than before, while any surplus sold over and above the quota would have its price marked up by 50 per cent. Higher prices were also to be paid for vegetable oil, a vital staple. Shortly afterward, the government also raised the prices of meat and fish – and paid city dwellers a few yuan extra each month to compensate them. The financial burden which fell on the government with this new subsidies policy was enormous, and it promptly led to a sharp round of inflation.

The peasants also benefited from the restoration of free markets, both in the rural areas and in the cities, where they could name their own price for their surplus products. The leadership held that it made no sense to continue the dogmatic opposition to peasant self-enrichment, or to ask the peasants to produce more if they were not encouraged to share in the fruits of their labour and skill. They looked above all for results – hence Deng Xiaoping's famous maxim, 'It does not matter whether the cat is black or white, as long as it catches mice.'

These changes in official policy towards the peasants – seen as vitally important to the growth of the entire Chinese economy – were a shattering repudiation of Mao's ideas on the subject. The Maoists' hostility to the idea of letting the peasants think too much about their own prosperity was rooted in their political outlook. During the period of land reform in the late 1940s and early 1950s, the chief targets of official policy, and the designated villains of the show, were the landlords and the so-called 'rich peasants' (kulaks). Many landlords were shot after being dispossessed, and 'rich peasants' with the most land, animals, and farm implements were forced to surrender them to the collective as a means of sharing them with the 'poor and lower-middle peasants' – Mao's definition of the rural proletariat.

It was reasonable enough for the Party to assume that the better-off peasants who were dispossessed in this way would be disgruntled and prone to counter-revolutionary activity, sabotage, and even collaboration with the Taiwan-based Nationalists. The Party made it a matter of dogma that the families and descendants of such people would be unreliable. Someone whose father, grandfather, or even uncle had a 'rich peasant' background was subject to severe discrimination, unable to obtain higher education or a responsible job, or join the armed forces, or even marry if the Party thought the match ran contrary to class loyalties.

Right up until 1978 this discrimination was still common in the villages. People who had once been 'rich peasants' – by now middle-aged or elderly – in many cases had spent the last nearly thirty years working at menial jobs for low rates of pay, sometimes not even allowed to join in the work-points system of income division. Their children, by now grown up, lived in fear of left-wing political movements sponsored from Peking, in which they were often chosen as the main targets and scapegoats. If anything suspicious occurred in the village, such as a fire or a crop failure, they would be the first to come under suspicion and perhaps be accused of sabotage – a crime which, in extreme circumstances, could carry the death penalty.

The post-Mao leaders, once they were firmly established in power, disowned this savage policy, saying that the sins of the parents should not be visited on the children. This was true progress in China, where severe criminal punishment in imperial days had sometimes been extended to include the family of the offender and even distant relatives. The let-up in persecution of landlord and 'rich peasant' descendants led in some places to anger and despondency on the part of the 'poor and lower-middle peasants', whose interests the Maoists claimed to champion. They felt that their Peasant Associations – the vehicles of most important political movements in the villages – no longer had any important function. The Party press had to explain that although class struggle of the type favoured by Mao was over, there would still be a need for political activity to expose and punish embezzlers, speculators, and profiteers in the villages.

The other big issue in the debate about commune organization concerns the amount of private production and trade the peasants are allowed to carry on. Apart from the allotted production task on a stretch of communally owned land, each peasant family – with few exceptions – may farm a small plot, either outside its house or somewhere else in the vicinity of the village. A typical private plot measures about 13 metres square (1,300 square feet); its size varies in accordance with the locality, the quality of the land, and the number of people in the family. Among principal products from these plots are pigs, chickens and eggs, fruit, vegetables, and tobacco. The peasants may also grow some hardy crop such as sweet potatoes on hilly land, uncultivated by the commune, and gather wild plants or trap snakes and tortoises on totally non-arable land.

Some of the joint income from these activities may be consumed by the family – such as tobacco for Grandad's pipe – but most of it is for barter or for sale. Following the Cultural Revolution, frequent attempts were made by local officials to suppress this type of activity. Rural free-trade fairs either were abolished or were organized in such a way that the authorities set the prices and made such trading relatively unprofitable for the peasants. Inevitably, this gave rise to black-marketeering and petty speculation.

Since 1977, the suppression of free-trade fairs has been denounced as anti-economic and dictatorial; the peasants are again encouraged to sell and barter products among themselves, as well as taking them into the cities for sale. At first the authorities were reluctant to permit free peasant markets in the cities, fearing speculation and soaring food prices. But the system's good points – especially the immediate improvement of urban food supplies – were soon recognized. The State continues to exercise some supervision: for instance, by laying out areas where peasants can trade and by supplying official scales on which the weight of products bought can be checked for a cent or two. The individual peasants' cash earnings from these markets are an important source of current income.

The Deng leadership has fully recognized the importance of private sideline production in meeting the national demand for more food, but it has more sweeping long-range schemes to improve food supplies to the cities. As opposed to communes, more capital is to be invested in state farms – large concerns where the workers receive cash wages instead of work points – to grow grain and vegetables and raise livestock in areas which were previously uncultivated. Especially suitable for such schemes is the big northern province of Heilongjiang, named after the 'Black Dragon River', which the Russians call Amur and which marks the border with the Soviet Union. Heilongjiang was settled with Chinese peasants only in the past century or two, having originally been the home of the semi-nomadic Manchus, the founders of China's last imperial dynasty. The province still has much land which could be brought under the plough. The climate is less harsh than in Inner Mongolia, Xinjiang, or Tibet – other places where there is much unused land at present suitable only for pasturage. But serious dangers have been noted in the hasty and indiscriminate cultivation of parts of Heilongjiang: excessive lumbering is destroying the forest and creating soil erosion problems, grain stalks are being burned instead of being turned into compost, and even the precious nightsoil

– the agricultural lifeblood of China proper – has been wantonly thrown away.

Chinese economists have calculated that to modernize and mechanize their country's agriculture would cost a staggering 1,000 billion yuan (US$ 555 billion at 1981 rates of exchange). The country's entire gross national product is put at only around 300 billion yuan, so the enormity of the problem is clear.

Left to themselves, the peasants of China could eke out a survival existence on the land now under cultivation, if they could be persuaded to practise effective birth control. But the peasants do not exist in a vacuum; they are the providers of basic necessities for the entire nation, the people who make it possible for China to be a world power. And the peasants in turn need from the cities supplies of machinery, electric power, fertilizers, pesticides, modern medicines, clothing, and consumer goods. The Party's problem has been to find exactly the right equation in the exchange of goods between the countryside and the cities, so as to motivate both sides to work at optimum efficiency levels. The decision to increase greatly the price for farm products paid to the peasants, which was announced in 1979, shows the Party's awareness of the need to close the gap in living standards to some extent, and to do this by levelling the peasants' incomes up, rather than – as Mao would have done – levelling the city incomes down.

Chinese agriculture and the life of the peasants will remain backward and under-productive until well into the twenty-first century, even if China is not involved in any large-scale war. This may be a bitter pill for the nation to swallow, but at least social stability will be maintained and the worst extremes of poverty and starvation held at bay. Full-scale industrialization will have to come one day, for every nation must have its industrial revolution if it is not to go under in the international power game. But industrialization is not an immediate cure-all, and a nation firmly rooted in the soil, as China is, has a better chance of survival than nations which have outstripped their own natural resources and may be tempted to launch themselves into ruinous wars to grab new markets and sources of raw materials.

4.   *Function, Roles, and Attitudes*

The most determining feature of the Chinese people's attitude to the world around them is their total commitment to life as it is – if necessary, with an extra commitment to make it better than it is. At worst, they will hope to create conditions in which their children or descendants can have the good things they did not have. Their modern civilization is based on the most forthrightly materialistic value system in the history of mankind. If they see pie in the sky, they immediately start figuring out how to get it down on to the dinner table.

This attitude towards life makes the Chinese super-conscious of the functions of things. Their material circumstances and their own diligence and skill are the sources and instruments of well-being; the trick is to find the inner working relationships of things and manipulate them to make life better for oneself and one's family or social group.

In this world view, all human activity – religion, sex, war – consists of functional acts aimed at achieving something. Only the arts are considered to have intrinsic value, and they are chiefly reflections of the real world or an imagined world, not abstract patterns. The Chinese have little of the European or Japanese concept of action as its own reward, or the mystical appreciation of pain and death as transfiguring experiences. Action must have a purpose, the Chinese feel; there is nothing ennobling about pain, and death is an infernal nuisance which can have value only as a symbolic act reinforcing an argument (such as suicide in the face of persecution). Most Chinese, seeing a Hindu holy man stick a knife through his cheeks or walk on coals, would conclude that he was either a fool or a fraud, who was transgressing against nature and against the body given him by his parents.

No generalization about a nation and its typical attitudes can be true of all its people. Especially in the case of the Chinese, typical attitudes may be eroded and changed by long residence in other countries and prolonged contact with foreign cultures. But the central concept of Chinese society is functionality.

Starting with birth, a Chinese life is aimed at several indispensable purposes. The aim of having children – apart from whatever feelings of joy or gratification are involved in the process – was traditionally seen as ensuring the continuation of one's own identity. In the context of ancestor worship, this meant being looked after respectfully in one's old age and worshipped after death. In the modern atheist–socialist context, it means making a contribution to the human edifice which represents the joint creative achievement of the nation. Through the continuation and flourishing of China, a Chinese life is validated and secured, and not to have children is nowadays seen as a lesser disaster than it would be in the old-fashioned concept of family life.

The subsuming of the family system into the wider context of society – as under socialism – increases the number of possible lifestyles and in theory offers everyone a satisifying existence. The secret of validating life is to 'make contributions': blind, crippled, or deaf-mute people will not be selected for higher education, but they will be given work to which they can easily adjust and regarded from then on as one hundred per cent normal. In exchange for their contribution to society, they are life members of a billion-strong club – the nation.

In this social ethic – rapidly being made obsolete in the newly beauty–conscious, fashion-conscious cities of China – people were not to be admired for accidents of birth such as beauty or some great talent, unless they used it in the interests of the group or nation. There was an anti-beauty cult in Maoist China: indisputably plain peasant girls and downright ugly old workers were used for the cover pictures of magazines, as though proclaiming the essential inwardness of human beauty.

Nowadays a new cult of comeliness evident in the rash of television, film and fashion magazines is rationalized as serving useful purposes, such as the modelling of garments for export. But actually the change in the early 1980s has been more fundamental. Young Chinese women have lost their shyness of wanting to seem pretty, and are wearing skirts, dresses and high-heeled shoes with obvious relish. The old Eve was not to be so easily put down.

A woman writer in a Chinese fashion magazine has explained it sensitively and well: she said beauty was not just external, and what looked good on one woman could look awful on another. The secret of good dressing, however modest, was to suit the clothes to one's looks and personality.

The concept of functionality is still evident in attitudes towards love and marriage. The long tradition of arranged marriage – perpetuated to some extent in modern China by the Party's self-appointed right to pronounce on the 'suitability' of proposed matches – means that choice and taste can be overridden by the need to marry someone thought 'suitable'. In the old-style arranged marriage, it was of minor importance whether love did or did not grow out of familiarity; the gratification of love was not the prime aim of marriage, which was defined as family alliance, finance, and posterity. In the socialist marriage, what matters is political right-mindedness and shared endeavour on behalf of society. This is considered as good as love – if not actually the highest form of it.

Of course there used to be, and in some places still are, arranged marriages in Europe and even America. But the European tradition of courtly love and choice of marriage partner is so integrally a part of the Western culture that the act of elopement, for instance, is seen as romantic and glorious, capable even of being forgiven by the parents. Such an act in China would have been seen previously as merely a form of extreme disrespect to the parents and would have made a couple virtually unfit for life in society (the worst punishment a Chinese person can incur). In modern socialist China, children who have reached the approved age for marriage are too old to be completely subservient to their parents, and so the idea of elopement is irrelevant. But if the parent substitute – society, as guided by the Party – should disapprove of a marriage, a couple will simply ruin their lives by going ahead with it. Until the end of the 1970s the Party still arrogated to itself the right to tell young people whether their class backgrounds made them a 'suitable' couple. Only quite recently has the Party consented to drop that right, and it is a matter of speculation whether it really will.

Young people in China nowadays have the right to marry for love, and many do so; but the weight of accumulated prejudice about the familial/social importance of marriage lays on them a burden to ensure that their union follows a course approved by society and useful to it. In the Euro-American ethic, by contrast, marriage is seen as a private affair into which society has no right to stick its nose.

Action is functional, in the Chinese world view, and people – actors – are literally all playing roles. Role-playing starts from a very early age. This is one reason why Chinese children are on the whole so remarkably docile: they are acting the role which parents and society prescribe for them – to be obedient and cute – and are trained from infancy to restrain their tantrums or let them be subdued in the pillow of all-encompassing maternal care. Children pass from the almost unbelievable warmth and security of parental and grandparental love into a social world in which an equally solicitous but more remote figure – the kindergarten teacher – takes over and supervises their adjustment to the experience of coexisting with other similarly secure and behaviour-patterned infants. Nobody accepts that a child can be 'bad' – only sometimes a little naughty (*taoqi*). Naughtiness is expected from time to time, but within strict limits, and children who show more than a very few small anti-social symptoms will quickly feel isolated from the totality of the kindergarten class – the group in which they live most of their waking lives. The other members of the group will not be impressed by or secretly admire a child who is bold enough to be naughty; they will disapprove of the disruption of their own security. The importance of social role-playing is emphasized by the ceaseless acting, dancing, and game-playing. A naughty child may be reminded that he or she is not 'living up' to the role assigned in a classroom play.

Imagine a large room with trestles all around the walls and down the middle. On the trestles some sixty children are sleeping side by side, so close together that they must frequently touch. Some lie with their feet facing towards the heads of the others. It is broad daylight. Outside in the kindergarten courtyard, a few of their own age group are entertaining a group of twenty to thirty foreign visitors wearing outlandish clothes with elaborate cameras around their necks. The noise of the childish lion dance is deafening. Foreign tourists keep coming and going at the door of the room where the other children are snoozing. In an adjacent classroom a group of children is playing 'musical chairs' to harmonium accompaniment. Through all this noise and distraction, the children lying on the trestles are mostly quiet. Many are sleeping. Only a few poke their heads up to glance at the foreigners, then turn coy and snuggle down again. Not a voice is raised in complaint or self-assertion.

Where in a Western country could one encounter such a scene? Would people in the West want their children to be so docile?

As the assigned role becomes wider and more complex with the passing of years, the childish personality fills out to fit it. Schoolbooks and blackboards take the place of kindergarten games. Sports, music, drawing, political education – these define the limits of the new role to be played. Every effort is made to fill a child's day with activities, and little time is left for random play or just lazing around or roaming the streets with friends.

Along with political education comes indoctrination into group ethics. All the teaching materials have a moral: 'Imitate Lei Feng' (a model soldier), or 'Love the Party', or 'Serve the people'. Deviance from a set pattern of growing up is not regarded as a healthy sign of individualism; it is treated as a dangerous symptom of anti-social attitudes and dealt with gently but firmly by the teachers, who will not hesitate to call on the parents to talk things over.

A documentary film by a European film-maker in the 1970s showed a Chinese class discussing the reasons for an incident in which some schoolchildren had become too boisterous during recess – a boy kicked a ball after the whistle had sounded to call him and his friends back to class, and the ball knocked off a teacher's cap. Obviously stage-managed, the class discussion which ensued showed the importance which Chinese educators attach to making children feel responsibility for their acts. Practically an entire lesson went by before the teacher was satisfied that all those involved had thoroughly examined their motives and attitudes and made a resolution to behave better in future.

Emerging into adulthood, a Chinese personality is fully equipped for the lifelong roles to be played: study hard and get a good qualification, respect one's superiors, marry at the right age, have a suitable number of children, perform socially useful acts, follow the Party line in everything, be content with one's personal lot. Everybody must belong to some group – in modern China, the *danwei* or 'unit' – that is, the place of service, work, or study. Without a *danwei* a person's existence is barely recognized. A foreigner ordering a taxi by telephone in Peking used to have to specify his or her nationality, and this could cause complications if the car was ordered from premises occupied by someone of another nationality. A shop I used to frequent started off by issuing receipts made out to 'a friend from Britain'. Later they simplified it by writing 'a foreign friend' – and eventually just scrawled 'friend' on the receipt. The foreigner's *danwei* was seen simply as the state of being foreign and friendly – but *danwei* he must have, like it or not.

The importance of belonging to a social group, in place of the old extended family, implies a commitment by all members of the group to make it secure and prosperous. At the national level, this commitment takes the form of a search for panaceas – cure-all remedies for social and economic ills. In the nineteenth century, China responded to the challenge of European civilization by borrowing techniques from Europe without ever really mastering the method behind them. The restructuring of the Chinese intellectual tradition to accommodate Western science was disrupted by war and revolutionary upheavals, so that by 1950 the fundamental question about the modernization of China – how to master Western techniques – was still unsolved.

The Communist Party believed that in adopting Marxism–Leninism it was applying scientific method to the solution of social problems, whereas the real reason for the success of Marxism–Leninism in other countries has not been its scientific method, which is highly questionable, but its impact as a set of moral statements about society and its ruthless methods of control. When it came to Chinese society, the statements which needed to be made were different from those made about Europe. Maoism – an emotionally charged system of ideas disguised as scientific method – can be seen as an outgrowth of this misunderstanding.

Throughout the first three decades of the People's Republic, policy at the top swung wildly between the extremes of 'self-reliance' and heavy dependence on outside advice and aid. Until 1977 many Chinese people – and quite a few Europeans and Americans – believed that, in Maoism, China had found the key to modernization. If they were right, they were never given a chance to prove it, because the post-Mao leaders decided that this system of ideas was either faulty or too difficult to put into practice, and they discarded it.

Something common to both Maoism and classical Marxism–Leninism is the reliance on purposive violence to bring about change in society. The maltreatment or killing of all suspected of being political opponents is routine in socialist states, as it was under the Chinese empire. But violence, like most other things in China, is seen as essentially functional. It is the way of enforcing decisions whose correctness is considered to be beyond question.

In Confucianism, the only sanctioned form of violence is that of righteousness, whether as judicial punishment or as opposition to invasion or tyrannical rule. In this conception, violence is not admired for its own sake, as in the macho tradition of the West. The only emotive responses to it are a sense of vindication (if it is thought to have been justified) or revulsion and contempt (if it is not). The military officer in the Confucian scheme of things is always morally inferior to the scholar-administrator; similarly, in modern China it is said that 'power grows out of the barrel of a gun, but the Party wields the gun'.

The Euro-American ideal of violent sport as an integral part of moral training, and an important aspect of the mature character, is quite foreign to the traditional Chinese ethic. A well-bred man in China did not necessarily expect to be able to defend himself physically, whereas in the Western tradition that was often assumed, and a 'gentleman' should be able to handle a gun, a sword, or at least his fists. The favoured sports in modern China are of a relatively non-violent nature: table tennis, swimming, gymnastics. China's main contribution to the martial arts of the Orient is *kung fu*, a form of self-defence which contains strong elements of balletic ritual, and which even so is not encouraged in modern China – only in Hong Kong and among the overseas Chinese communities. In the People's Republic the only 'martial arts' widely taught are the so-called *wushu*, completely stylized and choreographed sets of movements, and the still less pugilistic *taijiquan* (shadow boxing), whose relationship to fighting techniques is remote.

There is an old tradition of samurai-like 'knights errant' in China, but it is a minor one largely ignored by the Confucian value system, which does not greatly admire martial chivalry. The aim of war is to win or at least scare off one's opponent through bluff. A prisoner of war is either to be despised or converted to one's own side, as in the ludicrous episode at the China–Vietnam border after the 1979 war, when released Vietnamese prisoners contemptuously threw away the bedrolls and other gifts presented to them as goodwill gestures by their Chinese captors, before they crossed back into their own country.

On the occasions when one sees Chinese quarrelling on the street, the shouting and furious finger-wagging will go on long after the same argument would have led to blows in Euro-American cultures. And as often as not, the sheer expenditure of energy on mutual abuse satisfies the feelings of both parties, and one of them will gradually retreat, still hurling curses. If violence injures the person or damages the clothing or property of one or both parties, the dispute is immediately escalated to a higher level, in which a torn shirt or a small bruise will become an object of endless recrimination and self-justification – indeed, it may become the centre of the dispute, with the original issue fading into the background.

Such admiration for violence as there is in China belongs to the popular tradition, not the 'high' Confucian tradition. Tales of great military heroes of the past are still widely read and are influential in building the various forms of Chinese world view. But on the whole people read them while they are still young, and only a great military leader like Mao would go on paying close attention to their message for the whole of his life – seeking stratagems and tactical inventions which can help defeat even a modern enemy.

Much more important than violence, in the defences of the modern Chinese State, is secrecy. This is one of the outstanding features of all socialist states, and in China it has been compounded by the traditional mistrust of foreigners (which at one point in Chinese history was taken to the extreme of forbidding the teaching of the Chinese language to them). From the arrogance of the old imperial attitude, which held that Chinese culture was a sacred mystery beyond the reach of all but a few of the most gifted and privileged foreigners, the Communist Party has shifted to the role of custodian of all secrets which foreigners might use to harm its own authority or subjugate the Chinese people.

The general public has mostly collaborated in the Party's attempt to keep foreigners from learning more about China than they are supposed to. Through a complex, nation-wide system of background briefings and hearsay, the Party has established a remarkable degree of discreet communication between the leaders, the officials, and the masses, nearly all of whom assume without question that it is bad to let outsiders know too much about the way Chinese society works.

For most of the 1970s, foreigners living in China were met with a stockade of pious lies whenever they tried to obtain information which for one reason or another, often ludicrous, the Chinese thought might be used to discredit them or their country, or was simply embarrassing. There was also the powerful sanction that, if such information did get out, the Chinese person responsible for releasing it would be subject to severe punishment or reprimand. A group of British newspaper editors and proprietors shown around the offices and printing plant of a large Shanghai newspaper in 1975 were not permitted even to take away souvenir copies of that day's edition – 'because it contains information about local conditions which you might think typical of the whole country'.

Foreigners visiting places in China are often irritated by what they can sense is the obvious stage-management of their visit, with controversial wall posters torn down in a hurry, apartments spruced up, special food brought in, and people likely to be questioned by the visitors being minutely briefed on how they should reply. To some extent, this is simply a matter of national pride, equivalent to the attitude of a housewife who polishes the furniture before guests arrive. The guests would be thought intolerably rude if they commented, 'I don't suppose your house is always this clean,' and sight-seeing groups in China may be regarded as rude and importunate if they should say, 'I don't suppose you always eat this well.' In this way, the natural discretion and good manners of the visitors are used to manoeuvre them into a position where awkward questions are least likely to be asked. It is a misguided policy, however, because it leaves the visitors with a sense of having suffered an insult to their intelligence and creates not goodwill but irritation.

In any case, the Chinese resent attempts by foreigners to tell them how they should run their country. A foreign diplomat in Peking was once complaining to Chinese officials that he could not simply go down to the railway station, buy a ticket, and go anywhere he pleased in China, without obtaining prior permission.

'It's reciprocal,' said one of the Chinese.

'What do you mean, reciprocal? In our country, you can travel anywhere you like without special permission!'

'That's reciprocity,' was the irrefutable answer. 'In our country you obey our rules, in your country we obey yours.'

One of the biggest surprises for most Westerners visiting China is to find that the people – contrary to the 'blue ant' image put about in the 1950s and 1960s – mostly do not work nearly as hard as do their kin in places such as Hong Kong or Singapore. Any Hong Kong manufacturer will confirm that 'illegal immigrants' who have sneaked in from across the border and found jobs in the British territory need several months to adjust to the pace of work in Hong Kong. They are simply not used to expending a large amount of energy over a sustained period in the interests of making money. One reason is that hard work makes people hungry, but in China the grain ration does not immediately change to compensate. People in the heaviest manual jobs need a good 30 kg (66 pounds) of rice or wheat a month to keep up their energy level, if – as is mostly the case – they are not able to eat large amounts of other calorific foods such as meat and eggs. A person in a 'white-collar' job may need no more than about 15 kg (33 pounds) of grain a month. But whatever the ration intake is, people appreciate that to work harder will simply make them hungrier.

Another reason for the lethargy one senses in hotel attendants, drivers, construction workers – even in the peasants, at times other than the busy seasons of harvest and sowing – is the fact that the socialist system has not until recently emphasized the link between effort and earnings. If a person works hard, he or she may win praise from the local Party branch – but praise is not the same thing as income. Under the post-Mao leaders, vigorous efforts are being made to persuade people that the harder they work, the more they will be able to consume and spend; an entire system of industrial wage bonuses is in effect, but its implementation is still faulty.

At the same time, the Chinese are capable of impressive bursts of mass effort when they are sufficiently motivated – whether by enthusiasm, by fear, or by group spirit. The huge irrigation programmes which have made possible the doubling of grain output in the past three decades are a tribute to what the Chinese can do when they put their minds to it. But the more usual over-manning of machinery, idling around, taking smoke breaks, and attending endless unproductive political meetings – all of which are prominent features of Chinese factory life – help to explain why Chinese industry lags so very far behind the productivity levels achieved in capitalist Japan and Hong Kong.

One can make a case that in capitalist countries workers are exploited and have to work hard to earn their crust, whereas under socialism man has been granted the dignity to work at a natural pace without going in fear of destitution from one day to the next. But the Chinese, when motivated, are such exceptionally good workers that it is their disorganized and underemployed situation in the People's Republic which seems unnatural. The old truisms about exploitation of labour under capitalism have been reversed: the factory worker in China is much more closely chained to his or her job than the worker in an advanced capitalist country – if only because secure industrial jobs in China are so scarce, and so highly valued by the people who have them, that few people would think of giving one up in the hopes of finding something better. There is hardly any mobility of labour between different Chinese cities, except in rare instances when a worker wants to move from, say, Peking to Tientsin (few would wish to) and finds a person of equivalent qualifications in Tientsin to swap jobs with.

As for the dignity of labour, it depends on the worker's belief in the usefulness of the job being done, not just the income from it. When quality control standards are lax – and this is one of the biggest problems of Chinese industry – the worker has less incentive to turn out a perfect item. The knowledge that an item is being hopelessly overproduced through bad planning, or that demand for it is so intense that the consumers will accept almost any standard of quality, makes a worker inevitably lose interest in a job and become slack and lethargic.

This is the source of much misunderstanding about the nature of Chinese propaganda. In any day's output of words in the Chinese press, broadcasting, and news agency services, there will be a certain number of items about such-and-such a province over-fulfilling its grain output quota, or so-and-so-many miners meeting their coal-production target two months ahead of schedule. When they are not simply the result of falsification by local officials, these news items are significant precisely *because* they are news; it is relatively rare for quotas and targets to be greatly over-fulfilled (if they are, it probably means that the original planning was faulty in setting a less-than-feasible target). Perhaps the weather has been better than forecast and produced a bigger harvest. But to include upbeat news on such events in routine bulletins – something which hardly happens in the Western press – is a way of bringing to people's attention the fact that the overall output situation is poor or mediocre, and it would be a very good idea if *more* provinces or coal mines could pull their socks up and do a better job of meeting the State plans.

The same thing applies, in principle, to the constant trickle of news stories about selfless people who have gone out of their way to act in a generous or public-spirited manner. The Chinese have a strong anti-Samaritan tradition; there has long been in China a superstitious belief that to aid a stranger in trouble may bring bad luck. Thus in both Hong Kong and the mainland, it is quite common for the victim of an accident to lie helpless in the roadway, or drown in a lake, before someone finally fetches the police or an ambulance. There is an intense reluctance to get involved in inauspicious situations or overstep the limits of one's strict obligation to society. The *People's Daily* in February 1980 upbraided civilian onlookers who had actually jeered at some soldiers trying to rescue a young man who had fallen through the ice on a lake.

A colleague of mine in Peking once came out of the Central Telegraph Office, after filing a story, to find that his small car would not start. A group of young Chinese were coming down the pavement towards him, and he asked them to give him a push. They looked astonished at the request and shook their heads. Losing his temper, my friend summoned enough Chinese to say indignantly, 'Chairman Mao lives just around the corner from here. What do you think he would say if he knew that you had refused to help a foreign friend to get his car started?' The young people instantly became very grave and said, 'We must consult about this', and went into the telegraph office. Fearing that he might have gone too far by mentioning Mao, and not wanting to be berated for taking the great leader's name in vain after the young people had 'consulted' whoever it was they had to 'consult', my friend gladly accepted the offer of a push from another foreigner who was driving past and made off before they returned.

But when the word has gone out that foreigners should be helped to 'foster friendship' between them and the people of China, the Chinese are capable of the most tremendous burst of altruistic effort. Our removal van arrived outside our new flat in Peking on a cold winter's day. As happened frequently, the lift had broken down – and we were living on the sixth floor. The team of workmen from the Diplomatic Service Bureau set to, carrying heavy boxes and crates on their backs up six flights of stairs and never pausing except once for a cup of tea. Within a single forenoon, the van was unpacked and the waste packing materials cleared away, with all our possessions safe on the sixth floor, and the men went off with a cheery word.

The act of helping – like so many other things in China – is functional. Either a 'foreign friend' is deserving of help, and therefore should be helped to the utmost, or it is a matter of indifference whether he or she need be helped, in which case blank passivity will meet the request for aid. It all depends whether the act will meet a requirement on the part of the helpers – for instance, making a good impression on someone from a country which China is wooing. The young people outside the telegraph office, by contrast, did not know my friend's nationality. He was, in fact, Canadian, and I suppose he should have appealed to the memory of Dr Norman Bethune, the Canadian doctor who died while voluntarily treating wounded Communist soldiers in the late 1930s. But most Canadians in China are so heartily fed up with the tale of Norman Bethune – which is rammed down their throats at every opportunity – that he balked at this. Or maybe he just did not think of it. So as far as the young people were concerned, he could have been a Soviet 'social imperialist', and helping him would be a matter for some such official organ as the police, not an act which should be lightly undertaken by mere members of the public.

Maoism, while calling for absolute self-sacrifice on the part of individuals serving the Party, does also call for a greater degree of mutual help than was customary in traditional China. But it does not set altruism up as an absolute good, only as a means of strengthening the popularity and the control which the Party commands in society. To popularize heroes such as Lei Feng – a young soldier who died in an accident, leaving a diary which became famous because of its loyal sentiments – is a means of popularizing the Party. And to print stories about selfless or heroic deeds (preferably performed by Party or Youth League members) is a way of reminding people just how big is the gap between the ideal of public-spirited behaviour and its actual implementation in daily life. That is what makes them newsworthy.

An important aspect of the Chinese sense of humour is farce, which, though sometimes obscure to people from other countries, contains all the elements of punning, satire, and sudden juxtaposition which go to make up the Western sense of humour. A few examples:

A famous scholar, known for his drinking habits, was visited by a friend who asked him why he was sober that day. 'I've decided to give up drinking until my son returns home,' replied the scholar. 'Where has your son gone?' asked his friend. 'To the shop to buy more wine.'

Another 'oldie': Mr A had a fight with Mr B and bit off his nose. Mr B took him to court. 'I didn't bite off his nose,' said Mr A. 'He bit it off himself.' 'A man's nose is located above his mouth,' said the magistrate. 'How could he bite it off himself?' Mr A: 'He stood on a chair to get at it.'

A modern joke: Commune Deputy Wang had just sent his report to his superiors. They asked him, 'Who was in charge of the work on the machinery spare-parts factory you mention in your report?' 'I took care of it.' 'Who was in charge of the new experimental wheatfield?' 'I was.' 'Who was in charge of planting extra tea shrubs?' 'I took care of it.' 'Who looked after the peanut crop last year?' 'I did.' 'In that case would you like to tell us why your commune's peanut production fell last year?' 'Oh, what a shocking memory I've got! I've just remembered that it was Deputy Secretary Zhang who took care of the peanuts. I don't know the reason for the fall in output.'

A speaker is addressing a political meeting. Someone asks him, 'Why don't you speak to the audience?' Answer: 'Because there are more people on the platform.'

'Daddy, I've just taken the TV to bits and put it together again.' 'Heavens, I hope you didn't lose any of the pieces.' 'Oh, no, I've got about a dozen left over.'

Parrot: 'I'm smart – I can copy what people say!' Official: 'I'm smarter. I only copy what the leaders say!'

One of the most important areas of liberalization in the post-Mao period has been religion. Buddhist temples, Islamic mosques and Christian churches, which had barely functioned in most parts of China during the Eleven Years, were reopened to the accompaniment of declarations by the Party about its intention to respect the religious freedoms of ethnic Chinese and minority peoples alike.

This is by contrast with the Soviet Union and Eastern Europe, where religion is sometimes (as in Poland) an important political current and always a signficant cultural one which causes problems for the ruling parties in those countries. The Soviet Union is constantly having to crack down on Baptists, Seventh-Day Adventists, Lutherans and Roman Catholics, to say nothing of adherents of the Orthodox Church. The problem, for the Soviet Union, is that religion still exercises a good deal of influence in the historic Russian heartland, and in Central Asia the Soviet Union has swallowed such vast tracts of territory that Islam has to be counted a powerful social force throughout the southeastern parts of the USSR.

For the Chinese, the problem is less troublesome. The only religion truly native to China is Daoism, a strange amalgam of philosophical concepts centring on the idea of inaction with superstitious spirit worship, alchemy, magic, exorcism, and other primitive religious practices. This is the only religious force in China proper which gives the authorities any significant trouble today – mostly in the rural areas, where shamans and quacks still covertly indulge in superstitious practices on which the Party sternly frowns.

Buddhism in China is a foreign import, albeit an old one. Its texts are abstruse, and written in a mystical jargon based on Indian languages. Over the centuries, it has often become mingled or confused with Daoism and debased almost to the status of another form of spirit worship. Though Buddhist monasteries were once a significant economic and social force in China, Buddhism exercised real influence at the imperial court only for short periods. By reopening monasteries which are of historic interest and allowing a few former monks to resume their life-style, the Chinese authorities are not laying themselves open to any real intellectual or spiritual challenge.

The most important religious influence on modern China has been Christianity, not principally through conversions but through the scientific and political ideas which were brought to China by the missionaries. Western medicine, Western ethical concepts, Western music, sport, and ideas of democracy – all were to a large extent imported by the missionaries, who saw them as useful tools in the winning of Chinese souls for Christ. Certainly all these aspects of Western civilization would have been absorbed by China sooner or later, but they would have taken a much longer time to spread from the accessible coastal areas into the hinterland had it not been for missionary zeal. Inevitably some Christian ideals became inextricably inter-mingled with the modernizing process of the early twentieth century and the attempts of Chiang Kai-shek, a Christian convert, to haul China into the twentieth century. It can be strongly argued that a good few of the basic ideas of Maoism – egalitarianism, good works, per-sonal example, frugality, self-discipline, prudishness, hard study – were in part at least derived from Christianity, whether directly, through missionary influence, or through the import of Marxism–Leninism, which was itself an elaboration of a tradition of Western thought originally rooted in Christianity.

The mission of conversion of the Chinese people to Christianity has in broad terms been a failure. Many reasons can be advanced for this: the fractious nature of the missionaries, with their bewildering profusion of mutually inimical sects and their opposition to old Chinese customs such as concubinage and foot-binding; anti-Western sentiments caused by economic exploitation and gunboat diplomacy; feelings of cultural and racial superiority on the part of the Chinese; and so on. A large proportion of converts were either 'rice Chris-tians' or people seeking the legal protection which they could obtain by adhering to a Christian church – especially the Catholic Church, whose bishops at one time were nearly as powerful as high Chinese officials.

On coming to power, the Communist Party took a two-pronged approach to the problem of Christianity, which was an irritant in the sense that it set up values rivalling those of Marxism–Leninism. While promising freedom of religion to Chinese converts, the Party soon ex-pelled nearly all foreign missionaries, after imprisoning and mistreat-ing some of them. The approach to Christianity was similar to that adopted in the Soviet Union: proclaiming freedom of religious belief, and freedom of the State to make anti-religious propaganda, while Christians were not permitted to proselytize or instruct children in the faith. At the same time, the Party promised a spiritual vision and eventually an earthly paradise, which were good alternatives to the promises of Christianity.

Most important, perhaps, was the fact that the new vision was offered to Chinese people by other Chinese people, sharing the same language and cultural background. This did away with the biggest single drawback of Christianity from the Chinese point of view: the fact that it was invented and administered by foreigners, and the convert might be mocked, reviled, beaten or killed for aping foreign manners.

The domination of the churches worldwide by Europeans and Americans was rubbed in further when the Vatican disclaimed the Chinese bishops appointed under the auspices of the Party: Chinese Catholics were presented with the unpleasant choice of risking papal disapproval by worshipping under locally appointed bishops or ceasing church attendance altogether. Adherents of Protestant churches could more easily withdraw their religion into their hearts and stop outward demonstrations of faith which made them targets for criticism and hostility.

In the late 1970s some churches were reopened, especially in big cities frequented by foreigners, such as Canton and Shanghai. The numbers of Chinese Christians appearing for worship jumped suddenly, but only from a matter of dozens to a matter of hundreds. The social and political influence of the Christian churches in China had become a page in history, whose relics were tolerated – as a courtesy to foreigners and as a good way of diverting any hostility which influential Christians in other countries might feel towards the maintenance of a policy of strict atheism.

The Vatican has at the time of writing failed to resolve its longstanding conflict with Peking over the appointment of dignitaries. Partly because some maintained links with the Church in Taiwan, the Chinese Communist Party ordered those churchmen who were still at liberty on the mainland to proclaim their independence of the Vatican and blame it for its 'hostile' attitude towards the People's Republic. In 1981 a Chinese bishop, Monsignor Dominic Tang, who had just been released after twenty-two years in prison, was allowed to visit Rome. There the Pope appointed him an archbishop – touching off a furious reaction from the Chinese authorities and (allegedly) from other Chinese Catholics. He was stripped of his bishopric, and while in Hong Kong was evidently deliberating whether or not to return to China.

Much has been written about the Chinese concept of 'face', and it is sometimes thought that to make too much of it underrates the changes in Chinese ways of thought since the imperial period. However, it is impossible to understand Chinese personal behaviour without attempting to understand 'face'.

'Face' is commonly viewed as a kind of conceit or vanity, a desire never to be seen as stupid or wrongheaded. As such it runs against the Western/Christian tradition of admitting one's mistakes and trying to do better in the future. The fact that the Communists have placed so much emphasis on the need for confession and self-criticism may indicate that they are trying to substitute a new personal code of values for the old 'face' code.

Actually, 'face' is a more complex concept than this. It is an unwritten set of rules by which people in society cooperate to avoid unduly damaging each other's prestige and self-respect. Naturally, people implacably hostile to one another may refuse to cooperate in this way and will do whatever they can to make each other lose 'face'. But in relationships which are only mildly antagonistic – for instance, in bargaining for a business deal – each side expects the other to take his or her 'face' into account. Thus if a hard bargain is struck, and one party seems to have suffered a tactical defeat, the winning party should make some token concessions to save the other's 'face'. Both sides, and probably any onlookers, know exactly who has won or lost in the actual bargaining, but the loser has also won a kind of minor moral victory by eliciting sufficient respect from the winner to qualify for a 'face-saving' arrangement. If no such arrangement is made, the loser may feel justly aggrieved and try to avoid dealings with the other party in the future.

The idea of 'being a good loser', considered important in Western ethics, is replaced with 'being a good winner' in Chinese ethics – not rubbing one's victory in or crowing over it. This system of interpersonal relations has been carried over into the sphere of sports (which only in recent times have come to be considered socially important in China). A Chinese football team which defeats a foreign visiting side will be effusive in its congratulations to the losers and modest about its own achievement in winning. This concept, while similar to that of the 'good sport' in the West, is based on the assumption that the visitors also consider 'face' important, whereas a hard-bitten professional team from, say, England will fully expect to feel disgruntled and humiliated if it loses an important match and may resent as patronizing too much condescension on the part of the winners.

The importance of 'face' in China helps to smooth out ruffled personal relations between Chinese and foreigners, because the Chinese will be pleased with a 'face-saving' gesture, whereas it may mean little to the European to make it.

When a person 'loses face', the solution is to put on an air as though nothing had happened, adopting a stony or blank expression. This way, some 'face' is salvaged. Generally 'face' is forfeited still more through loss of self-control or a display of frustration and anger. If the person who has lost 'face' can avoid further contact with the person who made that happen, he or she will usually take such a course. But if circumstances make it inevitable that the relationship should continue, the best course of action for the 'face-loser' is to revert to correct and polite manners, thus pretending that the painful episode never took place. For a person to sulk visibly for some time after 'face' is lost is merely a prolongation of the defeat in Chinese terms, while in the West sulking can be taken as a sign of perhaps justifiable outrage and may command a certain respect. Whereas in the West the solution might be for the original victor to make a conciliatory gesture towards the sulking loser, in China reconciliation is best achieved through a tacit agreement not to refer further to the painful incident.

'Face' is also the ability to fulfil one's social obligations, whatever they may be. Ray, a Chinese journalist in the office where I worked in Hong Kong, was leaving to emigrate. The office staff booked a room in a restaurant to give him a farewell dinner, then divided the bill among themselves. But because of the big disparities in earnings in Hong Kong, some of the better-paid staff members suggested that the lower earners be exempted from sharing the cost of the meal. A sharp-witted Chinese secretary put her foot down at once, saying, 'You cannot do that. It is their face towards Ray.'

Though in general terms it is considered 'face-losing' to lose one's temper, a controlled show of anger by a person in authority elicits respect. The typical case is the traffic policeman telling off jaywalkers or careless cyclists. He will almost certainly adopt a rude and overbearing style, in which the victim is at an extreme disadvantage – first for having been caught breaking the rules and second for not being in a position to challenge the policeman's authority. In this instance, the usual tactic will be to blush, put on a foolish grin, and escape at the first opportunity.

Grinning or laughing fulfils special functions in Chinese social life, in addition to the normal one of reacting to a humorous situation. Westerners are often shocked by the Chinese habit of laughing at death, injury, and personal misfortune. A person may say, 'So sorry I'm late, but my father has just died, ha, ha, ha!' Or when one traps a Chinese person in an argument and tries to gain an admission that he or she is in the wrong, the reaction may just be a wide, fixed grin. Laughter is also used to cover up embarrassment, for instance at indiscreet questions. An American or European travelling in China will probably come across the situation where a Chinese person, asked a serious question about, say, sex, will just laugh and laugh; it is a way of saying, You know I can't discuss that subject, so please let's talk about something else. The foreigner who has put the question may, however, become indignant and say something like, 'What are you laughing at? It's a serious question!' The reply is more laughter.

If you are driving a car in Peking and you narrowly miss hitting a cyclist who swerves heedlessly in front of you, you can blow your horn and even shout for all you are worth, but the cyclist will never once turn to look you in the eye. Aware of being in the wrong, the Chinese person prefers simply to ignore the whole incident. That is one form of 'face'.

'Loss of face' entails inescapable proof in the eyes of other people that one has done something stupid. While hurrying off to an engagement in Peking one day, I inadvertently went through a light and was immediately stopped and called over to the traffic policeman's booth.

I was late for my appointment and anxious to avoid a twenty-minute lecture on the rules of the road. Chinese pedestrians were gathering to watch the fun of a foreigner being told off. The policeman demanded to see my licence – and as I took it out, I unintentionally saved the day by dropping my wallet on the dirty pavement. Out of it spilled a large bundle of 10-yuan notes, quite likely a year's salary for some of the people standing around waiting for the fun. I bent down in confusion to gather the money up and thereby lost so much 'face' that the crowd giggled in delight and the policeman smirked and let me off. The delight of seeing a foreigner throwing his inconceivably large salary around in the gutter was quite enough satisfaction for all concerned.

5. *Behind the Bedroom Door*

An American woman visiting China in the late 1970s once profoundly shocked her official Chinese hosts by asking them at the dinner table, 'Do you let your children see you naked?'

Her embarrassed hosts hemmed and hawed for a while as she persisted with what, to her, was a perfectly simple question of child-rearing. At last one said, with the air of a priest bestowing absolution, 'When Chinese fathers and mothers take off their clothes, they close the bedroom door.'

Why are the vast majority of Chinese nowadays so prudish over questions of sex? Their literature contains a rich strain of sexual writing, both scientific and pornographic. But in China there is not and never has been a cult of the beauty of the unclothed human form. Take your clothes off to wash or to make love, certainly. But how eccentric to believe that clothing, which is conceived at least partly as an ornament, can be dispensed with and human beauty thereby enhanced! One of the most noted sexual fetishes of the Chinese male used to be the tiny bound foot – which cost a girl years of pain and misery to acquire – deformed and often malodorous in its enveloping bandages. No other part of the female body except the face commanded such rapt attention.

The mainstream tradition of Chinese art simply ignores the naked body as a suitable subject for painting or sculpture. Clothes are what dignify human beings and symbolize their superiority in the natural order. Different styles of clothing even today signify a person's status in society as clearly as a military uniform.

By comparison with the many ups and downs of sexual mores in Europe and America over the centuries, the Chinese have on the surface preserved a fairly consistent tradition of discretion – taboo, almost – with regard to these matters. Even many Western-influenced Chinese people in Hong Kong usually show malaise if sex is discussed on social occasions as freely as is now fashionable in the West. To use sexual swearwords is not considered trendy but the mark of a boorish and common personality.

In the People's Republic, most attempts to discuss sexual topics, other than with doctors or birth-control specialists, are met with blushes, embarrassed laughter, or irritation, as though at a flagrant display of bad manners. Sex outside marriage is considered taboo, though of course it occurs. Sex within marriage is regarded as functional, a matter of gratifying the body and producing children. The European and Hindu concepts of sex as the mystically supreme expression of love are little encountered in the Chinese tradition, ancient or modern. Love poetry exists in classical Chinese literature, but it does not occupy the sublime position accorded it in Western literature. And in the modern literary criticism of the People's Republic, one of the chief grounds for disparaging Western literature is that it 'takes love as supreme'.

Even love poems from ancient Chinese oral traditions were reinterpreted by Confucius and his devotees as sociopolitical or moral allegories. In the China of the most recent past, the mere mention of physical attraction between men and women – as say, in a Tolstoy novel – was denounced and banned as 'pornography'. All love was supposed to be intimately related to political attitudes.

Despite the less inhibited approach of earlier periods, there is little in extant Chinese literature or historical writing to suggest any great degree of permissiveness in ancient or traditional society, and over-fondness for women was regarded as the sign of a bad ruler. The written character for sexual licence 姦 (*jian*) is simply a stylized drawing of three women, which suggests that in antiquity sexual indulgence was regarded as the prerogative of men rich or powerful enough to have many concubines or female slaves.

Mencius, the most important early exponent of Confucius's ideas, once wrote a short treatise on whether it would be permissible for a man to take hold of his sister-in-law's hand if she were actually drowning at the time and it was the only way to save her!

By contrast, the plethora of pornographic and semi-pornographic literature which survives from the late Ming and early Qing dynasties (sixteenth to eighteenth centuries A.D.) never achieved literary respectability until the modern age, and scholars who used to read it did not advertise the fact.

Some of the 'bluest' things ever written anywhere are contained in the great seventeenth-century novel of manners, *Jin Ping Mei* (The Plum Blossom in the Gold Vase, translated into English as 'The Golden Lotus'). This novel – highly prized for its portrayal of the life of a rich family – is so pornographic that when it was first translated into English the most outrageous passages were rendered in Latin.

Numerous woodblock prints from roughly the same period show men and women in a variety of postures, including horseback performances and lovemaking in the open air – and not always restricted to two partners.

But traditional Chinese thought harbours many misgivings about the effect of sex on a person's health. The semen is seen as closely linked to a man's vitality, and a very widespread Daoist tradition advises men to avoid ejaculation, not so much in the interests of prolonging the pleasure as to strengthen their health. Buddhism – a later import to China – taught abstention from all carnal pleasures and helped foster the idea that over-indulgence in sex could lead a man to exhaustion, ruin and death. Chinese medicine abounds with herbs and potions made from all manner of substances to 'strengthen vitality'. In Peking or Canton today you can easily buy wines containing the extract of different kinds of animal penis or the embryos of unborn rats – which are certainly not drunk for pleasure. In Hong Kong even such Western products as stout and chicken extract sell best if they bear labels containing thinly veiled references to their effectiveness in preserving or restoring vitality, which in the Chinese view is closely linked with sexual power.

On top of these pseudo-scientific ideas about the debilitating effects of sex, the Confucian tradition set up the stable family unit as the basis of human society and was highly unpermissive except insofar as it allowed concubinage.

The traditional Chinese approach to love and romance is sentimental and delicate and less closely related to sexual expression than in modern Euro-American culture. The traditional hero of Chinese romantic fiction was a slender, pale youth with a gift for poetry. This idea has had its counterpart in various periods of European culture, but to modern Euro-American taste, such a hero seems effete. Admiration for macho values in China is mainly restricted to the popular or folk culture; in the 'high' culture of Confucianism, a man is more admired for his wisdom and learning and uprightness than for his strength and physical courage. The sturdy young worker and blooming young peasant girl of modern Chinese propaganda posters are the result of earlier borrowings from Soviet 'socialist realism', not a development from the Chinese tradition.

In the People's Republic, sex education is not considered a necessary part of the school curriculum, except in the birds-and-bees-and-perhaps-rabbits tradition of old-fashioned biology classes. The only manual of sex education published openly in China in the 1970s was a little paperback called *Problems of Hygiene in Adolescence*, which gave no advice at all on sexual intercourse or contraception – thought to be topics quite unsuitable for teenagers. The closest it came to discussing sex was in a short passage on masturbation, which the book condemned as 'sapping the revolutionary will' and 'irritating the cerebellum', causing impotence in young men and bleeding in young women. However, it did add that someone who was 'into' masturbation should not become obsessed with guilt. The book listed frequent washing of the sexual parts, physical exercise, and refraining from lying in bed in the morning, wearing tight underclothing, or sleeping under too many bedclothes as ways of conquering the habit. (Lord Baden Powell, founder of the world scouting movement, gave his disciples similar advice.)

Not even the socialist and revolutionary tradition of adult permissiveness has dented the underlying prudery of the Chinese. In the 1930s and 1940s, it is true, young leftist intellectuals in Shanghai and elsewhere were somewhat more permissive than nowadays, because permissiveness was seen as modern and progressive. But against this slender tradition imported from the West, the ancient non-permissiveness of a peasant society, regulating marriage in a planned manner, has won out. (This is in sharp contrast to conditions in the Soviet Union, where the revolutionary concept of free love has survived and created an immense degree of sexual freedom – which is not, however, allowed to appear in modern literature and is discussed only obliquely in the press.)

A Chinese official told me, 'Free sex is banned because it is harmful to women's liberation.' In the old days, women were subjugated partly by the freedom of the man to take a concubine and the scant legal protection of women's rights in marriage. What sexual permissiveness there was existed mainly for the pleasure of the man, not the woman. The 1950 Marriage Law, guaranteeing women's rights, is a piece of legislation of which the Party is particularly proud.

In the 1950s and 1960s, the Party organized the training of 'token' women in such male-dominated spheres as flying aircraft and working on high-tension power lines. The Cultural Revolution swept away the main organs of work for women's liberation, the Women's Federations. But in the Eleven Years women rose to a number of important positions through political skills – and perhaps through the support of Jiang Qing, a feminist who by all accounts wanted to be the first woman Chairman of the Party.

The Women's Federations were restored in 1973 and became active again from 1977 on, concentrating on such obvious subjects as birth control, hygiene, and pediatrics. Chinese officials admit candidly that women's liberation still has a long way to go in their country and that the Party's role should be to promote it and foster it, not pretend (as the Soviet Party does) that it is no longer a problem. There were only two women in the 25-member Politburo in 1981, 14 out of 205 full members of the Central Committee, and 37 out of 235 members of the Presidium of the National People's Congress.

As in all socialist countries, it is a moot point in China whether the employment of women in low-paid industrial jobs (especially neighbourhood cooperative workshops) is a liberating measure or a new form of subjugation. But there can be no question that women have immensely improved their social and economic position since 1949, and if they have sacrificed certain cultural and political freedoms in doing so, the men have sacrificed them too.

The right to choose a sex partner and enjoy lovemaking before marriage is very definitely not considered to be a desirable aspect of women's liberation in China. Inevitably – as in Victorian England – there are cases where passion overcomes the taboos, and young people have intercourse before marriage. They had better be sure to keep it a secret, though, for the girl may be harangued and persecuted by the Party cell at her place of work, while the boy could be sent to 'labour reform' camp. If conception occurs, the girl will be forced to have an abortion if the pregnancy is not already too far advanced. They might, however, apply to get married, providing they were of the officially recommended marriageable age – usually twenty-five for the girl and twenty-seven for the man – or lived in the rural areas, where the age limit is more flexibly interpreted.

On the communes there is greater opportunity for illicit sex, on account of the contours of the landscape and the lack of bright lighting in the evenings. In the cities, it is difficult to find anywhere private enough to indulge in sex outside marriage, though passion everywhere is ingenious. From Shanghai have come increasing numbers of reports of unmarried girls and women seeking abortions, while some who were afraid to come forward and ask for medical help have sustained injuries through home abortions using unsuitable implements.

Taboos on open discussion of sex in front of young people, sublimation, severe sanctions for transgression, long working hours and political meetings, lack of privacy – all these help to restrain the libido, as in a strict boarding school. On top of this, Chinese young people know that they will almost certainly marry in due course (nearly all men and women are expected by the Party to marry when the time is ripe) and the mystery will be made plain. The status value of having sex at an early age and bragging about it can apply only in delinquent gangs, because to boast to one's peer group at school or at work about illicit sex activity might lead to discovery by busybodies and punishment by the Party.

Among girls and young women, especially, physical attraction for a person of the same sex can be expressed harmlessly in holding hands, romping or combing each other's hair – again, something which was commoner in the West in the prudish nineteenth century than now.

Most Chinese people refuse to admit that there is homosexuality in China. It is written off as a decadent practice confined to foreigners. But a cursory reading of the Ming and Qing dynasties' popular literature will show this to be untrue. Literati of the time even gave sodomy an elegant euphemism: 'Playing with the flower in the back chamber.' The normal Chinese word for sodomy is *jijian* or 'chicken depravity', suggesting a peasant tradition of bestiality involving hens. There are plenty of gay Chinese in Hong Kong (which, however, still punishes homosexuality with imprisonment). Jean Pasqualini, author of *Prisoner of Mao*, recalls the summary execution of a labour camp inmate accused of homosexuality.

The mounting disorder in Chinese cities following the mass return of young people from the countryside was blamed for quite numerous instances of rape (including gang rape) which were reported in the official press from 1978 on. Rape is one of the accusations commonly levelled at officials who have abused their position, and to be forced to bestow sexual favours on commune officials, in order to live a little more comfortably, was one of the grievances of girls sent from the cities to the rural areas. There is abundant evidence of prostitution in Canton – whose proximity to Hong Kong alone does not explain away the phenomenon, but merely makes it easier to find out about. Prostitution is also found in industrial areas where many young workers are unmarried or living apart from their wives; coal-mining districts are especially prone to it.

One would hardly expect Chinese officials or the press to report on such practices as exhibitionism or Peeping Tom-ism. But the grounds of the old Summer Palace near Peking, a favourite picnic spot for some foreigners, were graced in the mid 1970s with the presence of a middle-aged Chinese man who would occasionally manifest himself on the top of a slope and masturbate openly on to the embassy ladies' cars. And at a concert given in Peking by the Vienna Philharmonic in 1973 my wife sat next to a young Chinese man who was apparently so aroused that he masturbated vigorously through his trouser pocket.

Knowledge of sexual 'deviance' in China can never be anything but scrappy as long as it is regarded by the authorities as a shameful secret whose very existence must be denied. I for one am quite prepared to believe that is has a lower incidence than in the West, where constant discussion of the topic may influence people to experiment with practices they might otherwise have shied away from or never even have thought of. In addition, marriage in China is taken very seriously, as a necessary patriotic act which must be honoured and protected.

The Party's ideal model for a modern marriage is roughly as follows. Two young workers of different sex get to know each other at political study classes and find that they share a common zeal for the achievement of the Four Modernizations. By encouraging each other to do well at work and study, they develop a deep and comradely affection. Having reached the proper ages, they agree to marry. The wedding ceremony is simple in the extreme, and they hold a small tea party afterwards for family and close friends, where a few peanuts and some sweets are served. The next day they return to work. After a year or two they have a baby and then decide not to have any more children. Both undergo sterilization and devote themselves to educating their child in the values of a socialist society.

Somewhat stark? It would be, if it were the common pattern. In fact, love and marriage and childbearing stubbornly refuse to fit themselves into the Party's ideal mould. People still fall in love across 'class barriers', marry for passion, spend lavishly on the wedding and honeymoon, bear more children than the national birth-control policy recommends, and refuse sterilization. They still often fail to bring up their children to accept wholeheartedly the prescribed set of social values, and they still fall out of love, quarrel and get divorced, or have adulterous relationships.

It is in the rural areas that the Party's prescriptions for the correct form of wedding ceremony are most widely flouted. The peasants still mostly consider it a disgrace and a humiliation not to throw a big party to celebrate the marriage of their children, and total costs may easily run into the hundreds of yuan – probably over a thousand.

First, the matchmaker must be paid. These experienced women are still widely found in Chinese villages. Although they have no official status, they can make a tidy income from their knowledge of families in different villages, their tact, and their negotiating skill. The authorities do not generally interfere with them. The matchmaker's fee will vary widely according to the amount of time and trouble needed to find a suitable partner, but it could go as high as 50 yuan (US$ 28).

Once a choice has been made, the young people and their parents are brought to meet each other. The young man's mother will carefully inspect the proposed bride and ask questions about her health, strength, and working skills. And the girl's parents will inquire none too obliquely about the financial standing of the young man's family, their annual income in work points and cash, the size of their private plot, and the number of family members.

If each side is satisfied, there will be a further meeting, and if neither of the young people raises serious objections to the proposed marriage partner, the amount and form of the bride money will be discussed.

Contrary to what a foreign visitor will usually be told when visiting a Chinese village, it is still normal and accepted that the family of the bridegroom should pay in cash, furniture, bedding, food, or even jewellery for the arrival of the bride to live in their home.

This is not a dowry, but the opposite. With the relative emancipation of Chinese peasant women by comparison with their previous condition, their labour power is assessed as a future contribution to the income of the husband's family. The wife will probably not earn as much as a man, but it will be enough to pay for her own keep and add something to the family's joint income. In most cases the only dowry to be provided will be some simple articles of personal use – combs, towels, a thermos bottle – which will be presented by her family, and which are the only things she will be allowed to take back home again if by chance the marriage is a failure and ends in divorce or separation.

Bride money varies widely from village to village. In places where there are large overseas Chinese communities, it could exceed 1,000 yuan (US$555). But in most parts of the country, where there are few or no remittances from abroad, the total in cash and presents will probably not be more than about 500 yuan – still a very substantial sum for a peasant family to have saved, but one which is generally considered essential to the dignity and proper order of the vital institution of marriage.

There are cases of extremely poor or politically motivated peasants who break with this tradition, but they are the exception rather than the rule. For instance, a young man who lived alone with his widowed mother in a village of Guangdong province was long unable to find a bride because of their inability to pay the bride money. After several years spent searching, they found a girl whose father, for reasons of his own, had decided to let his daughter marry without demanding any bride money. The girl offered him her own savings of 200 yuan ($111), but he refused them. On the day of the wedding, the bridegroom just bought a pound of pork, two pounds of noodles, and two pounds of biscuits and sent them to his new father-in-law as a gift in the guise of a birthday present. No guests were invited to the wedding, and no alcoholic drinks were served. The young couple had a plain meal of noodles and vegetables on their wedding night.

This wedding was considered by the Party to be so exemplary in its frugality that it was propagated in the provincial press. But the authorities are perfectly well aware that very few peasant families would be content with such meagre celebrations.

More typical is the 1970s wedding ceremony described as follows by a former resident of southern China. On the wedding day, the young couple went to a local police station where registration is performed on one day out of every five. They filled in a form, paying a registration fee of yuan 0.50 (28 US cents). The registering officer asked them – as a matter of form – whether the bridegroom's parents had made any presents to the bride's family, since it was 'no longer the government's policy' that bride money should be paid. The couple dutifully lied, denying that any payment or presents had been made; the registrar saw no reason to investigate further; and they became officially man and wife. But they did not sleep together that night.

The 'real' ceremonies began on the same day, when the couple went to the bridegroom's home to have tea with the parents and close relatives. Gold rings – family heirlooms – were exchanged. The bride went back to her own home before sunset.

On the morning of the third day after the official ceremony, the couple put on their best clothes and went to the home of the bride's parents, and from there to a restaurant in the local township, where a banquet costing roughly 4 yuan ($2) a head had been laid on for two or three dozen relatives and friends. (If the bride's family could not afford this, they would try to supply some tea, cakes, cigarettes, and sweets; the poorest families would just offer a few sweets.) The young couple both made short speeches, promising to work hard, serve the country, and practise birth control.

Wedding gifts – bedding, a wardrobe, some earrings – had already been sent to the bridegroom's family home, which was thoroughly cleaned, and lucky slogans written on red paper were hung by the door. (Political slogans are now often used instead of the traditional ones about long life, many children, and prosperity; the peasants do not seem to mind, so long as the paper is red and the general tenor of the slogans is benevolent.) The bride on this occasion went to the length of putting on a red dress for good fortune, and she was escorted to her new home by three middle-aged women, with one of them – the matchmaker – holding an umbrella for her. Another of the women carried joss sticks, which were lit on arrival at the house. Firecrackers were set off and another banquet was served, with fully ten tables of food for several dozen guests. Each family had been allowed to buy a generous extra ration of fish for the occasion. The marriage was consummated that night.

Three days later, the couple returned to the home of the bride's parents for a ritual visit. They brought gifts, a chicken and some sugar cane. This ceremony was intended to prove that the bride remained filial to her parents and would not forget them in her new home. Then the young couple took a week off from work (without pay) to spend their honeymoon in the big city of Canton. On return, they settled into the everyday routine of the commune at the bridegroom's family home and began to plan the setting up of their own home – in a new house which would cost about 1,000 to 3,000 yuan (US$555 to $1,665) to build and would be the final big expense of the marriage process.

As rural weddings go in China, this was a fairly lavish one, but by no means extraordinarily so.

In the cities, the ceremonies are usually simpler, and the ritual customs associated with ancient beliefs are likely to be dropped. But there will still usually be a hearty meal, toasts will be drunk and gifts exchanged. Many urban families do still pay bride money, but they are more likely to disguise the payment in expensive gifts: perhaps wristwatches, which are also commonly used as engagement presents or pledges of troth.

Simple or lavish, the marriage marks a tremendous change in the lives of the young couple (as is no longer necessarily the case in the West, where many couples live together before marrying). They are fairly unlikely to have had prior sexual experience – the bride especially – and her knowledge of sexual matters is probably confined to a heart-to-heart chat with some older woman, perhaps an aunt or a friend of her mother's. It is not considered proper to give sexual instruction to young people before they are old enough to marry, but the man has most likely picked up the basic knowledge from friends at his place of work.

Usually the couple will aim at having a child soon after marrying. Contraceptives are handed out free to married people who have had a child or want to postpone the event. I once acquired a jar of 1,000 oral contraceptive pills in the pharmacy of a commune in Jiangsu province, merely through asking to see them; the pharmacy clerk positively pressed them on me, as though I alone might be responsible for solving China's population problem! The Chinese have also experimented with oral contraceptives for men and 'morning after' pills for women and claim a fairly good success rate. Condoms are becoming less popular as chemical contraceptives catch on.

The Party's problem over contraception is not the provision of the physical aids but the difficulty of changing people's attitudes over the bearing of children and the size of families.

One of the biggest problems which the leadership has proclaimed its intention to solve is that of separated couples, who may number as many as 50 million people. Because of the shortage of industrial jobs and the relatively small number of posts available in scientific research institutes, it is common enough for qualified young people to be directed to work in different parts of the country, perhaps a thousand miles apart.

In the revolutionary period and the civil war, many young activists in the rural areas joined the Communist armies, leaving their families behind. After years of service they might be given responsible positions in the new military and later civilian administrations being set up wherever the fortunes of war had brought them. For a battle-hardened Party official, who might have learned to read and write during his service, it would often seem more attractive to take a new wife, preferably an educated city girl or a young worker, abandoning the old marriage. This practice was condemned by the Party and died out as the country settled down to a period of relatively peaceful economic construction.

Though it is the natural inclination of a young couple to live together when married, revolutionary zeal and romanticism could persuade them to adopt the more patriotic course of working in their assigned specialities, meeting only once a year. Separated couples are entitled to twelve days' leave each year to see each other, and if this holiday can be taken at the Chinese New Year, they can stretch it to fifteen days, minus the travelling time. The fares of whichever partner travels are supposed to be met out of official funds. This is one explanation for the huge numbers of people travelling at Chinese New Year, with concomitant problems of shortages of trains and tickets and the disruption of rail freight services.

Having indulged – probably for the first time – in sexual intercourse just after the marriage, the young people are likely to want more of it. So there is a clear temptation for either of the separated partners to seek sexual gratification extramaritally, with all this entails for the cohesion of the marriage. Such activities are frowned upon and may even bring legal sanctions; the death penalty for repeated extra-marital sexual liaisons is not unknown.

One reason for separating married couples is the practice of sending specialists and workers off to remote border regions to clear the land and build settlements. In cases where the partner being visited lives in a dormitory, the work unit may make available a single room for the time of the visit.

If the honeymoon or once-yearly bouts of intercourse result in pregnancy of the wife, she may have a hard time bringing the child up on her own, and unless there are very good day-care facilities at her place of work or residence she will hand the baby over to the grandparents. Although day nurseries and kindergartens are a vaunted feature of the modern Chinese social system, they are by no means to be found everywhere. Whether or not a factory can set one up depends on the accumulation of welfare funds, for which there are other demands, such as health care.

Although extramarital sexual liaisons are much more common in China than is freely admitted there, it is difficult for an unmarried couple to live together publicly. While it might be possible in the rural areas – where the officials are much less close to the people – in the city it would make life very difficult for some purposes, such as renting rooms. In practice the only ways in which an urban couple can live together without being married is to use an empty part of a friend's house or find quarters somewhere in the surrounding countryside where supervision is less strict than in a large apartment house.

Young people who want to live together without marrying have reasons similar to those in other countries: they do not want the responsibility of having children, or they feel they cannot afford a regular marriage, or they believe their careers may separate them in the end anyway. There is the added consideration in China that until quite recently marriages of people with 'good' (that is, proletarian or revolutionary class) background were discouraged if the proposed partner had a 'bad' background (if, say, the parents were labelled by some such term as landlord, rich peasant, bourgeois, or 'rightist'). In 1978 the Party announced that discrimination against young people on grounds of their family background was to cease, though doubtless some prejudice has lingered , and people may fear that a new leftist upheaval will revive the opprobrium attached to politically 'mixed' marriages.

In the armed forces, officers of battalion commander rank upward can have their wives with them. Private soldiers, NCOs and officers below battalion commander may not have married quarters. If their intended spouse should come to live near by, they may be criticized.

Divorce is made as difficult as possible. This is in strange contrast to the traditional socialist view of marriage as a free compact which can be terminated when it is no longer to the liking of those concerned. (In the Soviet Union, divorce is so easy that the rate of family break-up approaches the proportions of a national disaster.) It is doubly surprising that the authorities should be so anti-divorce, when the previous subjugation of women in the household was a major source of unhappiness, and one of the worst social evils of Confucian society. Perhaps the Party sees divorce as socially destabilizing – although Mao himself was divorced around 1940, and his former wife, Ho Zizhen, was still alive in 1980.

Closer to the truth, perhaps, is the almost mystical belief of the Chinese in the importance of solid social institutions. Precisely because the Party introduced a straightforward legal solution to the problems of women's status, the Marriage Law of 1950, it is felt that problems of man–women relationships are thereby solved once and for all, and that to persist in having marital problems despite the existence of the law implies a personal criticism of the institution of socialist marriage. Judiciary workers concerned with divorce may spend years trying to persuade a feuding couple to compose their differences and will grant a divorce only in extreme circumstances.

The resistance to divorce, in other words, is an affirmation of the perfectability of human society under the guidance of the 'right' political principles. To seek divorce is to affirm that an important piece of socialist legislation has not proved equal to the task of perfecting a particular area of social relations.

This is probably linked to Mao's ideas about the power of persuasion in dealing with social misfits – the refusal to belive that anyone, except the most hardened criminal or 'counter-revolutionary', cannot be brought to see sense through prolonged instruction in Marxism/Leninism/Mao Zedong Thought. If this is so, we may safely predict that divorce will become easier in China as the memory of Mao and the reverence for him fade from people's minds. Indeed, from 1980 on the courts have been more cooperative in dissolving marriages which have become a burden to both parties.

Every divorce has its special peculiarities, but here are details of one which is pretty typical. Wang, a worker in the big coastal city of Tientsin, got married to a woman from the north-east industrial centre of Fushun. (One of her motives in marrying, probably, was to escape the grime and pollution and low living standards in China's biggest coal-mining and iron-and-steel centre.) It took the wife two years, even after marriage, to gain permission to come to Tientsin to live, and by that time she had had a baby daughter, conceived during a visit to Fushun by her husband. She showed little affection for the child and resented doing household chores. The couple's life together became intolerable, and they agreed to seek a divorce. But the woman wanted to keep all the furniture from their apartment and take the baby girl too. Wang objected – and in any case their application for divorce was turned down by the district court, on the grounds that after only two years of marriage they would need to show 'serious political or medical grounds' to part.

After four years of marriage, the wife abandoned their home in Tientsin and filed for a divorce on her own. The court agreed to hold a hearing in the apartment, attended by welfare officers from the couple's respective places of employment. Two court officials, one of them a full-fledged judge, were present. The judge made it plain that there could be no divorce unless the couple would agree, then and there, on how to divide their domestic effects. The hearing was adjourned, and the welfare officers had a series of prolonged meetings with the couple, trying to persuade them to reconsider. But they stood firm, and a second hearing was eventually convened – again in the apartment. This time the wife, tired of the wrangle, agreed to accept her husband's terms. They decided on the spot how to divide up the property, the judge leaving the apartment only after everything was cut and dried. The mother was granted permission to see the child as often as her ex-husband would permit, but she had no rights over the infant, and he paid no alimony.

6. *The Enemy in the Womb*

The solution of many of China's most pressing problems has created a new monster, population growth. Improved medical services, an end to protracted civil war, and reasonably stable food supplies have led the country into a demographic crisis which must be solved in the near future if past achievements are not to be wiped out.

At a conservative estimate, the population of China today is increasing by roughly twelve million a year – nearly as many as the entire population of Pennsylvania, Australia, or the Netherlands. Far from making China stronger in relation to other powers, excess population will keep her perpetually in a backward state if drastic measures of control are not adopted.

Seen from any angle, the problem is frightening. At present, on average, Chinese women bear three children each in the course of their lives. The Party and government are insistent that this must be brought down to one child. Every imaginable social and economic sanction is being imposed to deter parents from having more than one, or at the very most two. The plan is to reduce population growth to 0·5 per cent by 1985 and zero in the year 2000. China's population by then should stand at about 1.3 billion, and some demographers are talking about aiming at negative growth from then on, bringing the population down below the 1 billion mark again – a project no other country has ever attempted.

Working against the birth-rate planners is an expected baby boom between 1980 and 1985, a result of the similar boom in the late 1950s and 1960s. Since it is axiomatic that poor people and peasants usually have more children than relatively well-off city dwellers, China is fighting an uphill battle in birth control, for 80 per cent of her people live on the land and are very poor by the standards of the developed world. But without reducing the peasant birth rate immediately, more and more resources will have to be ploughed back into simply feeding them, and most of China's potentially arable land is already under cultivation.

There are, however, some encouraging signs. The national birth rate fell from 23.4 per thousand in 1971 to 12 per thousand in 1978, a period during which more than 170 million birth-control operations were carried out.

Some Chinese sociologists are already worried about the overall ageing of the population which will occur if the birth rate is curbed. The planners have no answer to this, except to say that improvements in efficiency and standard of living will make it possible to support an older population.

Strange though it seems, it is only in the past few years that the Chinese leadership has acknowledged the drag which a growing population exercises on economic development. In the 1950s, when a renowned Chinese economist, Professor Ma Yinchu, vigorously propounded the need for birth control, he was fired from his post as president of Peking University as a result and fell into obscurity. (He was rehabilitated in 1979 at the age of ninety-eight.) The Party at the time proclaimed that 'people are the most valuable resource', insisting that improvements in the economy and higher production could support any level of population growth. From the 1960s on, considerable attention was given to birth control, but only 'in the interests of planned economy' and 'to protect the health of women and infants'. Birth-control work was disrupted for several years by the Cultural Revolution and then resumed.

In the late 1970s, after Mao's death, the obvious was at last admitted: growth of population was bringing to naught all attempts to achieve a faster rate of development and modernize the country.

Professor Wen Yinggan, an economist at Zhongshan University in Canton, sums up the problem succinctly: 'Quite a large number of people in the rural areas still do not have enough to eat, the people's living standards cannot be improved as they should have been, there are tensions in market supply, and the number of people awaiting employment has increased.' Hunger, poverty and unemployment – these are the prices China is paying for the greater security which the new society has established and the consequent surge in population.

Faced with this desperate crisis, the leadership has adopted a policy aimed at making it so unpleasant for parents to have more than one child that most of them will desist. The one-child family is being set up as the national ideal, in sharp contrast to the traditional importance which the Chinese have ascribed to having large families, with as many sons as possible.

The desire for offspring among the Chinese is not just the normal human instinct to procreate, or the economic need to create more hands for the tasks of growing food and providing clothes and shelter. The urge to have sons has been, since remote antiquity, the basis of the country's most pervasive religious concept: the worship of the ancestors.

In the traditional world view of the Chinese, birth is not the absolute beginning of life, nor death its abrupt end. A child is born into an immensely long chain of human lives, which stretches back longer than anyone can remember and is hoped to stretch on endlessly into the future. A new life is only an event in this process. Ancestor worship is needed for the spiritual wellbeing of the dead, just as the help and support of the dead is needed for the living, if they are to survive and prosper. Parenthood in the Confucian world view is a compact, both with those who came before and those who will come after. To decline to have children, or show disrespect to one's parents, is the worst moral transgression in the Confucian world order; to be deprived of parenthood is the worst disaster — though it can be remedied by adoption. To have no sons is a sign of failure.

Feelings so deep-seated will not vanish in a decade or two just because modern thinking denies the existence of ancestral spirits or the need to care for them. By a quirk of history, the Communist ethic of life and death slots neatly into the Confucian one: a good Communist sees his or her life as no more than a link in the chain of social development. To be praised and remembered is the only immortality which Communists are supposed to hold dear, and their defined aim in having children is to continue the cause.

The sheer size of the Chinese population problem puts it in a class by itself, creating the need for solutions which have never been tried elsewhere and which will need an almost religious devotion on the part of Chinese parents if they are to work.

China does not have systematic census figures of recent date. Informed estimates of her population vary between 990 million and 1.1 billion. As is usually true of developing countries, the growth rate in the towns is less than the countryside. Recent statements by the authorities have named Peking as having already a lowered population growth of 0.5 per cent, the national target for 1985. However, even such a big city as Tientsin had by 1980 not reached this benchmark in the agonizingly slow downward trend.

Among the other twenty-seven provinces, self-governing cities, and 'autonomous regions', the big western province of Sichuan has done best, bringing its increase rate down from 3.1 per cent in 1970 to 0.44 per cent in 1980. But not every part of China has been able to establish a downward trend in population growth. The rich southern province of Guangdong has seen its rate rise between 1978 and 1980. With rich soil and a warm, wet climate, Guangdong has managed to increase the amount of grain grown per head of population from 235 kg (517 pounds) in 1950 to 290 kg (638 pounds) in 1979. But since 1965 the population has been growing at an annual average rate of 2.2 per cent, while grain output is increasing at only 1.6 per cent, according to Professor Wen.

Guangdong's failure to keep grain output rising parallel with population growth is particularly alarming for the national leadership, because the province is a hugely important agricultural area, chief supplier of rice, pork and other foodstuffs to Hong Kong and Macau and the country's biggest earner of foreign exchange. Guangdong's people, through the nearness of Hong Kong, are more knowledgeable and sophisticated than those of any other part of China – with the possible exception of Shanghai – and know all about modern birth-control techniques. If Guangdong cannot turn back the adverse trend of the grain–population equation, the leaders in Peking must wonder what other province can do so.

In mountainous Jiangxi province, the pressure of population has been measured in terms of farmland per head of population, and the results are alarming: annual population growth is put at 1.97 per cent, with only two thirds of the married couples using any kind of contraception. So there has been a drastic decline in arable land per head of population – from 1 hectare (about 2½ acres) on average in 1956 to 0.65 hectare in 1978. This cannot go on without ruining most of the successes scored in fertilizing, irrigating and reclaiming farmland.

In the late 1970s, the Party took a big step. Instead of relying mainly on education to bring down the birth rate, it chose to go all out for a package of arm-twisting measures. The plan is to bind as many married couples as possible to a vow that their first child will be their last. If they give an undertaking to this effect – or better still, let themselves be sterilized – they will straight away be given material rewards and the child will enjoy every benefit the socialist state can supply.

Parents are most likely to agree to this if their first child has been a son. At a rally held in the provincial capital of Fuzhou in 1979, nearly 5,000 couples were commended for agreeing to have only one child. But among them less than 1,400 were parents of a daughter.

Another big obstacle is the fear of parents that, once sterilized, they will not be able to have more children if their single child should die or be incapacitated. Personal acceptance of sterility is also a psychological hurdle. Efforts are being made to spread knowledge of sterilization techniques which can be reversed in a later operation if the couple really need to have another child. Extra holidays and cash are given to people who undergo the operation. But it is still difficult to get all the new fathers to come in for surgery; they often have to be tracked down one by one, after they have invented all sorts of guiles to outwit the birth-control programme.

The inducements to birth control take effect before a couple has had any children at all. The first is the policy of late marriage. In the cities, this is fairly easy to enforce because living quarters are very cramped, and couples are more willing to wait a while so that they will have a place of their own soon after getting married, and not live for years cheek-by-jowl with their families and in-laws.

In the rural areas, a house can be more easily built on to or rearranged, so that a son can bring his new bride home. And peasant ways of looking at things tend to go against the Party's late marriage policy – so that a peasant couple marrying in their early twenties would not feel as anti-social, or downright odd, as they would in a city. On the farms, people's jobs are dictated by the weather and the time of year; the Party has less say about the kind of work a person will do than it has in the city – and therefore less leverage on individuals. (One of the reasons why the Party winks at the payment of bride money in the communes is probably the fact that it puts off the date when a family can afford to let its son or sons marry.) In the cities there are better recreational facilities and more ways of distracting young people from thoughts of sex and love, while the sheer boredom of rural life could drive them to marry sooner.

Once the couple are married, they are warned to adopt some kind of birth-control plan, but real pressure on them will not come until after the first child. Then they will be pushed towards promising not to have a second.

The most public-spirited (or politically ambitious) couples will take some form of open vow not to procreate any more or will give a promise in private talks with local Party officials or Women's Federation activists. They may be persuaded to sign a 'letter of determination', which will be printed in the local press or nailed up on a bulletin board at their place of work. A typical text is:

> We are resolved to break with the old traditional concepts and to have only one child. We guarantee that we will not have a second child and will teach our child well, so that he or she can develop in an all-round way, morally, intellectually, and physically, and become a labourer with socialist awareness and culture. Meanwhile, we can concentrate our energy and vigour on speeding up the Four Modernizations. We must make concerted efforts to fulfil the demand put forward by the provincial Communist Party Committee that by 1980 the rate of natural growth of population of the whole province be restricted to 0.9 per cent. We must endeavour to reduce it to 0.8 per cent and ensure that our municipality will attain the target of reducing the rate of natural growth of population to five per thousand by 1980.

Sometimes a big rally is staged in a theatre or outdoor stadium to congratulate young couples who have adopted a birth-control plan and show they want to stick to it. In the cities a more direct form of pressure has been used: couples wanting to have a child gather at a big meeting and with the help of local activists decide which of them should have one in the next year and which should wait. 'Permission' will be granted to those with no children or with the best records of public and private behaviour.

Parents who agree not to have more than one child are showered with encouragements and rewards. Their incomes are raised by about 5 per cent, and they are put high on the priority list for new housing – to the extent of giving them accommodation previously reserved for two-child families. This makes the sanction against having a second child doubly severe; not only are two-child families given no special priority for housing, but they may have to watch as a one-child family moves up the list over their heads and takes what would otherwise have been their apartment. This can only breed envy – and a vengeful malice if the 'abstaining' couple then break their promise and have the second child after all. But this is unlikely, as the urban mother with one child will in most cases be persuaded to have an abortion.

The only child enjoys the biggest benefits of the birth-control policy. Medical care will be assured to the greatest possible extent; the parents will not even have to pay for expensive medicines or for treatment which goes beyond the limit set by their local insurance plan. The child will be given priority treatment at hospitals and clinics, will go to the top of the list for a place in a kindergarten, and will be entered first on the rolls of the local primary school, while some children are forced to wait because of the shortage of classroom space and teachers. The child will be generally pampered and rewarded for something that was none of its doing.

But woe betide the family if the parents break the undertaking not to have a second child. They will be made to feel anti-social, unpatriotic, and a nuisance to their neighbours – especially if the Party decrees financial penalties for factories or other places of work which show a higher-than-sanctioned birth rate. Cash allowances for the family will be withdrawn, and all privileges curtailed. Medical benefits will revert to their normal level, and the couple may have to move out of their new flat to a smaller one. The second child will not be given any priority for kindergarten or schooling.

The penalty for insisting on having a second child is of a mainly negative nature; the family are simply cut down to their original social status. But if they go ahead and have a third child, they will quickly feel the Party's severe displeasure. Unless the third child was a result of twins born at the wife's second confinement, the earnings of both husband and wife will automatically be docked by 5 per cent, and this will continue until the child is fourteen.

The third child will go to the bottom of the list for a place in kindergarten or primary school, and the parents will have to pay *all* its medical expenses. If they get into financial difficulties, they will not qualify for the loans or subsidies which are usually available in such cases. Their food supply will actually be reduced, and the wife will not be given free maternity leave; she will have to regard it as voluntary leave and lose pay for the time she takes off work.

If the children become aware of these sanctions – and this will inevitably happen in a society where there is such a high degree of public interference in private life – the psychological effect may be severe. (How severe, we do not know, because the policy only went into full effect in 1980, but it seems sensible to assume that there will be unpleasant consequences.) Not only will the older child suddenly feel social approval drop away and revert from most-favoured status to that of the ordinary rank-and-file; it may also feel guilty and show hostility towards the new baby or babies, which have not only invaded its relationship with father and mother but also brought financial problems and social downgrading for them all.

7. *The Political Contagion*

Few people nowadays visit the Garden of Perfection and Light, a picturesque ruin in the northern outskirts of Peking. Unlike the well-preserved Summer Palace a few miles to the west, the Garden has been neither protected nor restored, and every year it settles a little deeper into the dry and grassy slopes on which it stands.

The form of the remaining marble columns makes plain that the pleasure houses which once stood here were not Chinese in design but European. Jesuit advisers at the court of the eighteenth-century Manchu emperor Qian Long (Ch'ien Lung) planned it as a showpiece of the Italian baroque. It had pavilions, colonnades, manicured gardens, and an elaborate water clock made with stone figures of the animals of the Chinese Zodiac.

In 1860 an Anglo-French expeditionary force pushed up from Tientsin, near the coast seventy miles from Peking, to exact reprisals for losses they had suffered in a skirmish with Chinese imperial troops. On reaching the Garden of Perfection and Light, the officers took first pick of its gold, jade and other treasures and then turned the rank-and-file loose to loot and demolish the most notable monument to European science and culture in the whole of China.

Picnicking at the ruin one day with friends, I saw an elderly Chinese man ride up on a bicycle, followed by a boy of about ten or eleven whose spindly legs could barely straddle the frame of his own machine. To my astonishment, the old man said loudly to the boy in English, 'Come with me, and I will show you what the imperialists did to Chinese culture!'

Forgetting my manners as a guest in China, I bristled and called to him, 'This was not Chinese culture. This was built by European priests for Manchu emperors.'

He halted, looked me up and down, and said, 'That is not true. It was built under the Ming' – the last native Chinese dynasty, overthrown by the Manchus in 1644.

Having just been reading about the Garden, and being fairly sure of my facts, I said, 'Rubbish. And anyway, do you think it is a good thing to teach racial hatred to children?'

The old man seemed disposed to stay and argue, but the boy, who had ridden on a few paces, turned and called to him in imperfect but still impressive English, 'Come away, he will only say you lies!' Whereupon they both rode off.

I have often thought about this disagreeable episode at the Garden of Perfection and Light – in Chinese, Yuan Ming Yuan – and its implications for the whole business of cultural misunderstanding and historic grievances between China and the West. Why were the two speaking English together, and not Chinese? What was their family relationship? Why was the old man so hostile to foreigners?

The most likely answer is that he had graduated from a university overseas, probably in the United States, and then returned to China out of a patriotic desire to serve the revolutionary regime which proclaimed the People's Republic in 1949. The boy – perhaps his grandson – was getting daily English lessons from him, as well as educative rides and walks around Peking. On reaching the Garden of Perfection and Light on that Sunday afternoon, he was irritated to see foreigners sprawling over the old ruins, drinking wine. So he made the discourteous remark to which I took exception, not because he was entirely wrong to hate the Europeans for their past acts of rapine but because plain good manners should have dictated that he speak in Chinese and so at least try to avoid giving offence to people who had never consciously done China any harm.

The incident was a telling encapsulation of the sore points in Chinese–Western history and the entire modern political process in China, which has been to such an enormous extent dictated by that nation's search for its true role in the contemporary world order. The old man's sense of cultural pride seemed in conflict with his recognition of the boy's need to grow up speaking passable English. His deepseated resentment induced him deliberately and gratuitously to insult some foreigners – whom Chinese people have usually taken pride in entertaining politely, as long as they show a modicum of respect for Chinese tradition and customs. The young boy was already conditioned to believe that a foreigner would never speak the truth, even on a point of historical fact. And here was the once rich and splendid China brought so low economically that her people had to go around on bicycles while foreigners parked expensive cars on her ruined sites.

The keynote of all these factors contributing to the old man's bad mood – and his young companion's morbid suspiciousness – was politics. The memory of historic wrongs done to China by other nations has been so closely interwoven with her people's political attitudes that xenophobia sometimes just comes spilling out and is turned on perfectly innocuous targets. But perhaps, thinking more about it, one should be astonished that foreigners on the whole are made so welcome in China these days; the old man's rudeness was striking because it was untypical.

China's history of the last three decades is an interminable recitation of political attitudes, political change, political purges, movements, censorship, spy mania – all the paraphernalia of a great but disrupted culture trying to find political solutions to its own problems of weakness and poverty. Occasional outbursts of xenophobia are just the froth on the surface.

Alone among Communist states of the postwar world, China since the victory of its revolution has continued to undergo violent political eruptions. In the Soviet Union and East Europe, political processes have on the whole been subjugated to the demand for unity and discipline. None of these states has come – like China – dangerously close to destroying its own ruling Party and the institutions of the State, not just in order to win freedom from a dominating foreign power but in order to strengthen and purify its own ideological foundations.

Now China is trying to de-emphasize politics, in order to concentrate on more day-to-day matters such as producing food and educating youngsters. Probably the post-Mao leadership will succeed to some extent in assigning politics a more modest role in the country's affairs. But it is hard to believe that the political ferment to which Chinese people have become so accustomed will just disappear.

Probably it will be guided into institutional channels, less likely there to spawn anything resembling the surprises and upsets of the past three decades.

One can understand almost nothing about modern China without knowing something of her politics. Unfortunately, for most people in the West, the Chinese political process is wrapped in mystifying jargon and often seems full of inconsistencies and contradictions, with those leaders who were down one moment up the next, and proclaiming virtually the opposite of what their rivals professed when *they* were on top. It has been complicated still more by being described and reported on too often by people who have some axe to grind concerning the politics of their own country.

Politics in modern China, as in no other country, has been dominated by one question: how should relations with the rest of the world be conducted?

This may seem strange, since in the two millennia of the empire the Chinese, on the whole, showed strikingly little interest in happenings beyond their own horizons. China was not a country, for most of her people, but a world, on which foreigners impinged only peripherally. Insofar as most Chinese people thought about other countries at all, it was usually with apprehension, because of the many attacks and invasions the empire suffered from Central Asian tribes. As long as the country was at peace, they were content to live self-sufficiently off the products of their own land and within their own cultural tradition. The geographical expansion of their state was achieved more by settlement than by conquest. How different this was from the history of other great empires, such as the Roman, the British, or the Spanish.

Actually, China's long isolation is the main reason why in the twentieth century she has been forced to make foreign policy a central theme of her statecraft. Precisely because she formerly scorned or ignored the achievements of other countries in science, technology, navigation, warfare, and economic and political organization, she was weak – despite her vast size – and in the nineteenth century narrowly escaped being completely carved up by the Western powers and by Japan and Russia.

The struggle to maintain independence and territorial integrity against the inroads of the foreign powers became a dominant theme at the court of the empress dowager Ci Xi (Tz'u Hsi, who ruled China from 1861 until 1908 and whom Mao's wife Jiang Qing is said to have secretly admired).

The main cause of the 1911 downfall of the Qing (Ch'ing) dynasty, founded by the Manchus 267 years previously, was the economic decline brought about by enforced trade links with Western countries – on terms of trade highly favourable to those countries – and the national humiliation caused by the loss of Chinese territory to foreign powers. By the end of the nineteenth century, Taiwan (Formosa) had been grabbed by Japan, Hong Kong and Kowloon by Britain, Shanghai jointly by Britain, France, the United States, and other powers, Qingdao by Germany, and all the lands north of the Amur River and east of the Ussuri River by Russia. Britain and Russia had upset China's traditional suzerainty over Tibet and eastern Turkestan respectively, while France had put an end to the tributary relationship of Indochina to China. Foreign missionaries, especially the French Catholics, acted almost like imperial magistrates in large parts of the interior, and China's maritime Customs were put under the control of an Irishman. The strength of the foreigners, with their superior military techniques and overweening self-confidence, enabled a few hundred of them in the besieged Peking Legation district to hold out for eight weeks against the combined assaults of the imperial guards and the fanatical Boxer sect in 1900.

China's failure to win back her lost territories and national dignity at the Versailles Conference which wound up the First World War touched off the most important proto-revolutionary ferment among wide sectors of the Chinese public – the May Fourth Movement of 1919, which still today is seen as a crucial event in the whole revolutionary process.

The strength of the Kuomintang (Nationalist) regime was sapped in the 1930s by its failure to cope with the Japanese policy of seizing as much Chinese territory as possible to fuel the Japanese economy – and this was a principal reason why the Kuomintang was unable to destroy the Communists even after the defeat of Japan.

The Korean War of the early 1950s profoundly affected China's development as a nation and her acceptability in the world community: her exclusion from all important world forums, including the United Nations, forced her to follow a policy of near self-sufficient growth, even while Soviet technicians were helping her build up her industry.

The mounting quarrel with the Soviet Union over points of revolutionary principle and mutual equality led to the withdrawal of the experts in 1960 and the loss of all foreign aid. This helped widen the split among the top Chinese leaders and can be seen as one cause of the Cultural Revolution, involving the purge by Mao of thousands of top administrators, educationalists and scientists who were unhappy with the enforced isolationism. There were plenty of other factors contributing to the Cultural Revolution, but it was in large part a violent assertion of Mao's faith in China's ability to develop her economy and technology without foreign help, and of his ability to inspire others with the same faith.

In the 1970s, China's decision to throw in her lot with the United States, in the global strategy of resistance to Soviet expansionism, led her back into the community of nations – including the Security Council, the General Assembly of the United Nations, and numerous international bodies from which she had been previously barred. This led to a massive growth of her foreign commercial, technical, and cultural ties and a rethinking of the rigid and xenophobic social attitudes enforced during the Cultural Revolution. By 1980, China had reverted internally to a social and economic structure similar to the one she had copied in detail from the Soviet Union – before her quarrel with the late Nikita Khrushchev from 1956 on left her disillusioned with Soviet 'revisionism'.

Of course China's internal politics have contributed to the form her foreign policy has taken. The interplay between foreign and domestic policy is complex, and impossible to portray as a one-way process. But by comparison with other large powers, China's domestic policy over the past century has tended remarkably often to be shaped by events on the world stage beyond her control.

The huge role played by politics in modern China is in marked contrast to the low level of political activity in traditional Chinese society. Under the empire, national politics were mainly a matter of intrigue at the court. The general public played hardly any role, being only too happy to stay away from the awesome and dangerous arena of court affairs. The emperor, as long as he ruled, demanded absolute loyalty. There was no glory to be found in defying him, but only disgrace – except in the case of unsurping kinsfolk or powerful military commanders in outlying parts of the country, who sometimes successfully ignored the emperor's commands and lived in virtually independent fiefdoms. But even they would usually put up a show of loyalty to the remote and semi-divine head of state, if only to legitimize their own local regimes.

China has no significant tradition of institutionalized political opposition, either parliamentary or feudal. Historically, to go into active opposition meant raising a rebel army – and this was done more often by leaders of peasant uprisings or religious sects, or by disgruntled petty officials, than by high officials or kinsmen of the ruler, as so often in Europe. Natural portents were said to accompany the birth of future emperors and the downfall of dynasties. The overthrow of an emperor – even by a peasant warrior – was proof that the dynasty had lost the support or 'mandate' of Heaven, and the victor could then respectably found a new dynasty with Heaven's blessing. The historical periods during which there were rival claimants to the 'mandate', each ruling a different part of China, were short compared with the periods during which only one ruler was universally recognized. Blood ties with ancient dynasties were unimportant.

The most admired form of political opposition was that of the high courtier – a man of learning, sagacity, and great probity – who would risk the emperor's wrath for offering frank and necessary criticism of the state of the nation and willingly accept disgrace and even death as the consequence of his outspokenness. Another way for a courtier to show disillusionment with the politics of the court was to retire to his country estate, or even to a hermit's retreat, and spend his days in writing poetry or philosophy, painting, playing musical instruments, drinking, or contemplating the landscape. There was no senate or parliament, not even the most rudimentary, and debate on affairs of state was often conducted in the emperor's presence among scholar-officials who talked mainly in allusions to past history, which was seen as providing guidelines for all matters of government.

Short of raising a rebel army, the only way in which an ordinary Chinese citizen could become politically influential was to take high honours in the very difficult civil service examinations, which emphasized literary erudition, elegance of style, and even fine handwriting. Sometimes there were test questions on current-day problems, but even the answers to these had to be dressed up in elaborate flattery of the ruler and reams of quotations from ancient or classical books. The high cost of such an education created a semi-hereditary official class.

Onto a society thus unused to the Western idea of politics was imposed a pseudo-Western parliamentary system and, later, the dictatorship of the Nationalist period, whose most important features were corruption and hypocrisy, inept military leadership, financial bungling, and – in the end – outright defeat by the so-called 'bandits' of the Red Army. (Even today in Taiwan it is mandatory to refer to the Peking government as the 'bandits'. Political absolutism is to be found on both sides of the Taiwan Strait.)

What kind of political system did the Communists offer China, after Western-style forms of government had proved so drastically unsuitable?

In the early 1950s, Mao and the other leaders copied political, social and economic institutions wholesale from the Soviet Union. And nowadays, since Mao's death, a Politburo containing a good number of survivors from that period is restoring the Soviet-style institutions which were attacked and dismantled during the Eleven Years.

The fact that latter-day Stalinism (with some modifications) is again being seen as the best tried-and-tested form of government for China is not entirely a coincidence. Stalinism owed much to the autocratic government style of the Tsars, who practised a form of despotism closer to the political systems of Asia than to those of Europe; various forms of what has been called 'Asiatic despotism' stretched from the Baltic to the Yellow Sea. So the Stalinism which was imposed on China in the early 1950s felt less unfamiliar to the mass of people than had the unsuccessful attempt at parliamentary democracy in the second quarter of the twentieth century.

The reversion to Stalinism was not, however, total. One of the most surprising things about the early years of Communist rule in China was its relative leniency and broad-mindedness. Emphasis was laid on the formation of a united front of all patriotic Chinese organizations and individuals. Big capitalists were welcome to stay on and manage their factories, in the interests of an orderly transfer to State control at a later date. Religious leaders were promised freedom of worship and belief, if they would only co-operate in the Party's efforts to root out opposition and impose order after the civil war. The main brunt of the Party's anger fell on the rural landlords, who were stripped of their lands and often severely beaten or shot 'to assuage the wrath of the masses'.

The early Maoist policy of 'uniting with all those forces that can be united with' – which even tolerated the existence of non-Communist political parties, albeit small and impotent ones – was reflected in the first State Constitution drawn up by the Communists and promulgated in 1954. (This constitution was replaced by more left-influenced drafts in 1969 and again in 1975 and 1978, but was expected to have some of its previous liberal provisions aimed at national unity restored in the early 1980s.) The 1954 version provided for indirect elections to a parliament, the National People's Congress, which in theory was given the power of enacting laws, appointing high officials of the People's Republic, overseeing financial and economic matters, and deciding on matters of war and peace. In practice, all these functions are carried out by the Communist Party, which completely dominates the Congress, but the body does at least provide a formal framework for a 'constitutional' state such as Deng and his supporters claim to favour.

Partly, perhaps, because of alarm at the implications of the uprising in Hungary and the unrest in Poland in 1956, the Chinese Communist Party decided to strengthen its own position by inviting criticism from the intelligentsia and other members of the public – the so-called policy of 'letting a hundred flowers bloom and a hundred schools of thought contend'. Most of those naive enough to offer the solicited criticism paid a heavy price, being labelled 'rightists' in the big rectification campaign of 1957–8 and in many cases being down-graded in their jobs or forced to cease publishing or teaching.

Ultra-left economic policies pushed by Mao brought China to the verge of starvation in 1958–61 – the so-called Great Leap Forward – and were abandoned from 1962 on, while Premier Zhou Enlai, Party Secretary General Deng Xiaoping and other top administrators tried to sort out the mess left by Mao's attempt to force the pace of socialism, especially in the rural areas. This episode split the leaders over questions of principle: Defence Minister Marshal Peng Dehuai was dismissed in 1959 for criticizing the ultra-left policies, and scores of other top officials were marked down for attack as soon as Mao could muster enough support to overthrow them.

Only eight years after its promulgation, the State Constitution was showing its inability to handle the political currents of the time. The freedoms it guaranteed on paper were quite blatantly set aside in favour of stricter national discipline and unity. Meanwhile, the group around Mao – who was in semi-seclusion from 1962 until 1965 – built up round him a personality cult which has been rivalled in modern history only by those of Stalin and North Korea's Kim Il Sung. Still, this period was one of relative calm and order, during which China sought to boost her economic development – sabotaged by the pulling out of Soviet experts in 1960 – and mounted a campaign of smile diplomacy towards the emerging countries of the Third World, with the aim of encouraging them to look to China for partnership or leadership in a global order dominated by the two super-powers, the Soviet Union and the United States.

In late 1965, Mao's group prepared the ground for the Cultural Revolution with an attack in a Shanghai newspaper on the writings of three top officials of the Peking municipal committee, followed up the next year by the dismissal of the mayor, Peng Zhen. This was the signal for a seemingly endless series of violent verbal and physical assaults on top Party and government administrators and intellectuals.

By 1967, Mao's group had taken over national leadership with the dismissal and denunciation of head of state Liu Shaoqi, Party Secretary General Deng Xiaoping, war hero Marshal He Long, writers Ba Jin and Lao She, regional Party bosses Tao Zhu and Li Jingquan, and scores of other prominent people, some of whom were never seen in public again. With them, one after another, went leading provincial administrators, scientists, popular writers, educationalists, musicians, actors, physicians, philosophers, historians and diplomats, as well as hundreds of thousands of less well-known people who were simply made vulnerable because their jobs gave them authority over other people, such as factory managers and schoolteachers. The Chinese *Who's Who*, had there been one, would have been reduced by more than two thirds of its entries by the end of 1967. All in all, the total number of people thought to have been branded 'revisionist' and severely persecuted by the Red Guards is estimated to be in the order of several million. But although many of them were beaten up and held in prisons or labour camps for years on end – some had their health so badly damaged that they died as a result, while others committed suicide rather than face further persecution – it is still remarkable how many of them did survive to be rehabilitated in successive waves in the 1970s.

The Red Guard movement, violent and cruel though it often was, had, like most political movements in China, an element of theatricality and exaggeration. This made it extremely difficult to know whether the hysterical proclamations coming over the national and provincial broadcasting stations at the time were overplaying or underplaying the degree of violence and disruption. It is beyond doubt that firearms were used in many places, and quite a few Red Guards and other activists died at the hands of their 'class brothers' in factional feuding which often seemed to be over no identifiable issue at all.

Foreigners had numerous experiences of the madness of the Cultural Revolution. The British embassy was burned by Red Guards in 1967, and its staff molested. In a more trivial but still indicative episode, a European ambassador was called out of bed in the small hours of the morning and summoned to the post office for a dressing down, because someone in his embassy had mailed a letter with a stamp showing Mao's portrait – and, alongside it, a stamp with a picture of an archer, whose arrow was pointing in the direction of Mao's head. Such lunacy did not end with the fall of Defence Minister Lin Biao, either. In the mid 1970s the British embassy invited some of its Chinese staff to see the dress rehearsal of a Christmas pantomime, 'Jack and the Beanstalk'. The senior Chinese staff members later lodged a complaint that the performance insulted the Chinese people – because the giant was shown wearing Chinese-style blue cotton trousers.

A satisfactory explanation has never been given for the mass hysteria which gripped China's youth, fanned by the propaganda of the Cultural Revolution group around Mao, his wife, Jiang Qing, and Lin Biao. Former Red Guards say they felt fired with idealism and tired of the ossified attitudes and privileges enjoyed by administrators and teachers. They genuinely believed that Mao was in danger from a big plot against him and that they must defend him – with their lives, if necessary. The exhilaration of humiliating teachers and public figures took on a momentum of its own, and the chaotic organization of the movement led to the formation of rival armies of young activists who were soon embroiled in complex quarrels with each other. For many Chinese men and women now in their thirties, the Cultural Revolution was the most exciting time in their lives. They could travel almost anywhere in the country to 'exchange revolutionary experiences' with other young activists – usually without paying for their train tickets or their meals, for most people were too frightened to deny them anything.

The Red Guards' days of glory were short-lived. By 1968 they had been largely brought under control by the Army, which took over the running of the country's administration and economy while the Party sorted itself out from the shattering blow dealt it by Mao and his group. Many Red Guards were shipped off to the rural communes to 'temper' themselves by joining in manual labour with the peasants. This was a rude shock for most of them, for the Cultural Revolution had been above all an urban movement and the Red Guards had little experience of the hard life of the country. Some did manage to make the adjustment, marrying peasants and settling down to a lifetime of farming. But most of the young people sent 'up to the mountains and down to the villages' dreamed for years of returning home and leapt at every opportunity to do so. A few escaped by being recruited into the armed forces. When the universities reopened in 1971, after a four-year closure, some youngsters won sponsorship for higher education from the communes where they were assigned, and where relatively few of the local young people had received enough secondary education to be even considered for university. Parents of 'rusticated youths' also pulled strings to arrange their offspring's return, either to attend college or to take jobs in their home towns again. But the policy of sending school graduates down to the countryside was continued, partly because of the shortage of jobs in the cities; it was not till 1977, after Mao's death, that the leadership began to wind down the unpopular rustication programme. By 1980 it had been virtually abolished, to the relief of parents and youngsters alike.

The social group who maintained the most cohesion and stability in the Cultural Revolution were the armed forces, on whom the ideological mastermind of the Cultural Revolution – Defence Minister Marshal Lin Biao, named in 1969 as Mao's successor – relied as his line of defence against any change of political fortune. From late 1967 on, army officers were appointed to thousands of key positions in China, from government ministries down, and troops moved into factories both to restore order and to get production going in places where it had come to a halt.

There is no way of corroborating the official story that Lin plotted to overthrow Mao, before being exposed and allegedly dying in 1971 in a plane crash over Mongolia while attempting to flee to the Soviet Union. Myth or history, this event spelled an end to the near-dictatorship which the Army had established in other sectors of society. From 1972 on, the khaki uniforms began gradually disappearing from the Revolutionary Committees, organs of administration set up during the Cultural Revolution to replace the old governing bodies. Party authority was slowly rebuilt to the point where the Revolutionary Committees were brought under the control of Party committees in local government, schools, factories, communes and other grass-roots institutions, and in 1979–80 they were abolished in favour of management committees and provincial and local governments. The latter were elected by universal suffrage in 1979–80, and for the first time there was a choice of candidates – a limited choice, it is true (with only about 20 to 50 per cent more candidates standing than there were offices for elections), but still a choice of sorts.

Within three years of Mao's death in 1976, the theory and practice of the Cultural Revolution were completely discredited in China, and nearly all the surviving victims of the movement had been reinstated in top jobs or rehabilitated – if only posthumously or in their retirement. Peng Zhen was brought back to draft the country's new legal code, and even former head of state Liu Shaoqi, the most reviled figure in the history of post-1949 China, was rehabilitated eleven years after his death in prison and turned into a heroic martyr figure.

The folk hero of the decade was Premier Zhou Enlai, who died in 1976 and who – it was widely believed – had succeeded in modifying the worst excesses of the Red Guards and protected many prominent people from harassment; in the Chinese ethic, Zhou was the 'bamboo' who could bend with the wind without breaking, while Liu Shaoqi and others were 'pines' who could not. The most popular man in China after Zhou's death was Deng Xiaoping, who was seen as Zhou's spiritual successor and protégé, as the most effective modern leader working for a rise in the standard of living, and as the person who would lead the country away from the frantic and disastrous addiction to mass politics to which he himself had fallen victim – not only in

1967 but again in 1976, when he was dismissed and indirectly blamed for the riots on Peking's Tiananmen Square.

To understand just how disruptive the Chinese political process has been, it is worth reviewing the events of the mid 1970s, a period when China was struggling to decide between the ideas of latter-day Maoism and the pragmatic line followed by Deng and his supporters, and especially the 'Movement to Criticize Lin Biao and Confucius', which dominated the political scene for three years.

By holding on to both his position and his reputation as a loyal follower of Mao, Premier Zhou Enlai had aroused the impotent wrath of the leftists' Cultural Revolution group, who would have liked to see him overthrown and disgraced like many of his eminent colleagues. When Lin Biao was – allegedly – killed in 1971, the extreme-left movement associated with him, including Mao's wife, Jiang Qing, seemed in danger of exposure and destruction. So they masterminded a series of interlocking campaigns whose aim was to distance themselves from Lin and direct the flak against Zhou again. Meanwhile, under Zhou's influence, the most extreme leftist platforms of the Cultural Revolution group were being undermined and eroded: traditional Chinese themes returned in a small way to art and music, there were openings for cultural exchanges with Western countries, Chinese students went abroad again to learn advanced technology, and the attitude towards foreigners was relaxed and liberal by comparison with the late 1960s, when they had been in almost daily danger of being mobbed and harassed on the streets.

In late 1973 the leftists slipped into top gear with a change of their campaign's name to 'Criticize Lin Biao and Confucius'. This movement was the epitome of all the counterproductive, sterile aspects of modern Chinese politics. It was obscure, ambiguous, disturbing to the general public, and intimidating to professional people and intellectuals. It got in the way of China's foreign relations and irritated foreigners who were otherwise well disposed towards China. It culminated in violent rioting, a change of leadership, and eventually the downfall and disgrace of those who masterminded it.

Confucius – the name is a latinized version of the Chinese Kong Fuzi – lived in the sixth to fifth centuries B.C. To the feudal rulers of the divided China of the day, and to his many pupils, he expounded the concept of the 'superior man', whose conduct expresses righteousness and benevolence, moderation in all things, and a fixed system of social relations which is supposed to provide the correct key for behaviour in all circumstances. With brief interruptions, Confucianism – and later elaborations of it – was the dominant system of thought and ethics in China from the end of the third century B.C. right up to the 1911 revolution and, for most Chinese people, well into the twentieth century. It was a determining influence in the cultures of Korea and Vietnam and in various guises strongly affected aspects of Japanese life and thought. Together with Hinduism, Buddhism, Islam; Judaism, and Graeco–Roman–Christian ethics, it is one of the most durable codes of human behaviour ever devised.

Widely admired by somewhat ill-informed European thinkers in the eighteenth century as a system of just and stable government beyond compare, Confucianism had become a dead hand on Chinese society by the time the European seafaring powers arrived in strength in the first half of the nineteenth century. (The Portuguese and the Dutch had preceded the others by nearly three centuries, but their impact on Chinese life and society was small compared with that of the latecomers, especially Britain and France.)

The importance ascribed by Confucianism to the need for human beings to model themselves on the virtues of a long-lost golden age held back social progress and the use of scientific thought to create industry and wealth. Through its insistence on stable family and social relationships and an overwhelming, even exaggerated, respect for the elderly, it stifled the spirit of enterprise and adventure in young men and subjugated women to an extent thought shocking even in the far-from-emancipated Europe of the day. It discouraged speculative thought and looked down on manual labour and mechanical inventions. In the first half of the twentieth century, there was every reason for it to be regarded as the biggest single obstacle to progress in China.

Nonetheless, Confucianism had its good points: care of the aged, mutual help in stable family units, admiration for uprightness and loyalty even unto death, a plain and moderate life-style, rejection of wild superstitions and barbaric practices masquerading as religion, and respect for principle. Confucianism saw the prosperity of the peasants and the justness of official acts as the key indicators of the strength and weakness of a dynasty and in theory, at least, despised mercantile self-enrichment. It revered music and arts and exercised a civilizing influence wherever it was spread.

The Communist intelligentsia – Mao Zedong among them – had long seen certain aspects of Confucianism as embodying some of the best national characteristics of the Chinese. China's early revolutionary struggles were closely associated with the need to throw off foreign domination, and the quintessentially Chinese creed of Confucianism was often a useful ally. In the 1950s, numerous Chinese intellectuals had been content to work for national reconstruction under the Marxist leadership of the Party, while themselves sticking to Confucian attitudes.

The propaganda onslaught on Confucius and Confucianism in the mid 1970s could certainly be shown to have a genuine political content and was partly aimed at reforming modern Chinese society by throwing out musty Confucian attitudes which were opposed to progress. But the useful social content of the movement was actually very small.

Its peak was reached early in 1974, when the campaign took on a specifically anti-foreign orientation, a device which successive generations of Chinese court intriguers have found useful in gathering support and making opponents out to be treasonable. The leftist propagandists turned their wrath on Italian film-maker Michelangelo Antonioni for a long documentary film he had recently shot in China, saying it demeaned the dignity of the Chinese people and made socialism out to be gloomy and squalid. Antonioni had even had the impertinence to show Chinese people using a public toilet! At countless meetings and rallies across the country, millions of workers, peasants, students, soldiers and officials – who had never until then even heard of Antonioni, let alone seen his film – were obliged to go through the motions of fierce anger at him for his 'slanderous' portrayal of China.

Still more ludicrous, in the eyes of Western people, was the attack on 'non-representational music' – that is, Western classical music. Chinese music normally has a descriptive or symbolic theme: a famous battle, feelings of grief, mountain streams, flying geese, and so on. The Western ideal of music in the abstract, with no recognizable associations, could easily be seen as odd by Chinese people. But when the campaign began attacking as 'bourgeois' the composers Beethoven and Schubert – for having written 'non-representational music' – the derision which greeted it in other countries, and among the foreign community in Peking, was tinged with anger.

The introduction of a cultural theme into the campaign made it plain that Mao's wife, Jiang Qing – a former film actress who had taken closer and closer control of Chinese cultural activities since the mid 1960s – was one of those behind it. (She had cleverly put herself beyond criticism – despite her known youthful enthusiasm for Western movies and Western music – by asking a visiting American orchestra in Peking to play Beethoven's Pastoral Symphony, one of the minority of Western classical works of music that is actually tied to a pictorial and narrative theme.)

Towards the end of 1975, there appeared the thesis – widely touted in the media – that there was a single 'unrepentant top person in authority taking the capitalist road'. This ominous theme was aired in wall posters stuck up in their thousands by students at the two big universities of the capital, the University of Peking and Qinghua (Tsinghua) University. The students at first confined their attacks to Education Minister Zhou Rongxin and other 'revisionists' in educational circles, but the deeper significance was made plain by the Party press, which forged ahead with its denunciations of the 'top party person in authority', and in February of 1976 students in Shanghai and then in Peking began cheerfully admitting in private conversation that their attack was aimed against Deng. Nonetheless, the official media still did not mention him by name, though they clearly indicated who was meant, by criticizing the 'top person' for his reputed attacks on Jiang Qing's revolutionary operas and the 'barefoot doctor' medical scheme. The atmosphere grew gradually tenser, especially since Zhou Enlai's death in February touched off a wave of near-hysterical public grief, and resulted in Deng's being passed over for the post of Acting Premier in favour of the younger and relatively obscure Hua Guofeng, a long-term favourite of Mao's who had made his career in the Chairman's native province of Hunan.

The explosion came on 5 April 1976, the traditional festival of the dead called Qing Ming. Monday-morning crowds passing Tiananmen Square saw to their astonishment and anger that thousands of tributes left there the day before in commemoration of Zhou had been removed.

Within an hour, thousands of people were scuffling with security forces, trying to force their way into the Great Hall of the People, and making impromptu speeches of loyalty to Zhou from the steps of the big Martyrs' Monument in the centre of the square. They cruelly beat and bloodied a student who was rash enough to criticize Zhou out loud, and around midday they burned several official cars and mobbed and resisted firemen who came to put out the blaze. In the late afternoon the crowds set fire to a small police headquarters in the corner of the square. But as darkness fell, most dispersed and went home, and those who remained were allegedly clubbed and dragged off by security forces. (Claims that many people were killed and injured have never been verified. I once challenged a young Chinese man who said he was in the militia at the time and 'had to wipe the blood and brains of injured demonstrators off the square', but he stuck to his story. Nearly all foreign correspondents in Peking visited the square on 6 April, and none saw any trace of blood or of a clean-up operation, on the contrary, the place was a shambles, with burned-out cars and charred pine trees, a gutted building and sundry debris, lying around as the rioters had left them.)

It is certainly beyond doubt that a number of demonstrators – perhaps as many as several hundred – were arrested and imprisoned, being released in 1978 when the official version of the riots was reversed to blame all the trouble on the purged Gang of Four. It would also seem plausible that some people who were known to have set fire to vehicles or to the police headquarters would have been shot, but if that is so, it is odd that their names have never been published by the authorities, to whom nowadays they should be heroes.

On 7 April, the Party and government denounced the riots and dismissed Deng Xiaoping, though without specifically blaming him for them. He was, however, allowed to keep his Party membership, 'to see how he behaves'. At the same time, Hua was elevated to the full dignity of Premier.

The importance of the riots lay not so much in the amount of damage or number of injuries as in the clear message which the general public delivered to the Party and the clique around the dying Mao: 'We want an end to incomprehensible political campaigns; we want better wages and a rising standard of living. We are grieving for Zhou because he wanted all those things, even if his hands were often tied. We know Deng wants to give them to us too. So take heed!'

'Spontaneous' demonstrations of support for Hua and denunciations of Deng totally failed to arouse mass enthusiasm. People on the streets paid no attention, or even turned their heads away, when trucks – with drummers, cymbalists, and red bunting with slogans – drove through the streets proclaiming support for the 'wise decisions' of the Party.

Throughout the summer of that year, Mao's health deteriorated visibly, documented by official pictures in the press and on TV. The Chairman was clearly not long for this world, and the country seemed to be biding its time in silence until his awesome authority would no longer stand in the way of the destruction of those who had usurped it for their own aims.

Mao died on 9 September, and just one month later Premier Hua and the military-bureaucratic group in the Politburo arrested Jiang Qing, Yao Wenyuan, Zhang Chunqiao, and the youthful Wang Hongwen, as well as Mao's cousin Mao Yuanxin, Mao's daughter Li Na, and others. Attempts to start an armed uprising in the name of Mao in Shanghai came to naught. Hua Guofeng was appointed to head the committee supervising the construction of Mao's mausoleum on Tiananmen Square and to edit the fifth volume of his *Collected Works* (which until then had gone no further than 1949).

Hua seemed to be the man of the hour, around whom the veteran army generals and experienced administrators had grouped themselves in opposition to Jiang Qing's attempts to make herself effectively head of the Party and State. The media were dominated for the next few months by lurid tales of her vanity, self-indulgence, extravagance and intriguing. It was claimed that she and Mao had not been living together for years, that he had warned her against political intrigue, and that she had tried to monopolize access to him and tamper with files in the Archive of the Central Committee. She was ridiculed in thousands of vicious cartoons, which showed her variously as a fox (the Chinese metaphor for an immoral woman), an empress, and a snake. She was accused of having forced peasants to cut down their trees so that she could take better landscape photographs, and of having made soldiers link arms in a cordon around her when she wanted to go swimming in the sea.

The accusations against Yao, Zhang, and Wang, by comparison, were less personal. Yao was ridiculed for his bald head and popping eyes and was accused of masterminding propaganda attacks on Party veterans. Zhang was said to have had a shady political past in Shanghai when he was a young man. Wang was derided for his vanity, self-indulgence, and attempts to create a paramilitary force to oppose the People's Liberation Army in the event of a coup d'état.

But with the gradual exhaustion of plausible accusations against the Gang, the leadership had to look to more solid means of legitimizing itself and putting China's house in order. Hua's position – never very strong because of his lack of an adequate power base – was bolstered by the publication of an oil painting showing the dying Mao handing over to him a slip of paper bearing the words, 'With you in charge, I am at ease.' In 1977, a Party Congress – the Eleventh – was called, and Deng Xiaoping was returned to his posts as Vice-Chairman, Vice-Premier, and Chief of the General Staff, while Hua retained the Premiership and the Chairmanship, as well as being Commander in Chief of the armed forces. Much speculation and debate surrounded the relative powers held by Deng and Hua, and a somewhat anaemic personality cult was built up around Hua, whose portrait now hung alongside Mao's in countless homes and offices. Chinese people, however, showed no enthusiasm for Hua, who was an unknown quantity, but instead gave clear evidence of their joy at the return to power of Deng.

Deng did not disappoint them. Paving the way with a series of long theoretical articles in the Party-controlled media, he began dismantling, stone by stone, the social system set up by Mao and his associates, in which political attitude and will were the true tests of leadership. The leftist economic policies were thoroughly discredited – an act which could only have the support of the mass of people who had seen virtually no improvement in their living standards in the past twelve years, and who were fed up with being given politics to eat, instead of food, and politics to wear, instead of clothes.

But it has not all been plain sailing for Deng. There is believed to have been strong opposition to his return to power in 1977, coming mainly from those leaders who feared he might exact revenge for the way he was treated in 1976. (Among those was allegedly Peking's Mayor Wu De, who had to take responsibility for the way in which the riots were suppressed and who was publicly vilified in the wall-poster campaign at Democracy Wall in late 1978 and replaced by Lin Hujia, a former mayor of Tientsin.)

The chief opponent of Deng, and the most dangerous, was General Wang Dongxing, commander of the 8341 Detachment, which guarded the leadership's Zhongnanhai residential complex in central Peking and which had in the past served as a kind of praetorian guard for Mao and his family and close associates. Wang was also in charge of the Party archives and thus to some extent a custodian of the secrets of the other leaders. As a turncoat who had backed the purge of the Gang, Wang attracted mistrust even from the right-moderate wing of the Politburo, headed by Deng. But his fatal mistake was to oppose Deng's anti-leftist political line from 1977 on, especially the thinly disguised onslaught on the cult of Mao and Mao's thought. Deng and his supporters clashed decisively with Wang at the Third Plenary Session of the Central Committee in late 1978, and from then on it was only a matter of time before Wang and the other remnant leftists on the Politburo were ousted.

The position of Chairman Hua Guofeng in all this manoeuvring was ambiguous from the start. As a provincial administrator in Mao's native province of Hunan (though himself a native of Shanxi province), Hua had early won the old Chairman's favour and from 1971 on spent more and more time in Peking, where he was made a Politburo member in 1973. In 1975 he was named Minister of Public Security and in January of the following year was appointed Acting Premier to succeed the deceased Zhou Enlai – a victory of the left-radical faction over Deng, who had seemed to be in line as the obvious successor to Zhou. When Deng was dismissed after the April riot, Hua was named Premier, but his relations with Jiang Qing and the other leftists deteriorated over the next six months to the point where, one month after Mao's death, he masterminded or went along with the scheme to overthrow the Gang of Four.

Although from Deng's point of view Hua ended up on the right side of the fence, he could not simply wipe out memories of his past close links with the left-radicals when they were dominant. His own political record marked him down as distinctly left-leaning. Hua retained the aura of an ideologist, but the mantle of Mao which had been laid on his shoulders was not necessarily an asset, as Deng's political programme gathered momentum. The hard-core leftists around Wang Dongxing would probably have been glad if Hua had thrown in his lot with them to oppose Deng and restore aspects of the leftist programme. But Hua – being one of the youngest leadership members (born about 1920) and a full sixteen years younger than Deng – was evidently not prepared to risk his future. While distancing himself somewhat from Deng's programme , he carefully avoided any appearance of conflict and appeared content to wait for a more stable period in order to make a bid for leadership.

By doing so, Hua played right into Deng's hands. The survivors of the last Mao politburo, with few exceptions, were disgraced and demoted, leaving Hua almost isolated. His main support apparently came from Marshal Ye Jianying, aged in 1980 eighty-two, and from some disgruntled army commanders who disliked the destruction of the Mao cult because it also tarnished their political image. Ye's functions were as close to those of a head of state as is possible in China, where the office was abolished with the downfall of Mao's most prestigious victim, the late Liu Shaoqi. In 1980 Hua had to resign his premiership to Deng's protégé Zhao Ziyang, a rehabilitated Cultural Revolution victim. While Deng and several other top leaders simultaneously renounced their vice-premierships, Hua was the main loser. Hu Yaobang, a Deng supporter, was named to the revived post of party secretary-general (held by Deng before he was ousted in 1966). In 1981 Hua was relieved of the party chairmanship and publicly though not vituperatively criticized for having tried to foster a personality cult for himself, and for having made errors in his political line (too leftist) and his practical work (impetuous and ill-judged). Hu Yaobang then became chairman, while Hua was humiliatingly demoted to the position of most junior vice-chairman.

Meanwhile another nail was being hammered into the coffin of Maoist leftism. Mao's widow Jiang Qing, together with Yao Wenyuan, Zhang Chunqiao, Wang Hongwen, Mao's former private secretary Chen Boda, and five military commanders including former chief of staff Huang Yongsheng and former air force commander Wu Faxian, were put on trial in Peking. They were accused of a variety of offences, including conspiracy to usurp power and (in the case of the military group formerly loyal to Lin Biao) to assassinate Mao.

Jiang Qing defended herself vigorously in the court, some of whose proceedings were televised, though much was never publicly disclosed about them. She tried to shout down the judges and prosecutors, sometimes saying she could remember nothing of the events cited, claiming poor hearing, and sometimes alleging that everything she did had Mao's support and approval.

Zhang Chunqiao uttered not a word from the reading out of the indictment to the passing of sentence on 23 January 1981. He and Jiang Qing were sentenced to death, the penalty to be suspended for two years to see whether they would 'repent'. The others drew long jail terms, shortened, however, by the nine years which Chen and the military conspirators had already spent in custody since their arrest shortly after Lin's death. The youthful Wang Hongwen, like most of the others, gave the court his full cooperation and confession, for which he was rewarded with a sentence of life imprisonment rather than death. Yao Wenyuan, who had stammered and babbled his way through the trial, was sentenced to twenty years.

Hated though Jiang Qing was, she drew some admiration for her defiance of the court, which she said had no right to try her. In the West, her case attracted the attention of militant feminists who denounced the trial as 'sexist' – somewhat ludicrous when one considers that nine of the ten defendants were men.

Though it exposed many of the crimes and inhuman acts committed during the Cultural Revolution in the name of political zeal, the trial was a sorry business when viewed in the light of the new legal code introduced a year earlier. The code specifically rejects the extraction of confessions to incriminate the accused person, but it was obvious that those of the accused who admitted all or nearly all the charges (i.e. all except Jiang and Zhang), were let off more lightly than they would otherwise have been. The pathetic, frail old men, their brains barely functioning after nine years' imprisonment and interrogation, shuffled out of the courtroom with a fair chance of being reunited with their families before they died.

The role of the defence was minimal, despite the guarantee in the legal code that prisoners 'have the right' to a proper defence. Defence counsel did hardly anything but make a short speech at the end of the proceedings relating to each defendant, acknowledging the justice of nearly all the charges, and pleading leniency on the grounds of their clients' good behaviour in court.

The trial left little doubt in anyone's mind that, apart from the alleged plot to assassinate him, Mao had been in command of the social and political upheavals of the Cultural Revolution, was well aware of what the Gang of Four were doing, and must bear at least heavy indirect responsibility for the many acts of cruelty it fostered. Hua Guofeng, at that time still chairman of the Party with Mao's explicit blessing, could only see his prestige and integrity tarnished since he was one of those who rose rapidly to power because of their willing collaboration in the Cultural Revolution. The trial reversed the verdict on the events of the Eleven Years – something about which Mao and his supporters had given clear warning and had tried energetically to avert. Leftism was on trial together with the ten accused, and the verdict was uncompromisingly thumbs-down.

The official balance sheet today alleges that 34,800 innocent people were murdered, forced to commit suicide or maltreated so severely that they died, while 729,511 innocent people were subjected to 'unwarranted persecution'.

Such a pedantic enumeration of the victims comes nowhere near describing the fear, misery, mental anguish, wrecked careers, suspension of independent thought, lack of material progress, and violation of the most private and personal areas of the lives of hundreds of millions of people throughout China. A leading Chinese sociologist, Professor Fei Xiaotong, summed up those years as 'a sea of blood and tears'.

One of the great bugbears of modern writing on China is the coining of terms to fit Chinese political categories. The Chinese, for example, have never accepted the word 'Maoist', referring instead to 'Mao Zedong Thought', which they define as Mao's adaptation of Marxism to suit Chinese conditions. They have, it is true, claimed universal validity for his Thought and have translated it into dozens of languages. But they have not, since the late 1960s, proclaimed it as the ideal system for other nations.

What Europeans and Americans mean by 'Maoism' is usually pretty plain: a far-left revolutionary radicalism, with elements of anarchism, non-Marxist stress on the importance of the peasantry, solidarity with developing countries against the 'two superpowers', extreme dogmatism based on theories whose validity would hardly stand the test of logical analysis, and a strain of revolutionary romanticism which came close to deifying Mao and proclaimed its own invincibility even against modern weapons of war. 'Maoism', as understood in the West, also aimed at social egalitarianism and frugality in the interests of unity and progress.

According to Mao's successors in the Chinese leadership, this extreme-left trend of thinking was not the dominant one but was a result of distortion and falsification by 'Lin Biao and the Gang of

Four'. Citing other writings of his – especially those contained in Volume V of the *Works* – they make him out to be a balanced and moderate thinker and still invoke his name as the authority for what they are doing in China today. This is not difficult, since Mao's thinking was often mercurial and seemingly contradictory, and he swung in different political directions during his long career.

The fatal weakness in the modern argument that Mao is the true originator of the present policy line is that it entails believing that Mao was either unable to read the *People's Daily* or was a prisoner of his own entourage, anyway since 1965 and arguably since 1958. It is totally implausible that a fit and active leader (who proved his good health by a long swim in the Yangzi in his mid seventies) could have let a small clique of people, including his wife, distort his policies to the extent that they actually reversed and sabotaged them.

So despite the claims of modern Chinese political theorists and some Western Marxists, I do not see how any reasonable person can believe that Mao's policies were usurped and perverted to the extent nowadays claimed. It is easy to believe that he was hoodwinked over minor matters and was not always in full control of the situation. But to cast doubt on Mao's approval of the entire set of policies associated with Chinese extreme-leftism seems to require an extraordinary degree of gullibility – or willingness to be persuaded.

The most frustrating thing about following Chinese politics is that the dominant movement at any one time represents itself in the light of high-minded determination to achieve prosperity and social justice; whereas, in retrospect, the Party historians reduce their political process to one of squalid intrigue and personal jealousy. Time and again Western analysts have been rebuked by the Chinese for reading too much personal and factional power struggle into the events of any particular period, yet when the next upset occurs and recent history is re-evaluated by the official media, it suddenly transpires that naked ambition and power struggle were what it was about after all.

This is disillusioning for Western radicals, who have tended to see in China the living proof that their ideas can work. A whole generation of Europeans and Americans have been influenced by the concept of a utopian China, where poverty is somehow or other not distasteful because it is noble, and where the personal freedoms which most people in the West take for granted may be denied to Chinese people, who somehow seem able to get along fine without them.

Leaving aside the question of whether this attitude does not contain a fair measure of quasi-racist condescension, it is dispiriting for China's admirers to be told every few years that the policies which seemed so hopeful and idealistic were actually just a cloak for the treacherous scheming of so-and-so. Party history has been rewritten so often that there is no more than a handful of veteran revolutionaries in China whose past deeds have not at some stage or other been vilified, chewed up by the propaganda machine, or passed over in silence.

The left-radical or Maoist vision of the politics of revolution and socialism is as pristine as the ideals of the early Christians. It proposes a society in which everybody – except a small handful of 'bad elements' – works selflessly and devotedly for the advancement of all. Laws, courts, political institutions and formal education become well nigh unnecessary in the glow of enthusiasm which suffuses the whole of society. The theories of one man and one school of thought become a substitute for nearly all other human philosophy, which is therefore banished from bookshops and libraries as unnecessary and potentially harmful. All work, art, music, dance, sport – indeed, all activities of mankind, from defecating to studying astronomy – become offerings of the individual to society and to the Leader, just as in the most pious forms of religion every act becomes an offering to the deity.

It can be objected that this is not socialism, which is classically defined as an economic condition in which everyone gives according to his or her ability and receives according to his or her work. Beyond this condition lies communism, in which people give to the limit of their ability and receive according to their 'needs', however *they* may be defined. The Maoist vision of socialism, at its most extreme, comes very close to the concept of communism – though in true communism there should be no need for the personality cult of a semi-divine leader.

This, indeed, is the snag in the Maoist social fabric. People are still earning widely differing incomes, from perhaps 300 yuan a year for a peasant to 4,000 yuan plus 'perks' for a high official. It has not proved possible to equalize incomes without destroying those differences of rank and privilege which (some would say) give a society structure and provide incentives for hard and productive work.

The tensions generated by the contradiction between the ideal

Maoist world and the world as it is – full of selfishness, inefficiency, crime, callousness, and stupidity – are given substance in the process called 'class struggle'.

To all intents and purposes, the old exploiting classes in China – capitalists and landlords – were destroyed or neutralized as social forces in the early post-revolutionary years. Can a person be considered a 'landlord' if he or she owns no land? Can someone be a 'capitalist' and 'bourgeois exploiter' without any capital or fixed assets and no chance of employing a labour force?

Maoism said yes, because landlordism and capitalism are, above all, states of mind. Even without land or capital, the reactionary forces in society will sabotage or slow down the progress through socialism to communism. Those forces are to be found at all levels, not only in society as a whole but even in the Communist Party itself, right up to the level of its top officials. Where old 'bourgeois' habits of thought have died out, new ones will be engendered, for an indefinite period in the future. Some will be the children of former 'bourgeois', who will carry on their traditions of shunning manual work and seeking personal comfort and ease. Others will be engendered from within the very bosom of the proletariat and the peasantry.

This almost Calvinist view of the endless possibilities for human vileness makes a strange contrast to the mood of revolutionary optimism which is supposed to fire the mass of the people under left-radical socialism. Out of it, sometimes, is engendered a form of dynamic energy which can work small miracles in terms of dams built, harvests saved, invasions repelled. But its life cycle is short, because most human beings are not capable of being *permanently* fired with optimistic enthusiasm about anything.

The disillusionment which follows the failure of a dynamic mass movement – like the Great Leap Forward or the Cultural Revolution – is fertile soil for the ideas which lie behind the kind of policies being promoted by Deng Xiaoping and his powerful group of supporters. These are essentially practical men, who know the value of revolutionary fervour – in the right place at the right time – but who also know the hopelessness of trying to dragoon ordinary human beings into unworkable utopias. Their concern is essentially the stable and successful running of a state machine, which makes them Leninists and Stalinists more than Marxists. They openly profess their admiration for Stalin – despite what they euphemistically call his 'excesses' – because he coped successfully with the problem of modernizing a large, backward country without benefit of foreign aid and showed how economic growth could be converted into national power and even invincibility. Those are attractive ideas for the Dengists, and if they reject the weapons of extreme terror and extermination which Stalin used, they will only see themselves as refining his methods with a characteristically Chinese subtlety. They may reason that China has had plenty of its own brand of political terror and need not go down that road again in the foreseeable future.

The crucial issue on which the Dengist statecraft may founder is its inability to cope with the problem of bureaucracy. Bureaucracy flourishes in any socialist society. One of the admirable aspects of the Cultural Revolution was its rebellion against bureaucracy and its attempt to run society directly through mass participation in government. The evils of Soviet-style bureaucracy – massive privileges for the ruling group, inability to cope with some of the simplest demands of the deprived masses (such as adequate food supplies) – are enough to drive any nation to the brink of counter-revolution. But China's entire historical tradition has been one of putting up with bureaucracy as a lesser evil than anarchy.

The Cultural Revolution showed that without bureaucratic institutions even the best-intentioned political movements turn into anarchy, strife and even civil war. To restore order, the leadership (such of it as has not been purged) has to call out the army, which imposes its own form of disciplinary bureaucracy without even having the specialized administrative skills used by civilian officialdom. A spell of anarchic revolt may be exhilarating for young people and may attack some fundamental faults of the socialist system, but in the long run it merely makes a nation more willing than before to put up with authoritarian rule – in the interests of stability and personal security.

This is one of the strongest assets of the Deng group's political platform: it stands above all for social order and discipline based on rational thinking. It rejects wild political theorizing or the violent mobilization of frustrated social forces (young people, indigent peasants) to produce change.

The big problem of the present-day bureaucracy in China is not that it has been restored to its former arrogance, but that its self-confidence has been so mightily shaken by the anti-bureaucratic currents of the Eleven Years that it has become nervous about taking bold decisions or telling people – with its previous high confidence – what they ought to be doing. In China, the phrase used to describe the attitude of bureaucrats who are afraid there may be another Cultural Revolution one day, and who therefore shrink from the leading role in society which they ought to be performing, is 'lingering fear'.

8. *Drugs and Dragon's Bones*

No area of Chinese-originated science has in recent times attracted more attention – or given Western specialists more surprises – than medicine.

The Chinese possess a unique, millennia-old medical science of great complexity. Though inferior to modern Western medicine in many respects, it can still produce astonishingly good results. And instead of discarding their ancient learning, Chinese doctors and researchers have begun a long study of the best ways to combine it with what has been learned from Europe and America.

It was only in the second half of the nineteenth century that Western medicine became widely used in China, mainly through the efforts of missionaries, for whom it was an obvious way to perform charitable acts and win converts. The huge improvements brought by anaesthetics, aseptic surgery and microbiology made possible unprecedented advances in public health – provided that the organizational framework could be built up. And Western medicines brought a growing number of chemical drugs which were unknown to the Chinese except sometimes in natural form, as the extracts of plants, animals, fish, birds, lizards, turtles, fossils of prehistoric creatures (known as 'dragon's bones') and products of the human body.

The reputation of Chinese traditional medicine suffered as a result of the new European and American techniques which could cure or prevent such killer diseases as malaria and measles. Western medicine became one of the most popular subjects for Chinese students to take up, either at mission-founded colleges and universities or overseas. By the middle of the twentieth century, Chinese medicine had sunk to its lowest point in the esteem of educated people, though many went on using it in the belief that it was less drastic and more suited to the Chinese physiology than the powerful new drugs with their tricky side effects. The common people, who had little access to Western medicine, also continued using the ancient remedies.

Medicine and hygiene were among the aspects of Western-style modernization which Communists and Nationalists alike considered to be an important part of the Chinese revolution. Satirizing traditional medicine, Lu Xun, the radical critic and author of the 1920s and 1930s, wrote a famous short story about a poor family which spends its savings on a piece of steamed bread soaked in the fresh blood of a beheaded criminal, as a cure for their child's tuberculosis (of course ineffective; the child in the story dies).

On coming to power, the Communist Party was faced with a grave shortage of Western-trained doctors. Some had fled to Taiwan with the Nationalists, or gone to America or Europe to practise, or decided not to return to China from abroad. Many of those who patriotically stayed on or returned were victimized in political upheavals – first in the 'anti-Rightist' campaign of 1957, then more severely during the Eleven Years, when they attracted the label of 'bourgeois experts'. Medical training programmes were badly disrupted by the Cultural Revolution, and hospital routine was sometimes wrecked by attempts to put doctors on an equal footing with nurses, orderlies and cleaners. Some doctors and specialists were persuaded or coerced into going to settle in the rural areas, where the shortage of equipment, drugs and up-to-date medical literature prevented them from using their training to the best effect. Others, idealistically accepting Mao's demand for greater attention to the needs of the peasantry, went voluntarily to work in the countryside.

Unable to meet the demand for fully qualified medical practitioners in the rural areas, the Party took the bold and imaginative step of introducing 'barefoot doctors' and encouraging specialists in traditional Chinese medicine to go on practising their craft and instructing young successors. When political conditions permitted, advanced research programmes were pursued in a number of spheres, especially the reattaching of severed limbs, and therapy and anaesthesia through acupuncture. Endemic diseases like schistosomiasis, or 'snail fever', were tackled through a combination of medical treatment, public health measures, and educating peasants. Extensive research on the properties of traditional herbal cures was carried out – with some impressive results – and a vigorous effort was made to provide better midwife services and mother-and-child care for peasants as well as city dwellers. The medical equipment industry was built up rapidly, so that only the more advanced devices had to be imported from abroad. Disease-carrying vermin, especially flies, were attacked in successive campaigns. Strong encouragement was given to factories and communes to set up their own medical insurance schemes.

Founded in the mid sixties, a year or two before the Cultural Revolution, the 'barefoot doctor' movement aimed to set up a large corps of lightly trained medical auxiliaries who could tramp the dykes and hillsides of their communes to educate the peasants in elementary hygiene and health care (moving latrines away from wells, for instance), besides treating minor ailments and referring more difficult cases to hospitals or clinics.

Two barefoot doctors – near-middle-aged women – whom I interviewed on a commune in Hebei province said they had originally been given three months' training at the county hospital, supplemented by another three months after they acquired some practical experience, and occasional refresher courses and briefings. They were trained mainly in first aid, hygiene and midwifery, and were given some theoretical lectures on acupuncture and other forms of Chinese medicine. But their knowledge of anatomy was sketchy. They had only one medical handbook between them. Their salary – paid by the production brigade on which they worked – was 40 yuan (US$22) a month, but there were moves afoot to cut their cash incomes and instead include them in the post-harvest division of grain and cooking oil among the peasants. Their 'surgery' was a room about three metres (11 feet) square, with a bare wooden couch, a desk, and an upright chair. Consulting hours were between 8 and 11 a.m. and 4 till 6 p.m., and they also made house calls and routine rounds.

Equipment in the 'surgery' consisted of about a dozen hypodermic needles, a stethoscope, a few thermometers, a sphygmomanometer, and – for midwifery – rubber gloves, forceps and a speculum. The medicine chest contained throat lozenges, vitamin tablets, glucose, cough syrup, aspirin and liver-extract capsules. They could buy penicillin, aureomycin, tranquillizers, sleeping pills and other commonly used drugs from the commune clinic, and they were reimbursed with funds from the brigade's collective medical insurance plan. The annual budget for drugs was put at about 125 yuan (US$69) for a brigade of some 800 people. Patients who needed prolonged courses of drug treatment, and who could afford to pay, were expected to foot their own bill. Contraceptives were distributed free.

Severe cases which the barefoot doctors could not handle were taken to the clinic or county hospital by truck, horse-drawn cart or bicycle cart. The more remote villages were over an hour's journey from the clinic. There was no ambulance service.

Asked about the incidence of diseases, one of the women said the ailments most commonly encountered were colds, influenza, arthritis, ulcers and rheumatism; sometimes arteriosclerosis, tuberculosis and cirrhosis; as well as endemic diseases like meningitis and hygiene-related afflictions such as gastroenteritis, dysentery and hepatitis. Asked how many people died of cancer, they said, 'None.' I got the impression that this meant cancer in an elderly person was regarded as 'death from natural causes' and would not be treated if there seemed to be no chance of an easy cure.

The barefoot doctor system has been widely admired by foreign visitors, especially those with experience in other underdeveloped countries. However, despite the near-miraculous results ascribed to it during the Eleven Years, it is only a stopgap measure providing elementary services on the basis that 'half a loaf is better than none'. It is also an economy measure designed to intercept patients with minor ailments who would otherwise be wasting the time of qualified doctors at the commune or county level.

Deng Xiaoping is reputed to have criticized the system by saying there must come a time when the barefoot doctors will 'put on straw sandals, and later rubber shoes'. Deng was not, of course, referring to the doctors' footwear (few of them actually go barefoot) but to the standard of their training and qualifications. It may be better to fall ill in a Chinese village than in an Indian or African village, but few people from developed countries would care to have even a minor operation in a Chinese commune clinic, where the dirty floor and walls rule out fully aseptic surgery, and the overall standards of cleanliness and maintenance of equipment – even to a layman's eye – leave a lot to be desired.

The unwillingness of qualified doctors to work in the rural areas is a longstanding problem which it has proved impossible to solve. A country practice in China is not the cosy, sociable position it may be in Europe or America. It is a long – sometimes lifelong – exile to crude living and working conditions, lack of medical literature and new equipment, shortage of drugs, and semi-literate, superstitious peasants for neighbours and friends. Obviously, it takes a great deal of dedication or Party pressure to make a doctor pass up the chance of using modern equipment and having access to the latest technical information in a big-city hospital somewhere, to say nothing of more comfortable living conditions and better food.

Doctors' salaries in big-city hospitals vary widely, from about 55 to 240 yuan (US$31 to $133) monthly, depending on their seniority and degree of specialization. Accommodation for a young married doctor usually consists of a tiny apartment of about 15 square metres (10 by 16 feet) at a monthly rent of 2 yuan (US$1.11), with charges for water, gas, and electricity of about the same amount. Grain rations are low – 15 kg (33 pounds) monthly per person – on the grounds that doctors do not usually do hard physical work. Other rations include 200 gm (7 ounces) of cooking oil per month, and half a kilo (about 1 pound) of sugar for each family. In common with most hospital employees, doctors receive free medical treatment – a perk of the job.

There is heavy pressure on hospital beds, of which there are little more than 1 per 10,000 people, even in the big cities. Inexplicably, there is a high ratio of doctors to beds, and doctors to nurses. Admission charge is usually about 1 yuan (55 US cents), and the charge for a non-specialist operation only about 3 yuan (US$1.66). Meals cost 0.50 to 0.60 yuan per day (28 to 33 US cents), but food is usually brought in by relatives. An abortion costs 2 yuan (US$1.11) but may be given free to a peasant woman.

In specialist hospitals, charges are higher and the cost of an operation may reach 80 yuan (US$44), with blood for transfusions being bought from the general public at a fee of 15 yuan (US$8) per 100 cc, the high price suggesting difficulty in persuading people to donate.

In most cases, a worker's stay in hospital will be heavily subsidized or paid for entirely by the insurance fund at his or her place of work, but the fund may only meet half the costs of hospitalization of a worker's dependant, the remainder being deducted from the pay envelope.

Funding systems are the key to China's relative success in medical planning. Instead of the government's providing free medical services for everyone, or imposing a nationwide medical insurance plan, individual work units have been persuaded to set up their own joint funding programmes. These vary greatly from place to place, but the general principle is the same: all who can afford it make a small annual or monthly contribution, and the factory or other work unit matches this out of its profits.

The amount of insurance is enough to see a person through a routine operation and one or two weeks' hospitalization, but beyond that the financial burden on the patient's family may become quite severe, especially if expensive drugs are involved. There is no standard benefit for disabled people, whose best hope is to be put to work in a factory or service unit designed for them – for example, blind people are trained as masseurs. 'Temporary workers' – peasants or young people who are taken on to help with a particular job or on a seasonal basis – have no access to the medical insurance fund and may have to pay all their own costs if they fall ill.

In the communes, the amount of medical insurance provided varies according to the prosperity and community spirit of the peasants in any particular team or brigade. Some brigades have no funds at all. Serious diseases will sometimes be treated free or with a subsidy by the county hospital if the peasant clearly cannot afford to pay, but this is not a systematized service. Every effort is made to return a patient to his or her family for care as soon as possible, thus freeing the bed for someone else.

Medicine in China is less socialized than in Britain or some other European countries where all available treatment is provided free of charge, except for the individual's contribution to national insurance. The standard of comfort, availability of hospital beds, and supply of drugs are much better in Western Europe than in China. Nonetheless, the Chinese system works well by comparison with many developing countries, where extremes of luxurious private care contrast with near-zero services in poor areas, and great economies have been made possible by the use of traditional herbal medicines and the invention of acupuncture anaesthesia, which although only partially effective costs no more than the price of a few needles and often a low-voltage electric current.

People in the West are mostly quite prepared to believe that some ancient Chinese herbal remedies may be as good as – or better than – modern synthesized drugs. But the idea that pain can be relieved and diseases treated with plain needles stuck into unlikely parts of the body still baffles us, and Chinese doctors and scientists are almost equally astonished by some of the results they have achieved. Still harder to believe in is treatment by moxibustion – burning the powdered root of the artemisia plant on or near the skin of a sick person – a technique which most Western doctors would reject as being no more scientific or beneficial than the former European practice of bleeding the patient.

Despite scepticism and exaggerated claims, there is by now general agreement among Chinese doctors – and amid a growing number of Western doctors – that acupuncture, in China at least, as well as being an effective cure for many ailments, is amazingly effective as a form of anaesthesia. The use of acupuncture therapy has become common enough in the West. But as an English surgeon said in Hong Kong, 'Even if I were prepared to try acupuncture anaesthesia on a European, I'd have a hard time finding anyone brave enough to be the guinea pig.' In 1980 two surgeons in Shanghai were permitted to publish a denunciation of the excessive use of acupuncture for anaesthesia. They said it was often only the 'sheer heroism' of some patients which made the operations attended by foreign doctors and other visitors successful.

There seems to be a good deal of psychological conditioning involved in acupuncture anaesthesia. About half a million operations are carried out annually in China with no other form of anaesthetics, and one benefit is said to be the patient's quick recovery and the lack of side-effects which may result from chemical methods. Western doctors have by now witnessed enough of these operations to confess themselves convinced of the efficacy of needling, if still baffled as to how it works. They have also reported that the anaesthesia is not total and may be quite ineffective for operations on some vital organs.

Some experts suggest that intense political indoctrination helps the patient ignore pain with the aid of numbing needles. But the former Mao cult has now been all but abolished, and political indoctrination has sunk to a low level of intensity compared with past years, yet acupuncture anaesthesia still works even in brain surgery, with the patient able to talk to the surgeons, guide them as to his or her sensations, drink tea or eat fruit while under the knife, and sometimes even walk unaided from the operating theatre.

Some Chinese doctors and researchers are embarrassed by the fact that this technique of proven efficiency is based on a theoretical system which bears all the hallmarks of superstition and proto-scientific speculation. Researchers either incline to the view that acupuncture is a hitherto unknown aspect of neurophysiology (and obviously has to do with the nervous system as understood in the West) or they accept the basic theories behind it, which are quite unprovable and even nonsensical in Western medical theory.

Some ancient Chinese ideas – such as the opposite male/female forces of *yang* and *yin*, or the concept of life as a form of energy in constant motion – look less unscientific today than they did fifty years ago. And the idea of the bodily organs as mere aspects of various functions, rather than the other way around, has its attractions. Nor is there any great objection to the Chinese view that medicine is a unity, in which acupuncture is only one form of treatment among the many. (The use of acupuncture for anaesthesia is a new science, for traditional Chinese medicine generally shunned surgery and was vague about anatomy.)

But how is the Western doctor to swallow a theory which ignores the existence of viruses and bacteria and links bodily functions in mystical associations with astrological concepts and primitive theories about the 'five elements' of wood, fire, earth, water and metal; a theory which has nothing to say about blood groups, brain chemistry, or the structure of cells, and which claims that the number of bones and joints in the body is equivalent to the number of days in a year? To place oneself in the realm of a theory like this means simply discarding everything previously learned about Western scientific method.

One of the most controversial aspects of Chinese medical research today is the question as to whether the 'meridians', or energy channels which are supposed to link the hundreds of prescribed acupuncture points in the body, actually exist, or whether they are just a convenient way of memorizing the points at which the needles should go in. But without the meridian theory, it is difficult to explain the effect of acupuncture in producing anaesthesia or therapy in some far-removed part of the body: for instance, placing needles in the arm and knee to treat a stomach ulcer.

Nor is it easy for any Western-trained doctor to concede that the most reliable method of diagnosis – as traditional Chinese doctors believe – is to feel the patient's pulse for anything up to three hours at a time. Or that gold and silver needles produce opposite effects (stainless-steel needles being conveniently dismissed as 'neutral').

I have personally had only one experience of acupuncture, and it was bad. I went to one of the best-known specialists in Hong Kong to obtain relief from the pain of a crushed finger. He prescribed a course of needling in the fleshy part of the hand at the base of the thumb lasting for about twenty minutes at a time, at a cost of US$20 per treatment. He did not X-ray the finger, which was later found to contain bone fragments and even a piece of leftover suture. The treatment produced a mildly pleasant warm feeling (electric currents pulsed through the needles, making the hand twitch rhythmically). It gave no significant relief, however, and a British surgeon told me later that nerve damage could spread down the entire hand if the finger joint was not amputated.

Conversely, I have had limited but encouraging experience of Chinese herbal medicines, including a highly effective lozenge for the relief of bronchial congestion (made on a base of mashed toad).

Sometimes the claims made for herbal and other 'natural' remedies in Chinese medicine seem extravagant, as in the literature accompanying a soluble extract of the flowers of the *tianqi* plant (*Radix pseudo ginseng*):

> This product ... can prevent, alleviate, or cure the following diseases: (1) facial pimples of puberty, boils, blisters around the mouth, etc.; (2) dizziness, nausea, vomiting, headache, palpitation, insomnia, emotional inquietude, etc., induced by hypertension; (3) heat on the palms, hot temper, grinding of the teeth during sleep, etc., caused by biliousness of the liver.

Most Chinese medicine comes in the form of pills – of which huge quantities have to be swallowed, sometimes thirty or forty a day – or infusions of herbs and other plants. Sometimes its alleged curative effects are based on similarities between the ailment and the medicine: for instance, deer foetus – and even human foetus – for gynaecological complaints.

It will be decades before research identifies and evaluates all the curative properties of traditional Chinese medicine. In the meanwhile, it has proved an admirable supplement to Western medicine – not least, perhaps, because most people in China have implicit faith in its efficacy.

9.   *The Responsible Comrades*

The Chinese are and always have been deeply concerned about the problems of day-to-day government and the people who carry it out. Their earliest written records are of acts of divination by priests, aimed at helping the ruler to decide on the most auspicious course of action at any time. Centuries before Christ, ancient Chinese thinkers were debating the problem of finding capable people to run affairs of state. With almost unbroken continuity, this debate has been handed down to the rulers and administrators of twentieth-century China.

The stereotyped image of a bad official in modern China is that of a middle-aged man wearing a tunic whose superior cut and fabric distinguish him from the workers. He carries a pen or two in his top pocket – the more pens, the more senior he probably is. He smokes one of the better brands of Chinese cigarettes; the sign of real vanity is to hold the cigarette between the index and middle fingers and point it up in the air when puffing on it, somewhat in the posture of a person about to throw a kiss, while holding the other hand behind the back. He drinks endless cups of tea and has crocheted antimacassars on the furniture in his office. He talks in political jargon and is incompetent at solving practical problems. He considers it a virtue not to know about technical subjects.

This stereotype – as held up to scorn in the Chinese media – is deceitful and cowardly, toadies to his superiors while bullying his inferiors, and angrily denounces any opposition to his own policies as 'opposition to the Party'. He is corrupt, thinking nothing of pulling strings to get his children into a university or obtain some other privilege. He spends much of his day shouting into the telephone or attending largely meaningless meetings with others of his kind. He squanders public funds on lavish feasts on the pretext of entertaining official visitors. He may even divert labour and materials to build himself a new house. He is always listening to the slightest murmurings of the political wind, ready to change course as soon as he feels it is the safest thing to do. He will not stand up for his principles, because he has none. He has several children – ignoring the national birth-control programme – and exacts sexual favours from women in return for influence-peddling. He will think nothing of having someone locked up indefinitely without trial, if he can find a pretext. He refuses to see members of the public who wish to complain about this or that, and he does not deal personally with letters or petitions.

The good official – as portrayed in China – is the opposite of this character in every way. He dresses plainly, so that he may even be taken for a worker, and does not mind wearing patched clothes. He keeps fit with a private exercise campaign, as well as taking part in group calisthenics, and at least tries to give up or cut down smoking. He drinks hot water without tea leaves and uses only the plainest wooden furniture in his office. He does not go on endlessly about politics (which has assumed the dimensions of a national disease in China), and he makes persistent efforts to master the technological side of the work he is supervising. He courageously criticizes his superiors when they need to be criticized and humbly listens to criticism from his subordinates. He never pulls strings or accepts bribes for private gain. He tries to reduce and shorten the number of time-wasting meetings called by his colleagues. He passes up the chance of better accommodation so that someone else may get a comfortable house or apartment before him. He takes a stand of principle on national and political matters (the hardest thing of all, since the definition of right principle changes in China almost from year to year). He marries around the age of thirty, has only one child, and is never unfaithful to his wife. He hesitates to use strong-arm methods or call on the local police to deal with bad elements in society, preferring to try to persuade them to see the error of their ways. He is constantly working long hours to receive visits and read letters from members of the public.

The average Chinese official – or 'cadre' – falls somewhere between these two extremes.

Anyone in China who does not do manual work, but rather exercises a profession or administers others, is called a 'cadre' (*ganbu*). This is different from the use of the word in other countries. Originally a term for the administrative staff ('framework') of French army regiments in the nineteenth century, it was taken over by the Soviet Union and is now used rather vaguely in Russian just to mean 'employees'. During periods of active revolution in some countries, it has been almost synonymous with Party member. But in China a cadre is not necessarily a Party member, and not all Party members are cadres. The simplest way to think about it is as a term for those who are called 'white-collar workers' in English – whether in China their collars are white or not.

That is the broadest sense of the word 'cadre' in China, but it also carries the connotation of seniority and authority – people who tell others what to do. Mere intellectuals, unless they also wielded administrative power, were for years dismissively referred to as the 'stinking ninth category' – an extension of the eight 'bad elements' in society: 'renegades, spies, people following the capitalist road, landlords, rich peasants, counter-revolutionaries, bad elements and rightists'.

The Chinese love discussing contemporary affairs by allusion to their national history, especially when the topic for discussion is as historically obsessive for them as is the question of bureaucracy and bureaucrats.

The founding of the imperial system in 221 B.C. led to the formation of a class of administrative officials who in later centuries were recruited by written examinations stressing literary talent and scholarship. Entrusted with the government of localities, regions, or whole provinces, these officials were rarely paid enough by the imperial court to enable them to maintain themselves in the style which their office demanded, so they financed themselves through levies, taxes, and bribes paid by the general public. This was thought quite normal and correct, and only if an official was too greedy in his exactions, or too cruel in his means of enforcing them, could he be reprimanded, demoted, or even executed on orders from the imperial court.

The multiple role of the official – as scholar, magistrate, administrator, and tax collector – has led to a peculiar ambiguity in the traditional Chinese attitude to the bureaucracy and its minions: the petty officers of the magistracy, who acted as a kind of police force in imperial times, were often heartily despised, but their authority was grudgingly recognized. The official at the top of the local administration generally commanded respect because he was by definition a scholar, and scholarship commands deep reverence in China – to the extent that it used to be thought unlucky to use printed or written-on paper for such purposes as wrapping parcels or lighting fires. The common term for the official was *lao ye*, 'old grandfather', signifying respect and sometimes affection. Since he acted as magistrate, he spoke for the law and the emperor, which enhanced the awe in which he was held. China has many tales of upright and just officials who unmasked villains and bullies and protected the weak and the poor.

Significantly, it was exactly over this issue – whether an imperial official could have been just and honest – that the first big literary debate of the Cultural Revolution took place in 1966.

Wu Han, deputy mayor of Peking and an author of some repute, penned a play entitled *The Dismissal of Hai Jui*, which dealt with the disgrace of an upright official by an emperor of the Ming dynasty (A.D. 1368–1644). The propaganda group around Mao fiercely attacked this play because it was thought to allegorize Mao's dismissal of Defence Minister Peng Dehuai, who had had the temerity to criticize the leftist Great Leap Forward in 1959. The grounds cited for the attack on the play, however, were that it suggested that 'feudal' officials could ever have acted in the interests of the common people. Marxist theory suggests that they could not, because they were prisoners of their own class background, and all seemingly benevolent acts were only calculated to soothe the anger of the masses and put off the day of revolution.

In the late 1970s the Party again turned to the history of the Ming dynasty to find an exemplary ruler who cut down on bureaucratic graft and privilege. The emperor Tai Zong, who founded the dynasty, distinguished his reign by measures aimed at wiping out the corruption and petty tyranny exercised by Chinese officials under the Mongol-dominated Yuan dynasty, which the Ming forces had overthrown. Tai Zong had a list of capital offences drawn up; it included the formation of cliques, flattery of high-ranking officials, going outside the city limits to welcome or see off a visiting dignitary, taking bribes, bearing false witness, and misappropriating grain. As is the practice in modern China, the gravity of the offence was measured by the amount of damage caused: a small bribe or misappropriation might be punished by a severe beating, whereas derelictions involving large sums would be punished by beheading. Some offenders were flayed after execution, and their skins stuffed with straw and put up in the offices of other officials, to serve as constant reminders.

With their victory in 1949, the Communists faced the same problem as Tai Zong: they had to set up an administrative structure of honest officials. Many of the experienced officials of the Republican period had fled with Chiang Kai-shek to Taiwan. Lower officials who had served the Kuomintang were thought unreliable, potentially traitorous. So the Communist Party established its own bureaucracy, based first on military commissars and officers from its own armed forces – many of whom turned civilian for this purpose – and, later, on straight civilians who had proved their loyalty and reliability.

For the mass of the people, this was substituting one bureaucracy for another. While the Party proclaimed the ideal of selfless service for its bureaucrats, it also called on them ruthlessly to suppress any signs of hostility towards its own rule – so that local Party officials throughout China were given the power of life and death over former landlords, 'rich peasants', or others regarded as exploiters, counter-revolutionaries, or spies.

When the first big wave of mob trials and drumhead executions in the early 1950s was over, China was once more in the hands of officials who believed that their credentials to govern were unquestionable, by virtue of their adherence to the Party – people who had tasted the absolute power of 'the dictatorship of the proletariat' and had become intolerant of criticism and increasingly inflexible in their methods of government. Over the next decade and more they became increasingly cliquish and dictatorial.

To some degree, this was what the Cultural Revolution was all about. To the extent that it was a spontaneous movement (and the degree of spontaneity is open to many qualifications, for it was also greatly manipulated from above), it was aimed at overthrowing and humiliating those cadres who had thrown their weight around too heavily in the past and who were now made to pay for it with curses and blows and humiliating 'criticism' rallies. It was also aimed at the intelligentsia, which traditionally in China has seen itself as the real elite. Lacking actual power to defend themselves, the country's teachers, scientists, doctors, artists, musicians, writers and others fared the worst in the early stages of the Cultural Revolution in 1966–7, especially those who had already been labelled 'rightists' for having had the audacity to respond to the Party's request for frank criticism in 1957. As well as being subjected to mass 'struggle' sessions, at which they were abused and pushed around sometimes for hours on end, many of them were obliged to do menial labour or were locked up.

Local Party and government officials, by contrast, still had their lines of communication with the Public Security (police) organs and the local army garrison. Though this did not save all of them from the Red Guard fury, many were able to keep their positions long enough to learn how to manipulate the rampaging youth groups and sit out the storm until the Army was called in to restore order in 1967. The problems of entrenched bureaucracy were in fact never solved by the anarchistic Cultural Revolution; all that was accomplished was that the bureaucrats became more devious in their methods of hanging on to power. With the gradual rebuilding of the authority of the Party and the government in the early 1970s, the bureaucrats became once again more self-confident – though still wary of being denounced as 'revisionists'. The same wariness persists today.

One of the most harmful tendencies among the cadres has been the formation of cliques, or factions. In the unstable political climate of China, the ostensible cause of this is the need to belong to some group which can agree on its policies and show a united front to resist criticism or erosion of its authority. But the urge toward factionalism probably goes deeper and is rooted in the traditional Chinese need to belong to a secure group – previously the enlarged family but now, with the gradual breakdown of the family system, a kind of artificial family made up of like-minded people at one's place of work. A provincial Party committee has defined factionalism in the following way: 'Not hesitating to create rumours and slanders, and reverse right and wrong and black and white for the sake of private interests, and the needs of one's own faction; if there is something to say, saying it to the faction instead of to the Party, and relying on one's "mountain stronghold" instead of the organization to solve any problem which arises; making use of each other, eating and drinking excessively, exchanging flattery and favours, and regarding the department or unit for which one is responsible as an independent kingdom.'

A typical abuse of a cadre's official position is to make it an excuse for setting up a sumptuous meal in a restaurant under the guise of holding a conference. A report prepared by the Party in the big north-western city of Lanzhou in 1979 praised local cadres for having cut down on their official entertaining – but disclosed that out of four meetings held in the recent past, one had still taken place in a restau-rant and had lasted two to three days! Singled out for praise were cadres who had come some distance to attend but who ate plain meals at the local government hostel, rather than discussing official business over dinner. This reduced the cost of each meeting by 200 to 300 yuan (US$111 to $166).

An important aspect of the cadres' work is to receive visits from members of the public and read letters from them complaining about this or that. As Wan Li, former First Secretary of the Anhui Provin-cial Party Committee, told his cadres, 'You are political weather stations. You must analyse the political situation and political climate and temper yourselves from the people's letters and visits.'

An especially bad habit of the cadres is to seek revenge against people who criticize them, rather than examining the criticism to see whether it is merited. This is called 'using a microscope on one's own faults, and a magnifying glass on those of others'.

An important dividing line between good and bad officials – in the Chinese view – is their willingness to hear criticism from any quarter and give it serious consideration. The bad cadre angrily rejects criti-cism and may try to retaliate with extralegal methods of persecution against the person who voiced it. A colourful modern metaphor for cadres of this type is that their faults are like 'the scabs on Ah Q's head'. Ah Q is an imaginary character in a brilliant story by the 1930s author and critic Lu Xun, a great favourite of the Chinese Com-munists because of the political support he gave them when their for-tunes were at a low ebb. Ah Q is a semi-moronic down-and-outer, full of absurdly pretentious ideas about himself: Lu Xun used him as a symbol of Republican China (1912–49), which was indeed a sorry mess. Ah Q's head was covered with sores caused by parasites, but he was so vain that he forbade anyone to mention them in his presence and would fly into a rage if they did.

For all their failings, the cadres are essential to the functioning of the Chinese economy and social system, and concentrating attention on some of their recurrent faults should not obscure the fact that a good number of them try honestly to do a good job, communicate with the general public, and build China up into a strong and prosperous country. Many have suffered quite severely for their political 'sins' or small self-indulgences, and while continuing to berate them for lethargy and pleasure-seeking, the Party leadership has also stated firmly that 'the policy on cadres must be implemented'.

This is a characteristically vague Chinese phrase denoting a very specific act: the reinstatement of cadres who suffered injustice or were wrongly demoted in the Eleven Years. In common parlance, to 'implement the policy' means to rehabilitate officials who were disgraced and to remove shameful tags from them.

Whereas in the West the typical fault of a governmental official is to 'pass the buck', in modern China it is a sort of inspired inaction in which decisions are postponed from month to month on the grounds that further 'examination' is necessary. Foreigners in Peking have endless anecdotes about the lethargy of the government departments with which they have to deal, whether to have a washing machine installed in their flat or to arrange the details for the visit of a VIP. As long as the Chinese side has not made up its mind fully and is not prepared to act decisively, there is an exasperating series of such clichés as *kaolü kaolü* ('We're looking into it') or *bu da fangbian* ('It's not very convenient').

Another technique of bureaucratic delay is to invent regulations out of thin air. During the 1970s, very few Chinese government regulations, and hardly any laws, were published and available to the general public, still less to foreigners; the main ones available were the Marriage Law and the Peking City Traffic Code. Whenever foreigners wanted to do something not covered by either of these pieces of legislation, they would be told it had to be done in this or that way – *anzhao womendi guilü* ('according to our regulations'). Embassies setting themselves up in Peking unreflectingly sign a document agreeing to adhere to the regulations of the Diplomatic Service Bureau'. But since no foreigner has ever seen these regulations, what it comes down to is a test of wills with the host organization. Usually the latter wins – for instance, in claiming massive charges for rewiring a newly built embassy, in which the original wiring installed by the Chinese technicians was quite inadequate for the air-conditioning load in the summer months, and in demanding double payment for the construction of a swimming pool, on the grounds that it may have to be filled in again later!

Just the same, when Chinese cadres decide to take rapid action, they can move at astonishing speed, and their system sometimes shows an unexpected degree of vitality and resilience. The Chinese are excellent at rising to occasions – for instance, in building the Mao Mausoleum in a mere eight months, or in ignoring their own bureaucratic procedures in an effort to get some major project off the ground fast.

What irritates most foreigners is the Chinese unwillingness to give a straight no in answer to an impractical or unwelcome request. Instead, it is *fuza* ('complicated'), or 'the responsible comrades are busy at the moment', or 'perhaps there is some problem about this'. But the desire to evade direct refusal is a cultural trait rooted in traditional Chinese ideas of courtesy and is found in many other countries as well. Foreigners should adjust their thinking to the Chinese attitude on this, instead of taking offence unnecessarily.

Cadres are also reluctant to discuss their private lives. I remember one occasion in Peking when a mild-mannered, rather shy cadre from the Foreign Ministry was sitting at the Western journalists' table during a banquet in the Great Hall of the People. He had let it slip that he had just got married, and because we rather liked him, we all jumped in to ask where his wife was working, whether they had known each other for a long time, where they had held the wedding ceremony, and so on. The bashful cadre showed mounting signs of panic at these well-meant questions and gave increasingly vague answers, until one of us asked him, 'Where is your wife from?' and he mumbled desperately, 'I don't know!'

That, however, was in the bad old days during the anti-Confucius campaign of 1973–6, when to be too close to foreigners was definitely not good for a cadre's career. Now one can sometimes forge more intimate personal relations with Chinese officials – but many underlying inhibitions are still there.

A big problem of the Chinese administrative hierarchy is that a generation gap tinged with bitterness sets apart those cadres who were attacked or thrown out of office – and even into prison – during the Cultural Revolution and only began drifting back slowly from 1972 on, with the trickle becoming a flood tide in 1977–9, after Mao's death.

These older officials feel they stood by their principles in the

Cultural Revolution (though in fact they may just have been trying to stay in office) and have now been vindicated, or – as the Chinese put it – 'made as bright as snow'. They have returned to jobs equivalent to or senior to their previous positions and taken control of cadres who ran the show in their absence – people who survived the Cultural Revolution because they were politically wily or received so-called 'helicopter' promotions, youngish cadres who succeeded in establishing themselves as true-red leftists and were thus given advancement ahead of the normal seniority system. Obviously, lingering enmities, desire for revenge, and a sense of 'we are the masters now' must afflict all but the most charitable of the returning cadres, their hands blistered from work in labour camps or on communes and many of them made extra grouchy by rheumatism, arthritis, stomach ulcers or other health problems resulting from their harsh treatment. Whatever lessons about humility they may have learned at the hands of the Red Guards, the temptation to revert to old rigid and disciplinarian methods of work is strong. This is a problem that will affect the Chinese cadre system for years to come, and it certainly militates against bold thinking and efficient work-style in the administrative pyramid.

Deng Xiaoping recognized this problem in the period after Mao's death, when he called on cadres to 'let the past be past, so that everyone can look to the future'.

Despite Mao's attempt to bring about modest and frugal habits among cadres and to reduce pompous titles, the addiction of officials to high-sounding ranks soon reasserted itself; in 1980 cadres had to be forbidden to call each other by any title except 'comrade'. Another complaint – as I was told by an unusually frank Chinese official in Peking – is that senior cadres often cannot be persuaded to retire, and they go on hogging jobs which would be done better by younger and more vigorous people.

Unwillingness to admit errors has also been blamed by the Chinese media for inefficiency in the bureaucracy. 'For example,' to quote the *People's Daily*, 'some comrades know that certain instructions or measures are inappropriate and impractical. But they refuse to make corrections, because these instructions or measures have been drawn up by them or under their guidance. They think that making corrections means climbing down themselves, losing face and impairing their prestige.'

After beaureaucratic rigidity, one of the main problems of the cadres is corruption. It is impossible to estimate just how widespread it is, by comparison with corruption in other countries and social systems. What can be said with certainty is that it is regarded nowadays as a problem of the first importance and is given extensive treatment in the official media.

One of the most severe recent cases was that of a woman called Wang Shouxin in the north-eastern province of Heilongjiang, who was said to have amassed a personal fortune of half a million yuan (over US$275,000) and to have lived luxuriously on it. Wang, formerly a cashier in a coal company, rose to prominence through political guile in the Cultural Revolution and became the uncrowned queen of the province's commercial affairs, throwing extravagant feasts with the excuse of 'sampling products' and providing herself and her friends with high-quality clothing for 'test wearing'. She was so influential that county-level First Secretaries used to meet her and see her off at Harbin Airport when she went on trips around China. She was tried and shot in 1980.

Giving lavish banquets is one of the most common forms of misappropriation of public funds – something like businessmen's expense-account lunches in the West, but viewed as near-criminal in China if it can be proved that the entertainment was excessive. After all, most Chinese have only just enough to eat. An official in the province of Jilin was accused of having spent 26,000 yuan (over US$14,000) in state funds during a mere twenty days of entertaining export corporation officials who were looking for saleable goods. The official, a deputy director of the province's foreign trade bureau, laid on what were described as 'sumptuous feasts', including a whole ton of famous Chinese wines (which are measured by weight), 60,000 of the best cigarettes and 12 kg (26½ pounds) of top-quality tea. When the case was exposed, indignant members of the public were quoted as protesting that the money thus squandered was equivalent to one month's entire earnings for 500 workers, or a whole year's earnings for 100 able-bodied peasants.

Military officers have been guilty of similar self-indulgence, and the most casual observer in any Chinese city, railway station, or airport can see that the armed forces are a privileged group enjoying benefits and facilities superior to those of the general public. For security reasons, cases involving corruption in the military are less often publicly described than those in the civilian sector. But one such case was reported from the south-western military region of Kunming, where an army commissars' conference disclosed that officers in the local command had been buying up more food than they were entitled to, illicitly improving their houses and neglecting to pay rent, using army cars for their private purposes, receiving gifts, seeking special treatment, soliciting good jobs and university places for their children, relatives, and friends, employing unauthorized servants, shirking labour tasks, and using public funds to give banquets and offer gifts.

Bureaucratic work-style is under heavy attack from the Communist Party leadership. The *People's Daily* says in a commentary, 'Their [the cadres'] usual methods are that when more views [i.e. criticism] have been expressed by the masses, they will hold a meeting and the leading comrade will make a speech. After a time, they will hold another meeting, and the leading comrade will make another speech. This goes on year after year. What about the problem? It is left intact, or very little is done ... According to their customs, the method suitable for management is to make a speech. Whether or not the problem is solved has nothing whatsoever to do with leadership.'

Misguided zeal on the part of local officials is also condemned. During the Cultural Revolution in the late 1960s, Mao once casually dropped the remark, 'There is coal in my home village' (Shaoshan, in Hunan province). This inspired the local authorities to open a mine, under difficult geological conditions and despite flooding which put it out of action for six months at a time. The mine ran completely at a loss, but it was not until 1978 that the authorities finally got around to closing it.

In a similar though less drastic incident, after Mao's successor, Chairman Hua Guofeng, visited a piggery on a commune, one of the local activists collected up all the items he had used during his stay and then wrote to Hua, proposing to set them up as a shrine-like museum. Hua had him reprimanded, despite his own inclination to foster a personality cult round himself.

Mao, however, did not seem to mind these personality-cult shrines. At Qiliying commune in Henan province (once called Sputnik to honour China's erstwhile Soviet ally), the peasants set up a small museum containing the chair Mao sat in when he visited the commune, the mug he drank from, and so on. There was a little more justification in this case, perhaps, for Sputnik was the very first commune to be set up in 1958, when the movement got under way.

Premier Zhou Enlai was too astute to be caught in the trap of permitting a personality cult of himself, which would certainly have alienated him from Mao. While Zhou was still alive, I visited the Nankai Middle School in Tientsin, which Zhou attended as a youth, and asked whether they had ever thought of setting up a permanent exhibition of Zhou's days at the school. The principal, as though prepared for the question, said: 'We once asked Premier Zhou whether we might do this. But he replied, "We have the masses, we have the Party, and we have Chairman Mao. Why should we need an exhibition related to myself?"' Whether this was a case of genuine modesty on Zhou's part, or of his foreknowledge of the vast Mao cult which would exclude the possibility of all others, it certainly typified the extreme political skill for which, among other things, Zhou was admired.

The Chinese say a good official is one who 'has an official post but doesn't act like an official'. They condemn arrogant cadres by calling them 'people who put on airs'. A permanently contentious issue is the attitude of the cadres to the workers, especially if they are in charge of large numbers of them in a factory or a large service facility.

The Communist Party originated the idea that managerial staff should roll up their sleeves and do a day's labour each week or each month at the workbench, but those who still follow this practice seem to be few. Especially when the country is drawing up plans for a massive economic upsurge, a cadre will feel entitled to devote himself or herself fully to managerial work, rather than doing symbolic labour on the shop floor. But since there is no trade union movement in China (in the sense in which the concept is used in the West), there often are problems of communication, with the managers issuing orders, the workers failing – or passively refusing – to carry them out, and little or no feedback reaching the management.

Cadres are frequently blamed for misusing their position in order to obtain privileged status for their children. After a young man in Guangdong province was jailed for acts of assault he committed under the protection of his father's high Party and military rank, a special commission which was set up to investigate concluded: 'The parents had pampered the young man in normal times. This attitude of theirs towards him played an important role in turning him into a criminal.

They tried in every way possible to absolve their son of guilt or blame. They even disturbed and interfered with the interrogation work of the political and judicial organs. This behaviour shows that the "special privilege" mentality has been reflected in the problem of a cadre's son.'

Another *cause célèbre* was that of Zhang Longquan, a young man in Shanghai who in 1978 impersonated the son of a senior officer on the General Staff. He obtained free theatre tickets, use of a car, introduction to a girlfriend with a rich father, and innumerable gifts and invitations from local officials anxious to curry favour. When finally exposed and arrested, he is said to have made the immortal comment: 'I wonder if all these things would have been illegal if I had really been the son of a general?'

A centralized socialist state cannot be run without a large corps of officials; they take the place of industrial managers, financiers, city planners, educators, clerks, and other white-collar functionaries in the West. And the relatively high productivity of an industrial economy makes it possible for the state to support a much higher proportion of people who are not actually producing anything through physical labour. The gentry-scholar class of imperial China could afford to support only a small percentage of the population in official positions; the modern socialist state employs a considerably larger proportion of the population as cadres. When they exist in such numbers, the cadres are certain to create a whole stratum of social problems, which will not go away just because the leaders wave their wand and say: 'Avaunt!' The Party leadership in China – indeed, the whole edifice of Marxism and socialism – will stand or fall by its ability to motivate and control the bureaucracy, so there is every incentive to keep on fighting this seemingly uphill battle.

10. Laws, Lawmakers, and Lawbreakers

China marked her entry into the 1980s by presenting herself with a good start towards a brand-new legal system. Six codes – covering crime, judicial procedures, and elections to government office – took effect on the first day of the decade; a law on foreign investment and an experimental law on environmental protection had already gone into operation the previous year. Very broadly speaking, the new codes are based on Soviet law, which has its roots in the Code Napoleon and Roman–Dutch law. But legal specialists charged with drawing them up also studied the laws of different Western countries and even of the Kuomintang.

Astonishingly, China had come through the three decades since 1949 without any formal criminal or civil code. On winning power, the Communists were faced with the need to draft a legal system to replace that of the Nationalists. Party leaders could simply have copied the Soviet code word for word, as they copied so many other Soviet institutions in the early 1950s. But seemingly the Soviet model was not thought wholly suitable to the special conditions of China. The leaders chose a piecemeal approach.

In the nationwide upheaval after the civil war, the idea of a whole new legal system was given low priority. Fairly comprehensive laws were passed on special topics such as marriage and land reform, and the Party published several sets of provisional rules on the punishment of 'counter-revolutionaries', grafters, currency manipulators, and other people thought to be enemies of the new order, but the emphasis was on punishment and deterrents, rather than the rights of the accused or the niceties of court procedure.

In the absence of a detailed, published code of laws, China was administered mainly by a system of 'directives', numbered circular notices with various security classifications. These told of some political and administrative decisions of the top leaders and required the organs of Party and government at all levels to comply. In the words of the *People's Daily* in 1979, this system made officials 'dictatorial, patriarchal, lethargic, arrogant, and conceited'.

On top of the system of directives, law was subordinate to political campaigns and infighting among factions. The latest Mao quote in the *People's Daily* became the law of the land until it was replaced by another, even though nobody could prove the Chairman had ever uttered them. For example, if the Party media attacked 'capitalist' trends among the peasants, commune officials would chop down the villagers' private fruit trees and break up small rural markets where the peasants made a tiny profit from home-grown produce. If the Party denounced 'bourgeois' trends in education, university classes would be suspended for yet another orgy of political meetings, personal denunciations, and the writing of thousands of 'big-character' posters.

Chinese visitors to Peking in 1978–9 were told by friends and relatives that morale in the police had hit an all-time low, and this was compounded by the growing wave of public criticism of police strong-arm methods during the entire 1970s. Nor could the public forget that Chairman Hua Guofeng was Minister of Public Security throughout 1975 – and so could not escape blame for the state of affairs prevailing then.

Foreigners who had traffic accidents – very difficult to avoid in the chaos of Peking's streets – could be forbidden to leave the country for months on end while the Public Security (police) decided on how much compensation should be paid, or they could be summarily expelled from the country. There was no question of arbitration by a court – and if there had been, the court would simply have carried out the instructions of the Foreign Ministry or the police. The eventual decision would be strongly influenced by the state of China's current relations with the government of the foreigner involved.

In 1963, the thirty-third draft of a full-scale legal code was submitted to Mao and other top leaders for approval. Mao evidently did not give it his blessing, for it was not formally implemented – and in 1966 the Cultural Revolution swept away any ideas of legality or process of law. This draft was, however, used as a basis for the Criminal Law and the Law of Criminal Procedure which were put into effect on 1 January 1980. (These codes had been drawn up the previous year by a special commission of the National People's Congress headed by none other than Peng Zhen, the former mayor of Peking whose dismissal in 1966 was one of the first major events of the Cultural Revolution, and who returned to public life only in 1978.)

A new legal system was long overdue in China. At the height of the Cultural Revolution in 1966–71, the rule of law – such as it was – ceased to exist. From 1967 on the military virtually ran the country. Public order was slowly restored in the early 1970s, but justice was still largely a matter of discretion, with the courts mostly handing down verdicts determined by consultation with Party officials and the Public Security. It was impossible to buy the texts of legal codes in the bookshops or refer to them in libraries without special permission.

In retrospect, this is seen as a catastrophic period for justice in China. The Party journal said in August 1979 that during the Eleven Years 'people were randomly branded as "counter-revolutionaries", unlawfully arrested, and their property confiscated; large numbers of people were unjustly, falsely, and wrongly charged or sentenced; and democracy and the legal system were trampled underfoot.'

Testimony by numerous Chinese people – who are now much freer to speak their mind than before – supports this statement. Law became whatever the power-holders in Peking or in any locality wanted it to be at a given time. It was enforced through social discrimination, imprisonment, exile to remote rural areas, physical and psychological maltreatment, and sometimes execution of people who fell foul of the Party or the Public Security or incurred the wrath of petty officials. There was hardly any chance to appeal sentences, and most cases were tried without a public report on the proceedings. Officials carved out special privileges for themselves, their families, and their political followers, interfering with the work of the courts and securing immunity from prosecution for almost anyone they pleased.

This picture – being painted today by the official Chinese media – probably contains elements of exaggeration, as do most present-day criticisms of the last decade of Mao's rule, but in broad outline it corresponds with the picture given by ordinary Chinese people in intimate talks with foreigners.

A key to the system of arbitrary justice in the Eleven Years was the word 'counter-revolutionary'. Anyone who disagreed with the policies of the national or local leaders could be charged with being a 'counter-revolutionary' – a crime punishable by any means, up to and including death.

At the height of the Cultural Revolution, it was enough to make a slip of the tongue or the pen and refer to a political leader – particularly Mao – without the required degree of reverence, or accidentally break a bust of him, or smear his picture in a newspaper or magazine, to be accused of being a 'counter-revolutionary' and suffer vicious harassment by teenage Red Guards or be sent to a prison or labour camp.

Until the late 1970s, all crime was graded on a political scale. Murder was a crime, but its seriousness varied according to the current political atmosphere and the degree of political motive thought to be involved. During an 'anti-rightist' campaign, the son of a former landlord or capitalist who accidentally killed a Party activist or Red Guard in a mêlée would almost certainly be sentenced to death, whereas a political activist who caused the death of someone regarded as a 'bad element' might escape prosecution altogether.

Crime was treated as a transient phenomenon in the socialist society, allegedly caused by the survival of 'bourgeois' ways of thought. The social conditions which everywhere cause crime – poverty, ignorance and oppression – were not to be taken into account; to do so would reflect adversely on the management of national affairs by the Maoist-dominated Party. Crime was seen as part of the continuing 'class struggle'.

The discrediting of the concept of 'class struggle under socialism' in the post-Mao era led to disillusionment on the part of many activists, who felt deprived of legitimate targets for their zeal. Such people – who before had behaved as self-appointed defenders of the socialist system, informing on their neighbours or organizing mass meetings to criticize and condemn people thought anti-social or 'bourgeois' – lost interest in crime-fighting, once it turned into a simple matter of catching thieves and rapists. They felt the motivation for trying to clean up society had vanished together with its political rationale. 'Nowadays our hands and feet are bound,' one member of a People's Militia vigilante patrol told a colleague of mine in a provincial city.

After the fall of the Gang of Four in 1976, many policemen in Peking felt disillusioned by the re-evaluation of the politically motivated riots which took place on 5 April of that year on Peking's Tiananmen Square. Having skirmished with and arrested many demonstrators during the riot, the police and militia were informed in 1978 that these 'counter-revolutionaries' were now regarded as true revolutionaries and martyrs, defending Chairman Mao's ideals, not attacking them.

Astonishingly, in this judicial near-vacuum China remained reasonably stable and orderly in the 1970s, despite sporadic outbreaks of labour unrest and rioting. For this it had to thank its own millennia-long tradition of government through the subordination of the will of the masses to the authority of a semi-divine emperor, ruling through scholar-officials in accordance with hallowed precepts of social obligation and rank. 'Rule by men' was thought superior to 'rule by law', and the legal systems of successive dynasties never commanded the almost religious esteem in which the law is held in Western Europe and North America.

In traditional China, law was a set of decrees and statutes (reflecting the priorities of the ruling dynasty) and a list of extremely cruel punishments. People went to court only as a desperate last resort or because they were hauled there, for the magistrate, likely as not, would order one or both parties to a dispute, or a person accused of a crime, to be beaten almost to death in the interests of obtaining a confession of guilt or a settlement.

Similarly, in the China of the 1970s, the mere fact of being brought to trial would severely prejudice a person's case, since it was assumed that the police and the prosecutor would not have brought the action idly, or without being sure it was soundly based. The courts – to the extent that they functioned at all – were instruments of Party policy. People with a grievance would usually appeal to their local Party committee for redress, rather than going to court. People who were arraigned before the court for criminal offences would be always suspect thereafter (would, as the Chinese say, 'still have a tail'), in the unlikely event that they were acquitted. Innocent people jailed for investigation could become 'criminals' simply by resisting intimidation or not admitting guilt.

Court procedure customarily went along the following lines: first, the prosecutor read out the charge. Next, the judge interrogated the accused, and the prosecutor followed with a separate interrogation. The defending counsel or spokesman for the accused would then also ask questions, and possibly debate with the prosecutor during the summing-up. Normally no witnesses were heard. In theory, the accused could defend himself or herself at this stage and plead for leniency. Finally, the judge and two 'people's assessors' – laymen with some legal training who sit on the bench with the judge – withdrew to consider their judgement. There was no other jury.

In the vast majority of cases, the verdict would be 'guilty', with the sentence read out by the judge. Appeal must be made within ten days, to the next higher level in the four-tier court system ('basic', 'intermediate' and 'higher' courts, and the Supreme People's Court.)

Petty misdemeanours and civil disputes have been sorted out predominantly by a Party committee, a government ministry, the Public Security, or a neighbourhood committee. This to some extent has echoed the traditional Chinese system of administering low-level justice in the home or in the single-surname clan (the basic units of Chinese social organization until the mid twentieth century). A father whose son had got into trouble would traditionally have been expected to thrash him cruelly – even to kill him, if the business had greatly sullied the family's good name. Concubines and daughters-in-law were under the total authority of the first wife, if she had a strong enough personality to exercise it. Civil suits were conducted largely through bribery of the magistrate, who often had no significant source of income other than graft and 'squeeze'. There is a Chinese saying, 'The south gate of the *yamen* [magistracy] is open. With right on your side but no money, do not go inside.' It was a social order which worked tolerably well as long as most people understood and respected it and all knew their station.

In theory, it should have been feasible to replace rule by the emperor and his officials with rule by the Chairman and the Party cadres. Many of the attributes ascribed to Mao in the Cultural Revolution were semi-divine in nature. With the restoration of order, the Party cadres were expected – like the imperial magistrates – to be the 'fathers and mothers' of the masses, in a China where the family system was crumbling because of urban growth and industrialization. But Mao, never happy with peace and order, set the Party against itself, from the Politburo right down to the neighbourhood committee and even into the family – so that China split into feuding factions, all claiming deathless loyalty to Mao and inflicting indignities and injuries on those whom they denounced as 'bourgeois' or 'revisionist' or with any other such dimly understood catchword.

After Mao's death, the Party leaders decided to put a stop to this institutionalized chaos, which Mao had actually threatened to unleash on the country once every eight years or so. The new legal code is intended to be watertight and capable of dealing with all crimes and disputes. The law is to stand above all other codes, even the thoughts of Mao and the principles of Marxism. 'Those are not laws,' a Chinese official told me. 'They are guidelines to action. But all action must be within the law.'

The absolute authority of law is hard to establish in a country where it has until recently been subordinate to political ideology and the whims of the leaders. Some senior officials have misgivings, fearing the authority of the law may challenge Party policies and weaken the Party's leadership. The general public will take a 'wait-and-see-how-it-works-out-in-practice' attitude before accepting the efficacy of the new legal code, however many articles and commentaries are published to explain its principles and operation.

The task is only begun with the publication of a criminal code and codes of procedure. Before drawing up a code of civil law and a law of contract, the leadership will have to decide exactly what kind of economic and social system it wants – and this is still under intense discussion.

The absence of a detailed set of laws for commerce has caused difficulties in trade with Western countries, where even an insurance policy can run to several pages of fine print, and a contract to build a factory and take shipment of its products in lieu of payment might need an agreement as thick as a novel. The Chinese way, so far, has been to draw up lean, simple contracts and stipulate mutual goodwill and arbitration as the means of solving differences of interpretation. But this is just not good enough for Western company lawyers who are dealing with China for the first time and wish to plug every loophole in the relationship.

Legal codes governing foreign investment and taxation of joint ventures were published in China in 1980, but they were felt by foreign businessmen to be vague, and susceptible to variant interpretations. At the same time, the clamp-down on heavy industrial investment, new taxes on foreign enterprises; and the slow progress in construction of industrial estates in areas close to Hong Kong, cooled off the enthusiasm of many foreign firms for participation in joint ventures and other forms of economic co-operation with Chinese enterprises.

The new law-making process in China is – in theory – carried out by the National People's Congress, the rubber-stamp parliament which meets in session once every year or so to endorse the dictates of the Party. In fact it is the Party which has decided on the shape of the new legal system and is supervising its drafting.

Once the new laws are in force, however, the Party has said it hopes to distance itself from the judicial process, confining its role to one of observation and generalized supervision. The law is to be administered by the Public Security, the Procuratorates and the courts, and it is the expressed intention of the Party that they should mutually supervise and if necessary disagree with one another in the legal process.

It may be naive to believe that this is how it will be in practice. In the Soviet Union – still the most important working model of a large socialist country – the real authority of the courts is nil when a case before them has political implications. In a totalitarian system, there is nothing easier to subvert than a court. The Soviet Communist Party and the KGB (secret police) investigate the case and decide the punishment, which the court announces after the prosecution has made a politically biased speech and cursorily examined the accused; defence witnesses are seldom allowed.

However great the future temptations to subvert justice in the interests of Party rule and Party policy, the good intentions of the Chinese lawmakers for the 1980s are clear. A nationwide effort has been mounted to explain the new laws to the general public and quickly train up tens of thousands of new judges, police, prosecutors, procurators, investigators, defence attorneys and people's assessors. Cadres throughout the country have been told to put up 'blackboard newspapers' and introduce drawings, slide shows and even concerts to spread knowledge and understanding. Primary and secondary schools have been advised to organize classes on the law in their routine political courses.

An important aspect of the new laws is the accused person's right to defence. During interrogation – it is laid down – the suspect has now the right to know what charges are being preferred, to read through the written record in case of errors or omissions, and to submit a personal statement. During court hearings, the accused has the right to call anyone as a witness, to cross-examine witnesses, to argue the facts of the case, and to appeal (all of which was usually impossible during the Eleven Years). The accused may undertake self-defence or leave the defence to a lawyer, relative or workmate, or to a member of some mass organization such as the Communist Youth League or the Women's Federation.

In the past, defence lawyers have been in danger of being accused of 'protecting the enemy' if they too zealously defended an accused person. Defence was portrayed as a series of tricks, whereby a guilty person could get off scot-free by twisting arguments and distorting the facts. It could even be dangerous for the accused to put up too strong a defence; this could result in a heavier sentence for 'resisting and making sly denials', whereas an accused person who made a full confession and cooperated with the court might hope to be treated a little more leniently.

It has never, however, been mandatory for a court in China to take a lenient attitude towards someone who made a full confession. Plea-bargaining has always been at the discretion of the prosecution, and the bargain struck did not have to be honoured. Under the pre-1980 legal system, a person convicted of a serious crime, such as murder or espionage, would probably be shot whether he or she confessed or not. Recent trial reports from China confirm that this is still the case: an accused murderer is said to have 'candidly confessed' to the crime – and been shot immediately afterwards as the only reward for this candour.

The new laws – and this is an important point in China – specify that a person *can* be convicted and sentenced without any confession. Until now, enormous importance has been attached to confession, as a psychological rather than a judicial matter. It is rooted in Chinese legal tradition: under the empire, a court case was not deemed to have been satisfactorily dealt with by the magistrate unless one of the parties had confessed. Otherwise, doubt would always linger about the justice of the sentence. The fact that many confessions were obtained through beatings and torture mattered not a whit. Confession was the accused's submission to the supreme will of the empire and of heaven.

To Communists, confession is the total surrender of the mind. The post-1949 Chinese state has given great weight to confession, not just as a formality but as a real expression of the repentance and conversion of the accused and as an assertion of the absolute justice of the measures of Party and government. Confessions would be thrown back if they were thought 'insincere'; an accused person might have to spend months writing and rewriting a confession until the right mix of self-abasement and fact was found.

The new legal system bans the extraction of confessions under duress or 'by torture'. The word 'torture', in this case, probably refers mainly to mental intimidation and the imposition of severe physical discomfort – fettering, chaining and manacling, lack of sleep, hunger, long interrogations – rather than the pulling out of thumbnails or the racking of limbs. Severe beatings have been frequently reported, but no substantial body of evidence exists to show that torture in the extreme sense of the word has been a part of the modern Chinese judicial process, though in the absence of strict procedural rules it would not be surprising if instances of it had occurred from time to time.

Another important feature of the new laws is that the accused is given the right to refuse to answer any question unrelated to the case in hand. Even if he or she does answer such questions, the replies are not to be treated as evidence. One idea of this provision is to curtail the previous method of trying to prove any arrested person guilty of some crime – *any* crime – in order to justify the arrest. There is no *habeas corpus*, though an accused person is *supposed* to be arraigned within two days of the arrest (recent reports suggest this rule is being 'flexibly' applied).

Legal specialists Tang Zongyao and Sun Xian write in a commentary on this question published in Peking, 'Some Public Security officers realized that arrests or detentions had been unjustly executed, but they did not release the victims immediately. They tried in a thousand and one ways to prove that what they had done was "right". By bombarding their victims with all kinds of questions, they tried to extort confessions of guilt from the accused. Some other Public Security officers, who failed to secure convictions on major charges, then turned to minor offences to ensure that the accused was convicted.'

Jiang Hua, President of the Supreme People's Court, has stated that except in special circumstances – such as cases involving breach of official secrets – all trials are to be open and public. The accused is to be permitted to make a defence without being penalized for 'refusing to confess', as would have been the case quite frequently in the past. The courts are forbidden to meddle in pre-trial investigations, and every judicial decision must be the result of a trial. 'Struggle and criticism' sessions are not to be seen as judicial acts, and the accused is not to be paraded in the streets before the public (a common practice hitherto) or have his or her rights violated in any way. Jiang has also warned the judiciary not to cut corners in ascertaining the facts in cases before them just because of a heavy workload.

Jurors have had to be admonished against taking bribes or gifts from people connected with a court case. The Higher People's Court in Tientsin, a city with a notorious crime problem, has announced that such offences will be punished as corruption, and jurors discussing the case outside the court may be prosecuted for 'divulging State secrets'.

Lack of recent practical experience lies behind the poor knowledge of law and legal procedures among judiciary officers. According to official estimates, some two thirds of the legally trained people in China were appointed to courtroom jobs during the Eleven Years and after, a period when there was little firm basis of laws and statutes to guide their work. The other third, who were working in legal jobs before the Cultural Revolution, are considered to have become 'rusty' in their legal knowledge. Says Supreme People's Court President Jiang: 'The drive or enthusiasm that some comrades displayed in studying legal matters in the 1950s has almost spent itself.'

The practice of condemning people arbitrarily as 'counter-revolutionaries' just because they have done things which local officials or political power-holders do not like is now in theory banned. The new criminal code is in part intended to redefine 'counter-revolutionary' crimes. In the past, this tag was pinned freely on all sorts of offences which the authorities felt were harmful to the security of the State. Glosses on the new laws stress that in future it must be proved that an offender had a real counter-revolutionary intent when committing such a crime. Certain offences – such as conspiring against the government, spying, defecting, arson, or spreading seditious propaganda – are taken to have such a purpose, and the offender is severely punished, sometimes with death. But in cases of ordinary crimes, the courts are no longer allowed to bandy the phrase 'counter-revolutionary' around just to fix a stiffer penalty. Even the breaching of State secrets is not to be treated as 'counter-revolutionary' unless it can be shown that the offender intended it to be so, it has been stated in recent legal publications. Further, a person may be accused of being a 'counter-revolutionary' only after committing an obvious counter-revolutionary act; people may no longer be punished – as in the past – on the grounds that they were simply *considered* to have harboured 'reactionary' or 'counter-revolutionary' thoughts. If this side of the new laws is properly implemented, it will be a great step forward for justice in China.

Reports of crime in China multiplied hugely in the late 1970s. In part this was due to the more open information policy of the post-Mao leaders, who no longer saw much use in trying to hide all the unpleasant facts of life, either from the Chinese people at large or from the eyes of foreigners. But the surge in crime reporting in the Chinese media did also seem to indicate a slackening of social discipline, which was only to be expected in view of the massive programme of economic and cultural liberalization that was going on.

The decision no longer to force secondary school graduates into jobs in the countryside caused a surplus of unemployed youth in the cities, both among those who had recently graduated and among those who took advantage of the new mood to leave the gruelling conditions of the communes, state farms and pioneer brigades where they had been settled and return home. Many of them, unable to find regular jobs, formed street gangs which picked pockets, burgled property, raped girls and women, and feuded with one another. In the larger cities, bands of citizen vigilantes had to assist the police, militia, and armed forces in mounting patrols to keep down this sort of street crime.

There were also demonstrations and protests outside local government and Party offices, with young people clamouring for some form of recognition and support, ration coupons, jobs, college places – anything that would give their existences meaning. Some demonstrators occupied official buildings and ransacked files, held the staff prisoner in their offices, and smashed furniture and fittings. From Shanghai in late 1979 came persistent reports that one gang had occupied a large department store, killing and injuring some of the sales clerks and holding their position for several hours until the police mustered sufficient strength to overwhelm them. A foreign visitor to the same city saw two policemen on the street viciously clubbing a man with thick pieces of lumber. Official media in Shanghai said young women were becoming afraid to go to work on factory night shifts, for fear of being attacked on the streets.

This violence born of desperation was also felt in Hong Kong, where penniless young illegal immigrants from the mainland were thought to be behind some of the cases of robbery and assault at the apartments of both Chinese and European residents. On the mainland, railway lines and stations were frequent targets for gangs, as young criminals looted freight shipments and snatched illegal rides on trains.

Most of the crime wave has been hidden from foreigners living in or visiting China. Assaults and robberies committed against foreigners are treated with the utmost gravity, and even mentally deranged people who on one or two occasions have attacked foreign diplomatic personnel on the street have been shot. The simple presence of a foreigner is usually enough to deter people from arguing loudly, brawling, or molesting others, and the unpleasant state of affairs in the Cultural Revolution – when foreigners themselves could easily become targets of public rage and violence – has not recurred on any significant scale. Despite this, reports of stolen wallets, missing luggage, offers of illegal transactions, and other petty crimes involving approaches to foreigners and especially overseas Chinese visitors were so numerous by 1980 that they no longer aroused much attention, and foreign residents in China – for the first time since the 1950s – began to be careful about what they left lying around in their hotel rooms or in unlocked cars.

Despite the misleading appearance of calm, which most foreign visitors take as typical of the whole country, the official media relentlessly catalogue typical incidences of lawbreaking and disorder both in Peking and in the provinces. To estimate their extent is impossible, because there are no published crime figures, but it would seem that urban crime, while becoming a serious problem, is at nothing like the level common in European and American cities. But there is a persistent level of violence among individuals and groups in the rural areas, where the harsh living conditions fray tempers easily and clan feuds are a longstanding tradition.

Drug-related offences do not seem to be a significant factor. The near-elimination of drug addiction in China is undoubtedly one of the greatest achievements of the Communist Party. The supervision of all rural areas by brigade and commune officials makes it impossible to grow opium poppies except for pharmaceutical use. Soviet – and previously American – allegations that China grew poppies in its south-western region, and smuggled morphine and heroin out of the country to undermine the morale of the capitalist world, have never been authenticated by the British-led Royal Hong Kong Police, who are about as expert on opium-based drug problems as any force in the world. Significantly, most of the opiates and narcotics abused in Hong Kong come from Thailand.

Most crimes in China seem to be committed either for immediate gain – robbery, mugging – or out of passion or hatred. It has been well said of the Chinese that they have 'a high boiling point but an underlying hysteria'. It takes a lot to excite the average Chinese person to violence, but when the explosion comes it may be uncontrollable.

To give some picture of the law-and-order scene in Chinese cities, the following reports were collected from the official media, mostly over a period of about six weeks, in 1979.

Mao's native province of Hunan, in south-central China, seems particularly disturbed by disorderly conduct on the streets. There has been a spate of street gambling (all gambling is illegal in China). In the course of 'only a few days', police reported that they had dealt with as many as 300 cases of gambling in Changsha, the provincial capital. Other petty offences commonly encountered are peddling of quack medicines, fortune-telling by blind people, illegal lotteries, robberies, pocket-picking, assault and hooliganism. The crowded public buses and bus queues are the favourite place for pickpockets to ply their trade. In the province as a whole – with a population estimated at 40 million – nearly 4,000 criminal prosecutions were carried out in the first eight months of 1979. Almost 800 of these cases involved malfeasance by government officials and low-level cadres.

A gang of about twenty lawbreakers in Tientsin attempted to hijack a police vehicle which was ferrying prisoners from one place to another. Foiled, they went on a rampage, smashing windows and furniture and robbing and stabbing passers-by.

Crime reports in Canton for 1979 included the following incidents: a twenty-three-year-old man was sentenced to death for killing a man and a woman while trying to rob them. A forger was imprisoned for eight years for faking pork-ration coupons. A man was sentenced to death for teaching youths to steal. Sentences of between eight and ten years were handed out for street fighting and rape. A mass rally was held to hear sentences of between life imprisonment and one year being passed on nine members of a gang who attacked two young women on their way to the cinema, tearing off the trousers of one of them and beating her until she was covered in blood.

In the eastern province of Anhui, a criminal gang looted automatic weapons from a militia headquarters and wounded a fireman who tried to stop them. The weapons and ammunition were later recovered and three people arrested.

A public rally attended by some 5,000 people in the large south-western city of Kunming in October 1979 witnessed the death sentence being passed on a worker at a machinery plant who had attacked a doctor following an abortion operation on the worker's girlfriend. The accused was said to have hacked the doctor twenty-two times with a chopper, killing him, and then to have fled with the doctor's Swiss watch.

The steady stream of reports from the cities and provinces suggests that large-scale organized crime is not a serious problem. The gangs are crude in their methods and appear to have little systematic approach to lawbreaking. But the police are overextended and sometimes unable to cope even with daylight vandalism and assault. Rape is frequently mentioned; it is probably still commoner than the official reports suggest, because of the known tendency of raped women and girls to keep quiet out of shame.

The surge in illegal gambling will surprise nobody who has lived in a predominantly Chinese community such as Hong Kong. The Chinese are among the world's most compulsive gamblers, and the apparent elimination of this practice in the 1950s was another massive tribute to the moral drive and vigour of the Communist Party at that time. The closest a foreigner will usually get to seeing gambling in China is to come across groups of youths or old men playing cards, which surprisingly has not been treated as a 'bourgeois vice' and stamped out. The commonest game – inaccurately called *pu-ke* or 'poker' in China – appears to be a kind of gin rummy. If the players are keeping a tally in their heads for settlement in private after the game (a practice known as 'disguised gambling'), they need to have powerful memories and plenty of mutual trust. The game of mahjong, so popular in Hong Kong and in overseas Chinese communities, has long been banned in the People's Republic, whether because it is a tremendous time-waster or because it usually involves gambling. But for the police in Changsha to come across fully 300 illegal games in three days suggests something like an epidemic of gambling fever.

It is surprising how many recent reports tell of criminals with firearms. Some are home-made. There are, however, several ways in which unregistered firearms become available to criminals. For three decades, the Nationalists on Taiwan have been smuggling guns and explosives into the mainland for the use of saboteurs or dissident groups. As the Nationalists' hope of reconquering the mainland has faded, these weapons have probably fallen increasingly into the hands of common criminals. The Hong Kong police and customs have to keep a watchful eye open for shipments of firearms being brought in to be smuggled across the border into the People's Republic. In the Cultural Revolution, numerous army arsenals were looted by Red Guards and other warring groups – and the regular troops were reluctant to prevent this, because they had been told in Mao's name to 'support the Left' and were not always sure who the 'leftists' were. Inevitably, some of these weapons were never traced and returned, even after the Army stepped in to control the violence and restore public order in 1967.

It is likely, too, that some militia arsenals have been robbed of rifles; the arsenal I saw at a factory in Huhhot, capital of Inner Mongolia, was nothing more than a large cupboard protected by a padlock. Getting ammunition might present difficulties, but with millions of People's Militia undergoing small-arms training, it would not be impossible. And doubtless there have been cases of pistols being snatched from unwary policemen, as happens regularly in Hong Kong.

In dealing with criminals, the Communist Party has consistently striven to make the penal system one of personal moral reform. How genuinely this ideal has been pursued must have depended on the personality of the many prison and labour-camp commandants and warders. The granting of privileges to prisoners has been made dependent not just on their good conduct in observing prison rules and regulations but also on their 'political reform'. Enormous effort is invested in the attempt to drive a convicted criminal into a hell of personal despair and loneliness, from which the only escape is by genuinely 'turning over a new moral leaf' and wholeheartedly accepting the political line of the Party. Fellow prisoners have played an active role in this process, screaming abuse and taunts at a new prisoner to the point where it becomes impossible to know how much is play-acting and how much is genuine persecution. As a person gradually becomes 'reformed', he or she is expected to take part in the intimidation and indoctrination of new arrivals. The trusty system is widely applied in the appointment of cell leaders.

Physical conditions in jails appear to be reasonable, considering how low the standards of living are for the workers and peasants in the outside world. A former inmate of a large prison in Shanghai – originally built by the British there before the Second World War – gives the following description of it:

Prisoners are segregated in different cell blocks. Block One holds spies, murderers, and people sentenced to prison terms of more than sixteen years. Block Two is for burglars, pickpockets, and other minor criminals. Block Three is for 'counter-revolutionaries', former capitalists, rapists, black marketeers, and people with sentences of between ten and fifteen years. Block Four is for prisoners serving sentences of one to ten years. Block Five is for prisoners in poor health, and Block Six is for women prisoners.

The prison has a printing press and sewing shop, but only prisoners nearing the end of their term and with good conduct records are granted the privilege of working. The wardens are Public Security officers but are unarmed. (Most prisons have armed military guards at the outer wall.) In each block there are ten to twelve trusty convicts.

The day begins at 7 a.m., with roll call, time for washing, and breakfast of rice gruel (congee). Between 8 and 11 there are political and ideological lectures. From 11 till 1 p.m., lunch is served – rice with vegetables, a little fish twice a week – and there is a rest period. From 1 till 5 p.m. there are more lectures or, for those who are permitted it, work. Between 5 and 9 p.m., the prisoners are given supper (the same type of food as at lunch) and allowed some recreation. The usual 'recreation' is to study the *People's Daily* in groups of thirty; sometimes there is time to play a little chess. Lights-out is at 9 p.m. Once a week the prisoners are exercised by being allowed to walk around the cell block for half an hour. Prisoners with good conduct records may receive one visitor a month for fifteen minutes at a time. Once every two months prisoners may be allowed to play table tennis in the recreation hall or watch a highly propagandistic performance by a visiting drama troupe.

A bowl of water for washing is brought to each cell every morning by the trusties. There is a bucket for urinating and defecating. In summer, prisoners have a bath once a week, and in the winter once a month. Clean clothes are issued after the bath.

After ten years, prisoners with long sentences are sent to 'reform-through-labour' camps, or sometimes to factories where they can be 'rehabilitated through labour' and earn up to 30 yuan (US$17) a month, about half the average industrial wage. Labour camps are numerous; some estimates put their total population at several million. Less serious offenders are sent there directly rather than to prison. Life follows a prison routine, except that there is more freedom to move about – and there is work. The camps are sited near places where heavy labour has to be performed, such as irrigation projects and quarries. In the better camps, prisoners are encouraged to take pride in the national importance of the construction or excavation task they are performing. The most severe and persistent hardship is the inadequate food ration, only about half what an able-bodied peasant or manual labourer would get. Prisoners with good behaviour records are allowed to buy small items of food such as fruit, biscuits or sweets from time to time. The more lenient camp commandants also allow prisoners to receive food parcels from relatives.

The Peking city prisons administration has restored a system of visiting by relatives which fell into disuse in the Eleven Years, and which seeks to combine such visits with reform and rehabilitation of prisoners. Starting with the sock factory at which some prisoners work, relatives are taken on conducted tours of the penal institution and shown the various facilities. They are lectured on the need to reason with their convicted relatives and avoid simply abusing them for having brought so much trouble on the family. They are also briefed on the progress being made by prisoners in their programme of character reform.

Treatment of convicts in China has varied according to the political mood in the national leadership. In periods of political fervour – such as the late 1950s or during the Cultural Revolution – prisoners were treated with brutality and contempt, on the assumption that their very criminality proved their political rottenness, and regarded as enemies of the people who have been shorn of their Chinese citizenship.

The prison and labour-camp authorities pursue a well-planned and systematic programme of divide and rule among the prisoners, sparing no effort to make each individual prisoner feel responsible to and dependent on the State, not on the loyalty or friendship of fellow prisoners. Punishments and rewards are designed to split up prisoner solidarity through instituting a system of privilege. Prisoners are routinely expected to denounce each other and to participate in 'struggle sessions' against each other. Punishment for bad conduct can include reduction of rations, solitary confinement, chains, fetters and manacles, extra-hard work, and loss of visiting privileges.

Though these disciplinary methods can be expected to persist, the new legal code aims to safeguard the rights of prisoners as Chinese citizens. There has been much academic debate about the usefulness of curtailing the 'political rights' of convicted criminals even after they have been released. However, 'political rights' is a highly relative and fluctuating concept in China, and in times of conflict and stress, when the authorities have been cracking down hard on manifestations of social discontent, it has been difficult to distinguish any inviolable rights for the Chinese citizens.

Peking jurists Li Buyun and Xu Bing have addressed themselves to the problem of convicts' rights, pointing out that 'enemy of the people' is a political and not a legal term. 'Chinese citizens who have committed crimes still possess the Chinese nationality,' they argue. 'They still have certain rights and duties and are still citizens of our country.'

Under the new legal system, the rights of prisoners regarding income, property, education, marriage, and family are to be protected more effectively than before, when a convicted prisoner could easily suffer confiscation of property, and his or her spouse would initiate divorce proceedings to be free of the social stigma.

Li and Xu also say, 'Criminals have the right to education. Prisons and reform-through-labour organs have the duty to organize the criminals to study politics, culture, science, and technology. Many criminals break the law because they do not pay attention to studies and are used to wasting time. To change their bad habits, we must let them study.'

The same high moral tone is seen in the unique Chinese system of suspended capital punishment. Criminals may be executed for a whole list of offences, including murder, rape, armed robbery, espionage, sabotage, and malfeasance or black-marketeering on a large scale. But sometimes the court may impose a death sentence with a two-year suspension. During that period, the criminal will be expected to reform thoroughly; if there is no evidence of reform at the end of the two years, the criminal is shot.

Methods of execution are largely the same everywhere in China, with small variations. The hands are bound and the victim told to kneel. A soldier with a pistol or rifle and bayonet prodding the person's neck fires one shot, and then Public Security officers or a doctor check that he or she is dead. The relatives are later allowed to claim the body.

Sometimes there are group executions, carried out by members of the Public Security's special Judicial Squad, simultaneously firing into the back of the necks or heads of a row of victims. A *coup de grâce* is normally administered. Prisoners are not usually hooded or permitted to face the executioner.

It is still common practice to hold mass rallies when the worst offenders are sentenced. The participants cheer the sentence and roar abuse at the person sentenced. Death sentences are carried out immediately, but not in public. Official media say that the sentencing rally 'makes the criminals tremble, and educates the masses'.

Foreigners in Peking were horrified in late 1979 to see a television news item showing all but the actual shooting at an execution. The film clip showed the victim being brought to the execution ground, and then his body being tossed off a truck somewhere.

Public executions were on the whole curtailed after the land reform movement of the early 1950s, when the humiliation and killing of landlords was considered an important part of the political indoctrination of the peasants. A former Red Guard told me, 'When I was a little boy, I was always running off to see executions and getting splattered with blood. Whenever there was some big political movement or hunt for counter-revolutionaries, they would just send down to the local jail for the person with the most severe sentence, bring him out, and shoot him.'

In the case of political prisoners going to their execution, it is common to put a noose around the neck, which is pulled tight on arrival at the execution ground – to prevent the condemned person from crying out or shouting a political slogan. (It is highly embarrassing to shoot someone who is in the act of shouting 'Long life to the invincible thought of Mao Zedong!') Martyr-heroine Zhang Zhixin, a Party member who had dared to criticize Jiang Qing openly, was widely reported to have had her larynx punctured without anaesthetics on the day before her execution. (She was also once taken to the execution ground in the belief that she was about to die, made to witness two criminals being shot, and then taken back to her cell.) Sometimes plastic foam or some such thing is stuffed into the condemned person's mouth to prevent crying out.

Justice stands at the crossroads in China. The new legal code has provided the framework within which a free and impartial system may be implemented, but it gives no democratic safeguards against the subversion of the system through political coercion or simple unfairness. If, by the witness of her own leaders, China's recent past has been scarred with countless mistrials and perverted judicial acts, can the system be so quickly reformed and so thoroughly safeguarded that these things will not happen again? Optimists and pessimists will draw their own conclusions.

11. *Classrooms Under Siege*

Ideas about education in China and in the West showed a remarkable convergence in the early and middle 1970s. Visitors to China who were taken to see schools and universities were often impressed by the concept of combined study, practical work, labour assignments, and sociopolitical instruction which had been instituted after the reopening of middle schools and universities in 1970.

The Chinese theory of education which emerged from the cauldron of the Cultural Revolution was not concerned with creating elitist intellectual groups but with helping the great majority of pupils learn to live in society, be satisfied with their role in life, and be of service to others. The institution of a school system to implement this ideal – still a subject of controversy in the West – was achieved, it seemed, with no more than the overthrow of the old educational system in 1966–7 and the passing of a four-year moratorium during which teachers, parents, pupils and students were indoctrinated with the ideas of community service and the levelling out of gaps between workers and intellectuals.

The Chinese school curriculum of the early 1970s contained, it is true, too much politics for the taste of most Western teachers, and many would have had misgivings about the amount of school time devoted to repetitive physical work. The availability of books and teaching aids was, and still is, woefully inadequate, and classroom discipline stricter than most modern educators would recommend. But the basic ideas behind the Maoist educational system seemed progressive and – to many Western-trained teachers – preferable to the emphasis on grades and examination results common in the school systems of the developed countries. It was the more surprising, then – for people who thought China had solved the basic problems of education in a remarkably simple and straightforward way – to be informed by the post-Mao leadership that the whole system was actually in a hopeless mess, turning out huge numbers of illiterates and semi-literates, and that the only way to reform it was to go back to the pre-1966 system of emphasizing factual knowledge and checking pupils regularly by formal examinations.

Why did the Chinese leaders call an about-turn in the educational policies put into effect under Mao and admired by leftist educators in other countries?

On the traditional Chinese scale of priorities, education ranked only one notch below rice. To have a well-educated son was the pride and glory of any family that could afford the tuition fees and the long years needed to impart enough knowledge of China's classical literature and philosophy to enable a young man to compete in the civil service examinations.

This style of education was heavily dependent on rote learning. The need to memorize thousands of written characters – many of them with several different meanings – and be able to recite by heart the contents of the most important classical works too often deprived young minds of the ability to innovate or think independently.

Nor were they expected to do so. The aim of imperial government in China, and therefore the aim of education, was to preserve a stable status quo and, if possible, teach young people to adopt the reputed values of the Ancients.

Essays and philosophical works, poems and medical treatises – all gained distinction through their learned allusions to older books. Little attention was paid to scientific education, and the only physical accomplishments thought necessary for a gentleman were riding and perhaps a little archery. China was a closed cultural world in which education was a kind of street map to be committed to memory, not a catalytic agent for the mental development of people who would try to change society for the better.

The emphasis on rote learning has carried over into modern China, partly because it is still essential for learning the Chinese script and partly because modern education means absorbing much foreign-originated knowledge, especially languages and natural sciences. A typical modern Chinese student regards education as a process of *gongdu*, or 'assault by reading', similar to our concept of cramming. It was highly convenient for the Communist Party to take over and develop an educational system based on rote learning, for this made it easier to fill the pupils' heads with the dogmas of Marxism–Leninism, whether they were understood or not. Significantly, Confucius's idea of education as a process of studying, revising and repeating has been revived in post-Mao China, despite the attempt to discredit Confucianism in the last years of Mao's life.

The emphasis on learning by heart was visible even in the Cultural Revolution, when young people learned to recite the quotations from the *Little Red Book* of Mao's thoughts by memory – sometimes even backwards, just to show off their perfect mastery of them. This was paradoxical, since one of the ideas behind the Cultural Revolution was to get away from the old formal style of education, and stress learning through practice and from the example of the workers and peasants.

School pupils in the late Mao period were exhorted to apply the philosophical principles of Maoism – even vague and abstruse concepts such as 'one divides into two' – to the solution of practical problems. They spent hours making simple industrial goods, and profits from the sale of these were turned over either to the State or to whatever factory or commune was in charge of the school (nowadays the Party recommends that those profits be channelled back into improving school facilities). They had to listen to old workers 'recounting their sufferings' (*shuo ku*) with tales of the evil social conditions of pre-1949 China. They also had to help clean up the school premises and adjacent streets and help the peasants in busy harvest seasons.

While most of this had some broad educational value, it detracted a great deal from the amount of time that could actually be spent studying – and anyway the Maoist theory of education gave a low priority to formal knowledge and despised examinations. The severe shortage of schoolbooks meant copying down much of what the teacher said in place of a textbook. A similar shortage of laboratory equipment and technical aids meant that science classes made only slow progress and were supplemented by simple experiments or observation programmes – for instance, growing vegetables or keeping records of local weather conditions.

In the early Cultural Revolution, the teacher was likely to be the first target of a rising Red Guard movement in any secondary school. The bestowal of real political authority on the 'little generals' by Mao and his group meant that teenagers with a quite undeveloped moral and ethical sense were given the green light to disobey, scorn, spit on, detain, push around, and even beat their teachers and school principals. Some were 'cowpenned' – forced to do menial labour under the pupils' supervision and subjected to taunts, insults, and physical abuse – while others had to attend violent and humiliating criticism meetings and write 'confessions'.

Teachers who escaped such treatment would nonetheless be reluctant to correct the pupils' homework – if they did any – for fear of being accused of the supposedly deviant view that 'knowledge comes first' (as opposed to political zeal).

Even when the first wave of Red Guards had been disbanded and packed off to the countryside for 're-education', the situation in secondary schools, which began to reopen their doors in 1970, was tense for the teachers. The intake consisted of pupils who had been too young to take part in the first rampage, but by observing their elder brothers and sisters they knew that formal education was politically tainted and that teachers who tried to be strict and demanding could be intimidated by the threat of denunciation. Most schools had young activists – generally pupils who were less academically gifted or diligent and therefore had a vested interest in resisting the domination of formal education. The image of them propagated in the Chinese 'new writing' is that of ignorant, semi-literate, untidy, insubordinate loons, who could barely write a sentence of correct Chinese but who took it on themselves to mouth Mao's quotations in defence of anything they felt like doing.

A schoolteacher accused of 'revisionism' in 1966–7 was quite likely to be sent off to some remote farming area to scratch a living alongside the peasants, if not to a labour camp or jail. Some trickled back with the first wave of political rehabilitees in the early 1970s, but the continued left-radical atmosphere in the schools made it impossible for many of them to resume teaching, and they were forced to look for other jobs.

In 1974, the nightmarish spectacle of another Red Guard movement – based on even younger children than the original one – was dangled in front of the nervous schoolteachers. A twelve-year-old schoolgirl, Huang Shuai, was given nationwide publicity and shown on television for having kept a diary in which she denounced her teacher for political deviance. To watch her fiercely shrieking 'Struggle! Struggle!' was hair-raising.

Huang Shuai fell into obscurity after a few weeks; although details of the affair have not been disclosed, it is widely believed that she was the daughter of a high-ranking leftist official who was collaborating in the attempts of the Gang of Four to resist further rehabilitations and push through a new programme of leftist reform. Author Liu Xinwu, who was once persuaded to interview Huang Shuai, described her as fierce and arrogant, flatly refusing to discuss any details of her one-child rebellion. After the fall of the Gang, some of the media hinted at a conspiratorial intent in her extraordinary rise to brief stardom, but the affair remained mysterious.

At about the same time in 1974, national publicity was given to the case of Zhang Tiesheng, a university student in the north-eastern province of Liaoning (a leftist stronghold at the time), who had handed in a blank examination paper at university entrance examinations. His case was seized on by the left-influenced national media, and he was widely praised for this gesture attacking the 'bourgeois' system of examinations. But three years later his act was denounced roundly in the Party media, and he was not heard of again except as a 'negative example'.

In a country where children were encouraged to rebel against their teachers and the university examination system was thrown into disrepute, it is hardly surprising that people left the teaching profession in droves, and new recruits were obtained mainly because the teacher training institutes could offer places to students unable to get into other institutions of higher learning. As the key links in the system of training and indoctrinating teachers, these institutes – especially in Peking, Shanghai, and the big north-eastern city of Shenyang, capital of Liaoning province – became centres of left-radical activity, and quite a few published their own political journals.

Another means of replenishing the supply of secondary-school teachers after the reopening of the schools was to siphon teachers off from the primary-school system – though their qualifications were inadequate for their new jobs and the primary schools suffered from their departure. In a logical extension of this practice, the senior secondary schools drew teachers away from the junior secondary schools, so that the nation's entire teaching contingent became top-heavy.

This has been a serious problem in view of the bottom-heavy structure of the schools themselves. Primary-school pupils, according to 1978 statistics, numbered 146 million, while secondary schools had 65 million and colleges and universities counted a mere 0.85 million (though this figure rose to over 1 million students by 1980).

With four fifths of the population living on the land, it is the rural schools run by communes and production brigades that will determine the overall level of education among young adults in the 1980s and 1990s. These schools are mostly financed by the peasants themselves out of collective funds, not by the State. The amount of money the peasants put aside to finance a school depends on the priority they give to literacy and other basic forms of knowledge for their children. Some evidently feel that the children's light labour in the fields – at perhaps four work-points a day, or nearly half an adult's rate – is of more obvious benefit to the family and the community. The government promised in 1979 to 'gradually increase' its investment in primary education, to the point where schools would be run mainly out of public funds. But this promise, contained in a sixty-article document released by the Ministry of Education, has made farming folk still less keen to spend money on building schools and employing teachers, when the State plans to take over the funding in a few years anyway. Money spent on schools has in places been resented as an unreasonable burden on the badly paid peasantry. Costs of building a 1,000-square-metre schoolhouse (about 50 × 200 feet) are in the region of 18,000 yuan (US$10,000) and 8,000 voluntary labour-days contributed by the peasants themselves.

The *People's Daily* explains: 'Since the State is still unable to finance the operation of all schools, it remains necessary to encourage the communes and production brigades to run their schools largely at their own expense.'

As a stopgap measure, communes and production brigades are encouraged to send mobile teachers out to give lessons to the children in the fields while they tend cattle, or on board boats where they are performing transport or fishing work, or at home in the early mornings and the evenings when they can be spared from farm work.

One big difficulty about persuading the peasants to spend more of their earnings on schools is that during the Eleven Years they could see plainly that their children were spending a lot of time learning about abstruse political issues irrelevant to their family life and relatively little time learning useful things such as reading or calculating with the abacus.

In theory, every child in China is supposed to receive five years or more of primary schooling. In practice, this is not so. To score even 90 per cent primary-school attendance among children in the age group seven to twelve is regarded as a really admirable achievement in the rural areas – and the few places which have done it are held up as national models.

A sizeable number of children drop out of primary school after one or two years, in order to take part in farm labour alongside their parents. Such children will be near-illiterate. According to an official report in 1979, 'The percentage of school-age children who go to school has declined in many places over the past few years. The number of school dropouts has increased, the number of students who complete the five-year course is reduced, and numbers of illiterates and semi-illiterates continue to appear among young people and children.'

Despite their problems, China's primary schools have much to be proud of. The great majority of teachers have an excellent reputation for dedication and an almost parental solicitude for the children in their care. Disciplinary problems are less often met with than in schools in the West, and even if the curriculum used to contain a lot of theory associated with the Mao cult, the teaching of basic reading and arithmetic skills is in most places being well carried out, in combination with measured amounts of playtime and physical exercise, hygiene training, and light work tasks.

The primary-school curriculum varies from place to place, but the Education Ministry recommends Chinese language, arithmetic, elementary natural science, one foreign language (in urban schools), politics, physical culture, music, and drawing. Pupils in the fourth and fifth grades of the five-year course are to do manual labour for half a month each year instead of study.

Rules of classroom discipline are simple – 'Respect teachers', 'Be polite', and 'Do not spit'. Chinese schoolchildren appear, on the whole, to be more docile than their counterparts in Western countries – as long as there is no political movement in progress to stir them up.

But the authorities are dissatisfied with the speed of progress in raising the standards at primary schools. A Peking city education conference in 1979 concluded that the quality of education was still 'low'. The main blame was laid at the door of the senior middle schools, which had tried to give advanced secondary education to too many pupils, and to too high a standard. Primary education had sacrificed staff and resources as a result, and so had the junior middle schools. 'One thing that deserves serious attention is that primary school education has not been truly introduced everywhere,' the conference's report said. 'In reality, it is constantly turning out new illiterates and semi-illiterates.'

The secondary-school system was much more disrupted by the Cultural Revolution and its aftermath in the Eleven Years than the primary system, where the children were deemed too young to be used as political activists of the Red Guard type. The weekly *Beijing Review* (formerly *Peking Review*), a publication for distribution overseas, put it succinctly in 1980: 'Teachers were unable to do their work properly; neither could the students learn as they should. There was practically no discipline, no regular system of examinations, no criteria for promoting students to the next grade or holding them back a year. This resulted in a drastic decline in standards and a wide gap in the students' cultural level.'

The recommended curriculum for the secondary schools, now being painstakingly reformed and reorganized, is a five-year course enrolling pupils at the age of twelve and giving three years of junior secondary schooling and, for those who elect to stay on, two years of senior secondary education. The subjects taught are politics, Chinese language, mathematics, physics, chemistry, biology, a foreign language (usually English), history, geography, basic agricultural knowledge, hygiene, physical education, music and drawing.

The sheer enthusiasm with which school principals have thrown themselves into the reconstruction of the secondary-education system is in itself a problem. Before 1966, Peking had only 120 senior secondary schools with some 50,000 pupils. By 1977, there were 884 such schools with 200,000 pupils. Far from seeing this as a step in the right direction, top education officials say it is having a deleterious effect on the whole secondary-education system. Many schools have adopted a 'cramming' policy, with the aim of getting as many of their pupils into university as possible, though only a tiny number of university places are available. Laboratories and libraries have been occupied for classrooms, with sometimes sixty or seventy pupils in a class. Teachers have been pirated away *en masse* from lower schools to teach courses for which they are not qualified. Even some primary schools have been upgraded to the secondary level. Not a single secondary-school teacher in the rural areas around Peking was a graduate of a university or college in 1979. 'The schooling system has been undermined through the withdrawal of resources from the bottom to produce better results at the top,' a former Peking school-teacher told me.

The answer proposed is to restore quickly the vocational and technical secondary schools which were mostly closed for a full seven years from 1966 on (the universities reopened after only four years' closure). It is planned to open service and tourism schools to help cope with the growing numbers of visitors to China. More agricultural schools will be set up to provide qualified agro-technicians for the suburban and rural communes, and special job titles will be restored, to show who has and who has not studied a technical subject at an appropriate school.

The practice of bestowing academic degrees has been revived in Chinese universities after a thirteen-year hiatus during which not a single person was given the title of B.A., M.A., or Ph.D. But the bottleneck at the top of the schooling system is more severe than ever before, with universities in Peking able to accept only 10,000 out of the 200,000 senior secondary graduates each year. Enrolment at technical and vocational secondary schools, meanwhile, fell from 40,000 before the Cultural Revolution to 10,000 in 1978. The proportion of university students to secondary technical and vocational students has dropped below 1:2, compared with 1:4 in Japan. Training of teenagers is urgently needed in such skills as carpentry, engineering, driving, finance and accounting, sewing and needlework, photography, typewriting, seal-carving, radio repairs, and arts and crafts, according to reports by Peking educators on this problem.

These disclosures about the severe lack of technical training facilities, even in the capital city, are in strange contrast to the image of the Chinese educational system which was propagated during the Eleven Years. No effort was spared in that period to emphasize that Mao's policy was to train young people predominantly in practical skills as well as politics – even if the pure sciences, like the humanities, suffered considerably as a result. It is now evident that this picture given by the propaganda machine was quite false and that the Cultural Revolution severely disrupted the country's training of basic-level technicians and skilled workers in all fields.

The importance of education as a key issue between the left-radicals and the right-moderates was pointed up by the fact that the leftists chose Peking University and the large scientific and technical university also located in the capital, Qinghua (Tsinghua), as the base for their 1975–6 campaign to unseat Vice-Premier Deng Xiaoping. Foreign correspondents and diplomats were bussed out to the university campuses in droves to see the thousands of colourful wall posters denouncing the then Minister of Education, Zhou Rongxin, and making thinly veiled accusations of revisionism and 'restorationism' (the radical catchword at the time) against Deng.

During those visits, it was possible to have long conversations with the universities' staff about the meaning of the leftist 'revolution in education'. Their basic theme was that political rectitude was the main criterion for a good student, an abundance of which would make up for any shortcomings in studies. To tell this enthusiastically to foreigners was a matter of sheer survival for any university lecturer at the time, but many of them have by now repudiated their former 'leftist' leanings and are working hard for the technological and scientific revolution called the Four Modernizations.

To visit any Chinese university, even in the later period of the Eleven Years, was a deeply depressing experience. The buildings were – and for that matter, still are – dilapidated and ugly, the grounds simply bare earth with a few trees and shrubs, the staircases and lecture rooms apparently unpainted for the past decade or more. But the worst thing used to be that they seemed half deserted; the visitor had the impression of being taken to just a few places where students and lecturers had been deliberately assembled in picturesque little groups to form a tableau of 'university life'. Totally lacking were the verve and bustle which one senses in a real working university. The guides would usually give figures of students and lecturers which suggested an astonishing ratio of about two or three students to one lecturer. But since, at any one time, an unspecified number of the teaching staff were down in the countryside receiving 're-education', and large numbers of the students were out doing so-called 'open-door schooling' – manual work in factories or on communes – it was never possible to pin down just how many people were occupying the premises and engaged in the process of education. In the libraries, the books were neatly arranged but redolent of that dry, dusty smell which signifies they are little used. A glance in the borrowing register on the back cover often showed that the last time they had been taken out was in the 1950s. Particularly incongruous (to my way of thinking) was the sight of a locked glass cupboard at the University of Huhhot, in Inner Mongolia, where an immaculate two-volume dictionary of the Icelandic language could be glimpsed.

The problems of the big fall-out rate at university entrance exams have been predictable. Failure to pass the highly competitive examination can induce despondency and depression in high-school graduates, and the students – trying anxiously to raise their academic standard by hard study at home – may hang around for a year or two until they pluck up the courage to take the exams. An official report drawn up in Tientsin in 1979 said: 'Some candidates who generally score quite high marks think that their teachers and parents and friends will find it difficult to explain should they fail the examination, and people will not even want to see their faces. Some become very miserable and pessimistic.'

The fresh emphasis on formal written examinations for university entrance has led to corrupt practices. A lecturer at a provincial university's department of foreign languages was exposed as having secretly changed part of his daughter's examination answers. And a middle-school teacher, by some freak of bureaucracy, was sent examination papers to check when he himself was a candidate at the same university entrance test! Not too surprisingly, he changed the mark he had been given by a previous adjudicator. He was dismissed from his job, from membership in the Communist Youth League, and from his university candidacy.

The low academic standard of many younger Chinese scholars – brought about by the anti-intellectual bias of the Eleven Years – has put the country in the embarrassing position of often not being able to find people whose knowledge is sufficiently up to date for them to communicate meaningfully with foreign colleagues. While in Peking in the mid 1970s, I used to troop along loyally to British embassy cocktail parties to give send-offs to Chinese 'postgraduate students' who were leaving for academic exchange tours in Britain. They usually turned out to be men in their thirties and forties (if not older), who had not been out of the country for years and had probably had insufficient access to Western technical literature in their fields of study. Their problems of communication in the West would be worsened by the fact that the interpreters who accompanied them seldom had full mastery of the technical vocabulary needed – though fortunately the 'postgraduate students' often turned out to include one or two people who spoke foreign languages better than the interpreters and were looking forward to the chance to use them again!

At the universities, Chinese students learning foreign languages rarely had access to texts written by foreign authors or containing information about the countries where the languages in question were spoken. The exercises and composition themes were mostly related to China and Chinese politics, so that the grasp of the language the students acquired was to a large extent useless when they had to begin using it on foreigners. A young English-language interpreter in Shanghai told me that the only book he had ever read in English was Edgar Snow's *Red Star Over China*, an enthusiastic account of the Communists during their 1930s sojourn in Yan'an, in north-west China. And even that version was probably heavily abridged to avoid mention of Peng Dehuai, Liu Shaoqi, Lin Biao, and other revolutionary leaders with whom Mao later quarrelled. According to a survey carried out in 1980, some 30,000 trained linguists in China were employed in jobs where their knowledge was useless.

Meanwhile, an active programme of student exchange with friendly countries has been pursued, belatedly making up for the loss of places at universities in the Soviet Union and Eastern Europe which was a consequence of the 1960 crisis in Peking–Moscow relations. Most of the thousands of Chinese students now going abroad each year – to Europe, America, Japan, Australia, New Zealand, and Canada – are studying languages and scientific or technical subjects, while the smaller numbers of students from those countries coming to China are interested in Chinese language, history, and literature. Only students from Third World countries – especially Africa – come to China to study technical subjects, and many of them are unhappy because of the austere living conditions and lack of chances for sexual relations. On several occasions there have been violent disturbances which brought an ugly manifestation of Chinese racism to the surface.

A few Chinese students abroad have been able to stay with families in their countries of study, which gave them a colloquial command of the language such as they would never acquire living – as they usually do – in specially segregated hostels under the control of their local embassy. One young Chinese man who had just come back after staying a year with a family in the north of England was invited to a social evening at the British embassy in Peking. When a woman diplomat asked him whether he had enjoyed himself, his reply was, 'Don't ask me, luv – I'm only here for the beer!'

12.   *The New Consumerism*

Muffled in scarves and padded overcoats, and jiggling on their heels against the cold of a bright winter's day, rows of young Chinese stand guard over their makeshift stalls and counters in Peking's newest shopping district, selling chipped cups and saucers, candied crabapples, lapel badges, and brightly coloured tablecloths. Several stalls offer pin-up pictures of favourite Chinese film stars, with the words and music of their best-known songs printed beside their portraits, and even small photos of Rita Hayworth in a swimsuit. One stall-owner has a whole boxful of European and American bathing beauties of the 1940s showing off their legs in luxurious settings. Things in China are certainly changing.

This is Qianmenwai, the entertainment quarter of imperial Peking, once famous for its theatres and brothels. By the mid 1970s, the Qianmenwai area had lost its colour and sauciness and become just a dark, grimy rabbit warren of narrow alleys. It still had some interesting shops, selling hats in the styles of ethnic minorities such as Mongols and Kazakhs, as well as secondhand rugs, and jars of special Peking garlic pickles. But it had been shorn of its character, with the waning of the old pleasure haunts, and the most sensual enjoyment to be had there was roast duck in the Peking style – with thin uncooked pancakes, raw scallions, and a savoury brown sauce – to be eaten in a tiny upstairs room over the kitchen of a venerable restaurant.

Now the ducks are roasted scores at a time in a soulless modern eating palace in another part of town, and the biggest incentive for foreigners to visit Qianmenwai is to buy a traditional Chinese musical instrument or a porcelain dinner service or just soak up impressions.

But for those with a taste for the bizarre, the new hawkers' market in the back streets provides endless fascination. And it is many times livelier in provincial cities than in Peking.

Under Mao, most petty trading and hawking was denounced as 'capitalist' and permitted only on a small scale, either in rural areas or in the more remote cities where foreigners rarely penetrated to witness it. Now it has become a major source of livelihood for the young men and women who flooded back from the countryside into Peking and other large cities after the Eleven Years, and the Qianmenwai district has turned into a street market almost comparable with London's Petticoat Lane or the Paris flea market. The variety of goods is not so great as in those places, but to anyone accustomed to the former blanket ban on petty trading in most parts of China the things being sold in Qianmenwai are truly amazing.

A big crowd collects around a man who is giving a sales patter about what looks like a slab of pink bubble-gum in a coarse paper wrapping. He grabs the long, blue padded overcoat of a passer-by and points out a stain of food or grease. Without further ceremony, he rubs it with his stick of what now turns out to be cleaning material – some chalky substance. Then he takes a toothbrush from a glassful of water at his side on the curb and vigorously scrubs the patch of fabric being treated. Scrubbing finished, he demands, 'Isn't that much better now?' The owner of the overcoat which has been the guinea-pig of the experiment looks doubtful, since the lingering mark of water makes it impossible to tell whether the stain has gone or not.

At another stall in Qianmenwai, two young men and a girl are presiding over a stand of cracked porcelain cups, plates and bowls. Across the street, a small crowd has formed around a youth who is chanting in a high-pitched, singsong voice in an attempt to sell a small needle-threading device. Alongside him, another is taking orders for the transfer of favourite photographs on to handkerchiefs. Someone else is hawking cheap rings with plastic 'stones'.

The density of the crowds around the stands – so thick that an army jeep has to nudge its way through at a veritable crawl – shows that the young entrepreneurs are fulfilling some deeply felt need in Peking. By hook or by crook they have got their hands on small goods which the public wants and will pay for.

Just how they obtain their wares is something of a mystery in a planned economy. Perhaps factories and wholesale departments are selling them off at knocked-down prices. Some of the goods may be stolen; other items have been bought up by 'scalpers' (racketeers making block purchases for resale) as soon as they appear in the shops.

In Tientsin, a major port city some seventy miles away, it is already common knowledge that scalping has become a major business occupation for young people with no other jobs to go to. Among goods affected are women's shoes, quilts, vests, children's jackets, trousers and brooches. The hawkers in Tientsin will mark up a pair of shoes from their original store price of under 14 yuan to 16.50 yuan (from US$8 to $9) – not a massive profit, but enough to make the operation worthwhile. An embroidered quilt is marked up from 10 to nearly 14 yuan (from US$5.55 to $8). Ingenious practitioners have been pushing so-called 'toothache remedies' – which turn out to be nothing more than shavings of kitchen soap! Other people have been telling fortunes, which is still a highly popular pastime in China. Elsewhere in the city, members of the public have complained that black-marketeers have been selling off lumber misappropriated from the State.

Petty trading has been discouraged for so long in China that members of the public who consider themselves 'right-thinking' express almost as much horror at it as law-abiding Americans do at drug addiction and crime in the streets. An indignant reader writes in the following terms to the Peking municipal newspaper, complaining about the unofficial market which has sprung up outside the entrance to a secondhand shop in central Peking:

They split up into seven or eight gangs, each consisting of more than ten persons, whispering to each other, chatting away, gesticulating and behaving in a generally shady way. According to my information, the things being traded by these people include cigarette lighters, sunglasses, trousers, shoes, jackets, army uniforms, and other daily necessities. They also deal in expensive goods such as wristwatches, cameras, calculators, tapes, rings, necklaces, tape recorders, bicycles, and motorcycles. Certain of them even peddle gold and silver dollars, foreign currency, photos of nude women, and foreign sex magazines. It really is a dreadful scene, with all sorts of weird things going on. Prices charged range from more than 10 yuan [US$6] to several hundred and even over 1,000 yuan [US$555].

The outraged citizen describes how he and a group of others have banded together to help the police in dealing with the trading gangs, whose adherents 'ride bicycles in a reckless way, behave with great arrogance, and pay no heed to admonitions'. In the course of a few days the vigilante groups succeeded in checking 170 people, confiscating some of the goods they were hawking, notifying their places of work so that disciplinary proceedings could be taken, imposing fines, and handing the most hardened offenders over to the police.

Faintly comic though it may seem, the indignation of solid Chinese citizens at witnessing petty trading on the streets is rooted in a deep fear of profiteers – who enriched themselves through exploitation and inflation in the Kuomintang (Nationalist) period before 1949, leaving many ordinary people with no means of livelihood. After this experience of a capitalist economic system, most Chinese people are security-orientated and very much afraid of inflation. So how can one explain the upsurge of all this private enterprise – some of it dishonest – in a socialist economy which is supposed to cater to everyone's basic needs in an orderly manner? Or the fact that the authorities seem unable or unwilling to cope with it?

While a certain measure of free enterprise is healthy, and obviously welcomed by the mass of the people on the streets, the State cannot long condone the speculation in scarce goods by scalpers or the diversion of State property to the black market. But the police seem reluctant to move against such abuses without specific authority from above.

The problem is a familiar one in all socialist countries. The supply of food and consumer goods is one of the basic yardsticks by which the performance of a government or ruling party is measured. This should be regarded as crucial in socialist states, where the leadership takes on itself the responsibility of supplying the needs of people which in capitalist systems are looked after by commercial firms.

The Soviet Union and the socialist states of East Europe all have problems with the supply of consumer goods and food, which year after year take a back seat in the national economic planning to heavy industry turning out steel, oil, chemicals, minerals, machinery and arms.

China, a much older state and culture, has a rich tradition of food-growing, skilled handicrafts and industries turning out a multifarious variety of fabrics, domestic utensils, carvings, medicines, wines, carpets, ornaments and works of art – everything which makes human life colourful and enjoyable. A mere three centuries ago, China had the most prosperous and luxurious trading centres and cities anywhere in the world, and her consumer goods – especially tea, silks, and porcelain – became so famous that the European powers literally blasted open her ports in order to gain access to them, as well as to find markets for their own products.

But the doubling of China's population between the eighteenth and nineteenth centuries – and again between the second and fourth quarters of the twentieth century – put a severe strain on the country's economy and on its ability to supply the needs of all its people. At the same time it had to invest heavily in the construction of a modern industrial economy and maintain huge standing armies.

The Communists, on coming to power, decided that the disintegration of the Chinese economy could be stopped only by imposing strict controls on production and consumption. The overpopulation of the rural areas and the mounting problem of poverty in the cities were countered through centralized economic planning – which sought to give everyone a sufficiency, if only a modest one, at the expense of luxurious consumption by a minority. In the process, the old skills and crafts and lore were in danger of being lost, as the tremendous variety which used to be the hallmark of Chinese consumer products gave way to a dull uniformity, and public taste was gradually reduced to the lowest common denominator: sheer necessity.

In the near-revolutionary upheavals of the late 1960s, it became a matter of political – and even physical – survival for people not to show any hankering for material goods or wealth. The shops dismantled their window displays to make way for political slogans, and people thought twice before putting on clothes of a different colour from their neighbours' or workmates' or blowing money on a dinner party.

In the early 1970s, a slow swing back towards colour and variety began. The shops gradually reassembled their window displays, old street names were brought back to replace the repetitive political names given them by the Red Guards, and people to some extent lost their fear of appearing to enjoy themselves or covet material possessions.

After Mao's death in 1976, the slow move back to consumerism became a headlong rush – rationalized by the idea that people need material incentives to work harder and produce more. Consumerism – which was utterly repudiated by Mao and his group – has reappeared under the banner of economic growth. Advertising has returned, on city billboards, in cinemas, on TV, and in the press. Small quantities of selected foreign consumer goods, such as Coca-Cola and Seiko watches, have been cleared for import into China – though mainly for enjoyment by foreigners or Chinese people who have access to foreign currency to buy them: for instance, those who have relatives in Hong Kong or farther afield to finance them.

Suddenly the abundance or shortage of food and consumer goods has become a key indicator of the authorities' success or failure. The Party – following Deng's philosophy that consumption is the main motivating force for mankind – has given more support to consumer goods industries and food supplies. In 1979 it was officially proclaimed that agriculture and light industry would be the main targets of State investment over the next few years, at the expense of heavy manufacturing industry.

Deng and his team certainly had the chance to show the merits of their new semi-free-enterprise system in 1979, when Peking suffered one of its most serious vegetable shortages in years, and the prices of meat and other important protein sources were raised by between 20 and 30 per cent. Bad weather was blamed for the failure of vegetable crops in the summer, and supplies were down by 30 per cent from the previous year. The Chinese cabbage was bitten by early frost, and much of it rotted instead of drying out gradually in the weak sunshine. Dried cabbage is one of the chief vitamin supplements in the northern Chinese diet in winter, and the piles of oozing leaves on the pavements – where the cabbage was laid out in the hope that it would dry – were a depressing sight.

To visit one of the official food stores at that time was to find half-bare counters, with some mouldy-looking dried fish, which Chinese shoppers sniffed at suspiciously before deciding not to buy any; twists of leathery, dried seaweed; hunks of pork fat, streaked with a little red meat; a huge ornamental display of Chinese cabbage which the saleswomen would not disturb even when the cabbage on the counters had run out; some wrapped candies, boiled sweets, and jars of preserves. The best things on sale were the live chickens and eggs, though the chickens were scrawny and Peking eggs often have a tainted flavour in winter.

But a visit to one of the thirteen new market areas allowed by the municipality for free marketing by the peasants from surrounding communes gave an utterly different picture. Suddenly you were in the middle of a working economy again. The peasants were selling a huge range of products. At a stall by the entrance to the market area, piping hot millet soup was being served with a kind of Chinese doughnut – though people who wanted a bowlful still had to hand over some grain-ration coupons. Nearby, a team of self-employed cobblers were stitching up broken shoes on ancient sewing machines. A girl who walked past with two walnuts in her hand was grabbed by an older woman who demanded, 'Where did you buy those?'

In the main market area, the peasants were selling millet, legumes, beans, pumpkins, fresh coriander leaf, celery, walnuts, leeks, chestnuts, peanuts, dates, crabapples, Chinese pears, tobacco leaf, fresh fish, live crabs and turtles, chickens, ducks, geese, eggs, popcorn, sweet potatoes, chillis, carrots, sweet peppers, oil and honey.

Such supplements to the city dweller's diet are welcome because of the rationing which is still imposed on basic foodstuffs and which varies in scope and rigour according to time and place. Chinese officials usually only admit that grain, vegetable oil and cotton cloth are rationed in the cities. Actually a wide range of goods can only be had with the blessing of a person's place of work or in exchange for ration coupons. For instance, the Peking Iron and Steel Design Institute authorizes its employees to draw between 4 and 17.5 kg of grain monthly (9 to 38.5 pounds). (People who do non-manual work are expected to eat less grain; a real steel-worker might get as much as 30 kg – 66 pounds.) The ration is divided between different kinds of grain – in this case, 20 per cent rice, 65 per cent wheat flour, and 15 per cent cornmeal – a good reflection of the tastes of people native to Peking. Each employee also gets 250 gm (almost 9 ounces) of vegetable oil at a cost of just over 0.40 yuan (22 US cents), 1 kg (2.2 pounds) of pork for about 2.30 yuan (US$1.28) and the same amount of eggs for 1.80 yuan (US$1). Included in the rations is a bar of kitchen soap at 0.20 yuan (11 US cents).

Fruit and vegetables can be bought freely, though there is usually little fruit in the official shops except apples and pears and sometimes mandarin oranges, melons, and persimmons in season; the peasant markets offer a wider choice, but it is expensive to buy there. People returning to Peking after trips to southern China bring huge bunches of bananas or lychees with them, as a treat for their families and friends.

Bean curd – a soft vegetable cheese made from soybean milk – is a useful source of protein, though it became scarce in Peking after the prices of various other foodstuffs were raised in 1979. Few dairy products are sold, except to foreigners and nursing mothers. Most Chinese people dislike them, unless frozen as ice cream on a stick.

Restricted though the modern diet is, it consists principally of fresh, unprocessed foods and is low in animal fats and sugar. Chinese city dwellers eat more healthily than most Russians, something to which their sturdy frames and good complexions testify. But because of grain rationing, they seem to be obsessed by food, which shows in the lighting-up of faces and increased animation as mealtimes approach.

The most important human requirement after food – clothing – is also scarce. The cotton cloth ration is nationwide, with only small variations: about 5 metres per person a year – enough to make one new suit of clothes and keep a little of the ration over for underwear or towels. Synthetic materials, which are not rationed, are rather expensive; so is wool.

With the relaxation of clothing styles after the death of Mao, city people are ingenious in the way they use their sparse supplies of textiles to put a little colour into their dress and even copy one or two styles common in the West. Up till 1977, it was still politically and socially risky to put on anything but the drab grey, blue, black or khaki tunic and baggy pants – with the exception that in summer young women were permitted to wear blouses and below-the-knee skirts and could in winter wear padded jackets with coloured patterns of a sober style.

The narrow ranges of colours and styles available has led to the extraordinary belief – propagated by short-term visitors – that 'all Chinese people dress alike'. This was never true; only the Western eye, accustomed to a much wider spectrum of style and fashion, finds that the Chinese form of dress is somewhat uniform and monotonous. Chinese people, by contrast, have always been able to distinguish differences of fabric, cut, and colour; these readily identify the social status of the wearer.

Certainly the Peking fashion scene is now more colourful than at any time since 1966. The biggest variety of dress, as always, is seen in summer, with the younger women wearing quite short skirts and sometimes (with an appealing insouciance) flapping them to cool their nether regions on a hot day. A few young men are copying aspects of Western dress: a coat and a tie, or stovepipe trousers, or (for a brief period) bell-bottoms, which the Chinese call 'trumpet trousers'. Wedding dresses can be hired.

The great fashion craze in Peking in the winter of 1979–80 was for long scarves of bright red, black and white stripes. The scarf counter in the big Hundred Goods Emporium on Wangfujing Street was one of the most frequented – and a woman sales clerk make a speciality of showing how scarves could be worn in different ways, for variety. The favourite among Peking women at the time was college-style, with the longer end of the scarf flung back over the outside of the coat.

It must be stressed that improvements in dress have been seen mainly in the cities, where only about 20 per cent of the population live. In the rural areas, as always, clothing is more ragged and worn, often patched together and tied at the ankles for warmth. Old men, shuffling around the communes or smoking their long-stemmed pipes in the sun, look as if they have been dressed off the nearest scarecrow.

Food and clothing aside, low-cost consumer goods and articles of everyday use are in fairly good supply in China, which is reflected in the fact that requests for gifts from relatives living in Hong Kong or overseas usually concentrate on up-market products such as TV sets and cassette recorders. By comparison, in Russia, there is a demand for just about anything that a foreigner can import, from saucepans and socks to fountain pens, pharmaceutical products, and liquor. A Muscovite wandering around the shops of Peking is in a dream world of plenty; the ladies of the Soviet embassy are often seen ordering luxurious coats at the fur store on Wangfujing Street.

Few Chinese people can afford furs, though sheepskins are common enough, especially among peasants and pony-cart drivers. But they *can* afford to buy thermos flasks, enamel basins, mops, baskets, kettles, crockery, blankets, transistor radios and all the humdrum items which make up the fabric of everyday life. Of course such things are easier

to buy in the big cities, since they are the products of light manufacturing industries; still, they are also usually available to any commune peasant who cares to take a walk down to the local township
and has saved enough money to afford them.

Shortages are particularly common in certain items – including light
bulbs, bicycle tyres (there is one bicycle to every twelve people in
China), plastic shoes, matches, nails, bottles, soap, sewing machines,
watches and record players.

People in China joke that their light industries are 'like a train
entering a station – making a lot of noise but moving very slowly'.
In the event of scarcity of certain types of consumer durables,
shoppers must obtain so-called 'industrial coupons' in order to buy.
But efforts are made to ensure that the 'open international cities' such
as Peking, Canton and Shanghai have better supplies, to maintain
China's prestige in the eyes of foreigners.

Recalling the 60 yuan (US\$33.3) a month is a fairly good industrial
wage in a Chinese city, the following list gives an idea of the prices
prevailing in a provincial capital (Harbin, in the north-eastern province
of Heilongjiang). A kilogram is 2.2 pounds, and a metre is just over a
yard.

	Yuan	*U.S. Dollars*
Bicycle	154.00	85.46
Biscuits	1.32 per kg	0.73
Sponge cake	1.90 per kg	1.05
Cigarettes	0.30–0.40 per pack	0.17–0.22
Cotton cloth	0.30–4.00 per metre	0.17–2.22
Nylon fabric	4.00–6.00 per metre	2.22–3.33
Salted fish	0.80–1.60 per kg	0.44–0.89
Wheat flour	0.35 per kg	0.19
Cooking oil	1.68 per kg	0.93
Pork	2.86 per kg	1.59
Pullover	6.00	3.33
Transistor radio	50.00–60.00	27.75–33.30
Raincoat	18.00	9.99
Razor blades	0.10–0.12 each	0.06–0.07
Rice	0.30 per kg	0.17
Salt	0.34 per kg	0.19
Soap (laundry)	0.90 per bar	0.50
Soap (toilet)	0.64 per bar	0.36

	Yuan	U.S. Dollars
Sugar	1.72 per kg	0.95
Green tea	20.00 per kg	11.10
Toothpaste	0.35 per tube	0.19
Vegetables	0.10 per kg (approx.)	0.06
Wristwatch	120.00	66.59
Cinema seat	0.20	0.11
Quick meal	0.40	0.22

One of the most indicative things about this sample shopping list is that the items on it are all fairly basic. No aftershave lotion. No lipstick, tights, aerosol sprays, blender-mixers or electric razors. None of countless things that people in modern Europe and America just take for granted.

When one says that people's *basic* needs are reasonably well looked after in China, the emphasis is on the 'basic'. Toiletries for men are hardly known and would be too expensive for most people even if they were available. Women's cosmetics are still mostly 'out', with the exception of some face creams and powders, though lipstick has appeared in Peking, for sale to foreigners, and Chinese air hostesses on international routes are allowed to make themselves up. Stockings are still plain and coarse, and many women prefer to wear socks. Aerosols are unknown. Chinese men often shave only once every few days (they generally have a less vigorous growth of facial hair than Europeans), so why waste money on an electric razor and batteries?

Shopping for most Chinese people is a matter of laying in the daily necessities, not succumbing to wild temptations whipped along by advertising. There are no self-service supermarkets with piped Muzak. All transactions are in cash, and credit cards are unknown except for use by foreigners and overseas Chinese (they can now be used in major hotels and branches of the Bank of China). Since private car ownership is out of the question for most people, the only way to get the shopping bag home is to hump it onto a bus or a bicycle. Packaging consists mainly of a twist of vegetable fibre; you bring your own shopping bag. And – some visitors from other countries will say – China is the better off for not wasting her resources on packaging materials to clog up the environment and prettify the product. That is all a matter of value judgement.

One of the great strengths of the Chinese economy is the huge army of skilled craftsmen in all parts of the country except those most recently settled. Though sometimes scorned as showing a 'small producer's mentality', production of traditional handicraft items or foodstuffs – with countless regional variations – fills many of the simple needs of the population. People use skills handed down over centuries and even millennia, creating a wealth of simple but sturdy consumer goods and relieving the State of the need to set up light industries to make them.

Walking down a Peking street in a busy shopping area, you may see – if you are lucky – an old man sitting in a shop window practising the ancient craft of coopering, or barrel-making. With no more tools than a knife and a primitive but ingenious drill operated by a bowstring, his walnutty fingers shape a perfect circle of light, flexible wood and knot it into place with lengths of natural fibre. It probably took years of apprenticeship to learn this operation, but he looks as if he could do it with his eyes closed.

Other traditional skills – knife-grinding, cobbling, mending pots and pans – are pursued by itinerant craftsmen who wander from village to village plying their trade or are employed at service centres in cities. Itinerant servicing was discouraged during the Eleven Years and attacked as a form of 'petty capitalism', but it is now revived and plays an important part in meeting people's everyday needs.

At the upper end of the consumer goods scale, the most sought-after items are watches – especially Swiss and Japanese watches, which are imported officially – and colour television sets.

TV programmes have improved greatly since 1977, and the demand for sets is almost approaching the proportions of a national mania. China has had to buy Japanese picture tubes in order to keep up with the demand, and Chinese people from Hong Kong and overseas who are visiting relatives and friends on the mainland are increasingly bringing in colour TVs – black-and-white is no longer considered very prestigious.

'I just can't keep up with their list of wants,' a Hong Kong Chinese woman said after returning from a visit to relatives in

Shanghai, with a shopping list as long as her arm for things to be purchased before her next visit. 'They think we're made of money. They want TVs, watches, bicycles, cassette recorders, make-up, records and tapes – they even know the exact model numbers of the things they want and the names of performing artists on records.' (In 'bourgeois' Shanghai, that is plausible.)

One of the most astonishing sights, whether in the cities of China or on a rural commune, is a dark, cramped room in a dilapidated old house – with a brand-new colour TV sitting proudly in a corner. In the rural areas, it is quite feasible that a family sitting around their set – purchased by a relative in Hong Kong – might have risen from the supper table unsatisfied because they had nearly reached the end of their grain supplies before the next harvest.

Chinese people going on visits from Hong Kong and Macau at the lunar New Year (still the main holiday) can often be seen carrying in sacks of rice exported from China in the first place! The big stores selling mainland products in the two colonies will pack up food hampers and take orders for Japanese TVs or China-made bicycles, to be forwarded to the purchaser's relatives. People catching the train in downtown Kowloon to go up to Canton for a few days often carry so many gifts and supplies that there is a trade in ancient-style bamboo carrying poles on the smart new station concourse.

It used to be China's boast that she had no inflation. This was not strictly true; retail prices rose by 10 per cent from 1960 through 1962, for instance. But during the Eleven Years prices were strictly frozen, which – in view of the economic chaos created by the Cultural Revolution – meant an inexorable spread of the rationing system to cover more and more scarce products.

It has been a cornerstone of Deng Xiaoping's economic policy that the State – without giving up its overall control of prices and wages – should encourage manufacturing enterprises to set their product's price at a level which would reflect the demand for it. The State showed the way in 1979 when it sharply raised the prices for meat, fish and poultry in the cities, while at the same time raising the wages of about 40 per cent of the urban work force and giving every wage-earner a 5-yuan monthly food subsidy. The beneficiaries of this arrangement were the peasants, who – despite all the solicitude for them expressed by the left-radicals when they were in power during the Eleven Years – are still far and away the least prosperous sector of the community, as well as the biggest.

To the dismay of the authorities, enterprises around the country promptly reacted by pushing up the prices of their own goods and services. Even some hospitals raised their treatment charges. Short measure, adulteration of goods, blurring of quality grades, and plain flagrant profiteering were condemned by a hasty series of admonitions from Peking to the provinces and from the provincial capitals to the towns and villages. Shop assistants who were found guilty of short-changing their customers were fined and had their bonuses docked. Investigators went around insisting that prices raised without due authorization must be lowered again to their original level, on pain of prosecution.

There was much speculation as to why the Party had thought it could raise the peasants' incomes at the cost of the State (which subsidizes the price of grain and oil being sold in the cities) – or at the cost of the urban consumer – without causing inflation. In some places there were even queer contrary phenomena: shops and stores covertly buying back products, such as eggs, which they had sold at the lower official price, in order to market them again illicitly with a bigger profit. Some unscrupulous shop managers and sales clerks helped themselves to as much as they wanted just before the price rises.

The increases in food prices were accepted by the mass of the people with resignation, though many whom foreigners asked about it at the time said they did not think the extra cash payments to workers would meet the difference. In the general euphoria about the new consumerism in government policy, people were probably content to adjust their food intake somewhat to eat more bean curd, oil and vegetables and cut down a little on meat, eggs and fish.

Inflation is not the only thing China is copying from the West in the 1980s. An astonishing sight today – at any rate, for people who knew China a few years ago – is the sudden upsurge of advertising on city hoardings, in cinemas and in the press: Japanese TV sets, Chinese watches, and American banks all make up a motley and some-what amateurishly designed splash of colour on the grey streets of the capital – to say nothing of Canton, where businessmen flock in from abroad twice yearly for the Export Commodities Fair and are now greeted with a chorus of advertising slogans on walls and hoardings.

The puzzling thing about all this new advertising is: why are the Chinese authorities encouraging their people to spend money on consumer goods, when what the country needs most is to harbour its resources for investment and import of advanced technology and plant?

There seem to be several reasons. One is that the Chinese government is collecting advertising fees from the foreign firms involved and thus earning some extra hard currency. If most of the Chinese public do not have the means of buying the advertised product, well-to-do dependants of overseas Chinese do – and anyway it is not the government's concern whether the advertisers are getting their money's worth.

A reason to encourage the advertising of domestic products, as opposed to imported goods, is to help the State make bigger profits from the industries it owns and be able to plough them back into economic development. This is particularly so now that peasant markets have been allowed to flourish and there are more non-State-owned small industries; the State and its industrial concerns are effectively in competition with them for the money in people's pockets.

The new openness of China to foreign influence has been reflected in the partial lifting of the taboo on transactions in foreign exchange. Before, foreign exchange was controlled with the utmost rigour: not a penny of it was to be spent in China before it had been converted at authorized banks or hotels into yuan. I recall in 1972, when our delegation from *The Times* insisted on making a contribution to the costs of our tour, we decided on an appropriate sum, queued up at the hotel exchange office to change the requisite amount of travellers' cheques, received the bundles of crisp new yuan notes from the hotel safe – and then solemnly handed them back again to be entered in the books and replaced in the same safe.

With the exploding tourist trade permitted by the post-Mao regime, the encouragement given to overseas Chinese to visit, retire in, or invest in the People's Republic, and the sale for foreign currencies of foreign-made imports – such as whisky and wines and American cigarettes – those currencies have begun leaking into the economy at an increasing rate. Foreign currency is so enormously valuable in China's hived-off economy that some of it is certain to be diverted through deliberate misaccounting. By 1980, the authorities had become alarmed by this and the associated phenomena of black-marketeering, corruption and shady deals with residents or visiting foreigners. So it was decided to fence off the country as a whole from the insidious influence and severely limit people's access to foreign currency – as was the case before China suddenly opened her doors to the outside world in 1979.

Foreign currency certificates, resembling banknotes, were issued for the first time in 1980 – a practice copied from the Soviet Union, where such certificates are an established feature of the consumer economy. The method is to exchange foreigners' cash and travellers' cheques for special coupons which are marked with a face value in yuan and which entitle the holder to buy things not accessible to other people. This scrip-type currency is less versatile than dollars or yen or marks; it cannot be used outside China, so it is of little use to anyone plotting an illegal escape from the country. But as happens in the Soviet Union, some of this scrip eventually finds its way into the hands of local people and is highly prized, but those who get hold of it have to be careful how they use it, for fear of being investigated.

The big problem with the scrip coupons scheme is that it may increase inequalities of income among the local population. Some people – drivers, maids, interpreters – may wheedle scrip out of their foreign employers. Chinese students, journalists, diplomats and members of delegations travelling abroad can save up some of their foreign currency allowances, and when they return home with their little hoard the State may prefer to issue them some different kind of scrip from that used by foreigners, in order to preserve the distinction and keep tabs on everybody. This may lead to the setting-up of special shops or counters and the exacerbation of the problem of economic layers among the population: those who have considerable access to foreign currency, those who have a little and those who have none – the great majority. Writers, actors, dancers and musicians and others who receive fees or royalties for performing or having their works published abroad, all need their own special kinds of coupons, and inevitably much of this pseudo-currency will find its way on to the black market.

This, at any rate, is where the foreign-currency coupons system has ended up in the Soviet Union – as a disguise and instrument for applying social and economic discrimination among different types of citizens. Naturally, the Party elite soon start paying themselves partly or exclusively in scrip or simply set up secret shops where they can buy anything they want with ordinary currency.

Perhaps China, with its greater sensitivity to social inequity, will be able to avoid these side-effects of the system. But it has still to show that it can do this in practice, just as it has to show that granting higher standards of living to returned overseas Chinese or their dependants can be done without arousing serious resentment on the part of the mass of people with no such privileged status.

One encouraging thing about the State's new policy over consumer goods is that there is now official disapproval for people in responsible positions who try to cover up shortages in order to make a good impression on visiting foreigners or high-ranking cadres on inspection tours. The woman author Chen Jo-hsi, who spent seven years in the People's Republic during the Cultural Revolution period, has written a touching story about an old man who is allowed to buy a fish for his sick wife because the market has been specially stocked to impress some important visitors – only to have it confiscated as soon as the visitors leave. Many foreigners have had the strong feeling – difficult to verify – that commune stores they were taken to visit were artificially stocked and that some of the shoppers were mounting picturesque little charades of people buying things that were not normally available. Misguided attempts like this to represent living standards as higher than they actually are have done China's image much harm among people who know – from the personal testimony of those who live in or have lived in the People's Republic – that the supply and quality of consumer goods still leaves much to be desired.

Nevertheless, people's wants in any country are relative, and though most Chinese people would be glad of better food supplies and finer consumer goods in the shops, those over forty can remember the bitter years towards the end of the civil war, when a cold night might carry off dozens of undernourished street sleepers, and even people who did have a roof over their heads were often bankrupted by inflation, war damage, and looting. It is the younger generation – with no recollection of these things – who will become increasingly restive as their growing knowledge of the outside world brings it home to them that their nation still hovers only just above the poverty line.

13. *The Abacus Economy*

'Are the Chinese going to throw over communism?' This question, in varying forms, is being asked more and more often by people of other nations, at lectures, conferences and seminars – people who have a serious interest in charting the future course of the world's biggest nation.

There are good reasons for doubting China's long-term commitment to the European-originated idea of communism, an import modified by Mao and other Chinese leaders to fit what they saw as the country's special conditions.

The huge pictures of Marx and Engels which used to dominate the east side of Tiananmen Square in Peking seemed almost calculated to remind Chinese people of the foreignness of the ideology that rules their lives: awfully hairy, wild-looking Europeans, who in China only a few decades ago would have evoked straight away the epithet 'barbarian'.

The less fearsome-looking Lenin and Stalin, whose portraits used to hang on the west side of the square, were a lasting reminder that the Soviet Union was the world's first socialist state – and that in breaking with Moscow, China has asserted that the 'world socialist camp' no longer exists. (All four portraits were taken down in 1980 and restored only temporarily for special Party anniversaries.)

After its 1960 split with the Soviet Union, China broke relations with most of the other Communist parties of Eastern Europe and with the mainstream Communist movements in the Western world. Cuba and Vietnam have since also turned into enemies of China, and the only ruling Communist parties with which Peking had reasonably friendly relations in 1980 were those of North Korea, Yugoslavia and Romania. Even little Albania had fallen out with China.

In 1972 Mao had made friends with Richard Nixon – the sworn foe of communism, but nevertheless the best-liked American ever to have visited Peking. The high prestige enjoyed by Nixon in China was related almost solely to his decision to recognize the People's Republic, not to any naivety on the Chinese side about his political colouring.

Since Mao's death, China has begun a huge programme of cultural and economic liberalization, to the accompaniment of ever-friendlier ties with the United States, Western Europe and Japan, the bastions of world capitalism. Investment funds from capitalist countries, and from capitalist business firms among the overseas Chinese, have been eagerly sought to help along the country's modernization programme. Rigid political dogma and the personality cult of individual leaders have been pushed aside in the interests of better economic performance.

Communism, at root, is a statement about the economic nature of mankind. If China's economic policy diverges greatly from the ideas ascribed to Marx, Engels and Lenin, little will be left of communism in China. So it is the economy that must tell how well or badly Marxism has served China, and whether she will wish to follow it in the future.

If China's foreign relations in recent years have seemed to put her long-term commitment to communism in doubt, there are still stronger internal reasons why she may feel that Marxist theory has failed her in the attempt to build a strong and prosperous economy. After three decades of experimenting with socialist planning, she had not caught up either with the heavy industry, technology and military might of the Soviet Union or with the 'economic miracle' of Japan.

China's greatest asset, a near-boundless supply of human energy, has become a desperate liability, with population growth year by year wiping out the advances scored in the vital agricultural sector. The amount of food available per head of population in 1980 is little more than in 1955. Grain, cotton cloth, and numerous other products are still rationed. Meat is a luxury for all but a minority of Chinese living in the People's Republic. Housing is mostly crude or primitive, labour-saving devices in the home are almost unknown, and hardly anyone owns a private car. There is officially acknowledged to be a large and growing problem of unemployment, particularly among young people. Tentative moves to liberalize the economic system have resulted promptly in nationwide inflation. The country's foreign trade is about equivalent to that of nations which have only a fraction of China's population, such as Norway or Malaysia. And average *per capita* incomes are lower than those in Kenya.

Despite this list of economic woes, the post-Mao leaders seem still to hold to their faith in the basic ideas of Marxist socialism – and to believe that they can put things right by wiping out what they see as the mistakes made in the last two decades of Mao's life.

'Don't think we are going to become capitalists just because we take some useful practices from the capitalist system,' a pro–Peking Chinese journalist told me in Hong Kong. 'Nothing can stop us from building a socialist society.'

Still, China is anxious to learn what she can, from the West and elsewhere, to modernize her industry and streamline her economic management. 'The developed capitalist countries have a lot of useful experience, which may be of reference value to us,' the Communist Party proclaimed through its official journal in 1979. 'At present, our socialized industrial production still remains at pre-Second World War levels by international standards ... The capitalist system lacks planning and organization and causes great waste. Inside a capitalist enterprise, however, everything is carefully calculated. There is much in their method of management, shaped by experience accumulated over past centuries, which we can use.'

The root problem is that Stalinist state planning, which the Chinese copied wholesale from the Soviet Union in the early 1950s, has proved too rigid for Chinese conditions – but is too easily thrown into disorder if tinkered with.

'Our present economic management structure is basically modelled on the methods adopted in the Soviet Union in Stalin's days,' writes Xue Muqiao, a leading Chinese economist. 'The special feature of this structure is its undue emphasis on centralization and unification ... Its weak point is that it does not make allowances for the special needs of the localities and enterprises.'

But far from flinging the Soviet system out of the window, China's leaders in the post-Mao era have decided in some broad areas to put the clock back to about 1955, the year before relations with Moscow began to go steeply downhill after the late Nikita Khrushchev's denunciations of Stalin.

The problems Khrushchev faced in the Soviet Union of the late 1950s were quite similar to those confronting China today: flagging agriculture, lack of consumer goods, poor product quality and over-rigid planning in industry, excessive bureaucracy, and intellectual stagnation. Some of the latest methods being tried in China to cure these ills are reminiscent of Khrushchev's, though the personal hatred of him on the part of the older Chinese leaders makes it hard to discuss his historical role dispassionately in Peking.

It was in 1956 that Mao, in the course of one of the many twists and turns which marked his thinking, made a highly conservative statement on economic policy, 'The Ten Major Relationships'. In this speech, he faced up to the problems of China's lack of capital and proposed that the country build itself up by making the best of what it had, rather than rushing forward with ambitious industrialization schemes which it could not finance. He said agriculture and light industry must be developed as a precondition for the growth of heavy industry, established coastal industries should receive more investment than new industries inland, and the whole economy must be strengthened before there could be heavy spending on modernization of the armed forces.

Mao himself seemed to reverse his position on these questions in the Great Leap Forward of 1958–61, when industry was pushed frantically ahead at the expense of agriculture; again in the 1960s, when China developed her own atomic weapons and heavy missiles and built her own air force modelled on Soviet aircraft; and in the early 1970s, when emphasis was placed on building up new industrial centres inland, at the expense of investment in the big established coastal cities.

When Mao died, his successors laid great stress on his 1956 speech, which had never before been officially published. In mid 1979, the policy of downgrading investment in heavy industry – especially steel – was announced by the then Chairman Hua Guofeng, with the declared intention of boosting agriculture and light industry faster than before. At the same time, the screws were loosened on the Chinese intelligentsia, in the interests of encouraging more creative thinking and inventiveness. The underlying Maoist hostility towards imports of foreign culture, technology and expertise was dropped, while the country was thrown open to floods of tourists, politicians, and specialists from foreign countries – especially Japan, Western Europe, Canada, Australia and the United States.

The prevailing economic policy was dubbed 'readjustment, restructuring, consolidation and improvement' – the so-called 'eight-character policy', because each of the four Chinese expressions is written with two characters. This was nothing new, but the revival of a policy of the same name which was announced in 1960, when the damage done by the Great Leap was becoming impossible to ignore, and recovery measures had to be urgently drawn up.

By 1980 – despite the various changes of course which had taken place – there was no indication that the post-Mao leaders were considering dropping the most determining feature of socialism: public or collective ownership of the means of production. But they had clearly shown their determination to stress again initiative and self-interest among the workers, peasants and technicians, by directly linking their income levels to their productivity. This was precisely the policy which Mao's followers had bitterly denounced as 'revisionist' and 'capitalist' – so that, from a left-radical point of view, China was feared to be truly abandoning socialism and the dream of building communism.

From a Western point of view, it means no more than that China is attempting yet again to make socialism workable in her own particular set of national conditions. The latest Chinese experiments with socialism have aroused much sympathy and approval in the capitalist world, because they encourage commercial and cultural links between China and other countries and seem more rational than the wild ambitions of Mao's former group.

Foreign technology – once viewed with suspicion and resentment – is now welcomed as an indispensable aid. Old puritanical rules against the enjoyment of 'bourgeois' luxuries are being relaxed for those in China who can afford them. Political ideology and the personality cult of national leaders have been played down as a means of making people work harder. More Chinese people are going abroad to study and to be trained in modern technologies, and the gates of this once-cloistered country have again been thrown open to almost every kind of foreign visitor. A sincere and vigorous effort has been made to find out what other countries have to teach China about economic growth and modernization – while China herself hopes to avoid the complex economic problems and social ills of capitalist society.

By these means, the leaders hope, China will be able to overcome the chronic failings of the current-day Soviet system: its inefficient use of manpower, primitive market mechanisms, and disregard for basic human needs in terms of food and consumer goods, all in the interests of heavy industry and military might.

Japan represents an enigma from which the Chinese would like to learn more. Regarded until the late nineteenth century as a semi-barbaric country, sometimes hostile and sometimes 'tributary', Japan was never in the past thought capable of outshining China in any way. This made it all the more of a shock when the Japanese annexed Taiwan in 1895, sank the Russian battle fleet in 1905, seized China's north-east provinces in 1931, set up the puppet regime of Manchukuo, and imposed colonial rule on large areas of China until the end of the Second World War. On top of that, resource-poor Japan rose from the ashes of its wartime economy to build a thoroughly modern economic system, challenging the West, astonishing and worrying the Russians, and once more turning a speculative eye on China's huge human and natural resources – but this time with an eye on peaceful cooperation.

The Chinese could rationalize Western technological and military superiority in the nineteenth century by ascribing it to a kind of brutalized materialism devoid of the ancient ethical values of Confucian society. It is much harder for them now to rationalize the Japanese economic and technological success, since the Japanese have such a strong cultural affinity with themselves. This does not necessarily mean that China will end up by copying the details of the Japanese system. Despite the cultural link, Chinese and Japanese society and national psychology are vastly different from each other. Recently, China has shown more interest in what has been achieved in the United States – a country whose undisguised materialism appeals to the Chinese, because it is easy to understand – and in Yugoslavia and Romania, where the techniques of running socialist economies without large capital sums for investment have been experimented with in different ways.

Still, the Chinese cannot ignore Japan's success, despite the problems of urban pressure, inflation and labour unrest which the Japanese system suffers from. So they explain it to themselves as the result of careful attention to education and science, selective import and emulation of foreign technologies, and effective methods of motivating the work force to do its best. All these are integral parts of the policies being pursued by the post-Mao leadership in China.

In the meantime, China remains the country cousin of East Asia, with incomes and living standards far below those of South Korea, Taiwan, Hong Kong and Singapore, to say nothing of Japan. What are the flaws in the Marxist system of planning – or China's version of it – that have worked against the modernization and prosperity of a country which was once the richest and most inventive in the entire world?

Some Western specialists ascribe China's backwardness to the shattered state of her economy and social system after the Second World War. Others point to her century-long exploitation and subjugation by the Western seafaring nations and Japan. Others compare her favourably with India, where poverty and social disorder are much worse. Still others go along with the official Chinese line – that a handful of ambitious traitors have sabotaged the country's development in the interests of grabbing personal power.

Only now is it becoming possible, at long last, to build up a clear and detailed picture of what went wrong with the Chinese economy from the mid 1950s on. Since 1977, a swelling tide of facts and figures, devastating criticisms of the bureaucracy, suggestions, schemes and debates has burst out in the official press. And with the freer political atmosphere since Mao's death, Chinese officials and intellectuals are more inclined to talk frankly about their own problems and frustrations without the fear of being victimized for 'divulging State secrets'.

In their haste to find out just what went wrong, Chinese economists and political leaders have reversed – by almost 180 degrees – the view of their recent history which is propagated both for their own people and for interested foreigners. As short a time ago as 1976, the official line was that the economy had done splendidly in periods of fierce left-wing political activity (essentially 1958–61, 1966–70 and 1974–6), while stagnating and turning 'revisionist' in the intervening periods. The modern version, by contrast, is that everything was going swimmingly *until* 1958, when the disastrous Great Leap Forward narrowly missed wrecking the whole system; that the economy picked up again from 1962 on, thanks to drastic readjustments which were made to repair the damage caused by the Leap; and that chaos and anarchy again caused huge setbacks during the Cultural Revolution from 1966 until 1972 – when order was partially restored – giving way once more to factionalism and near-anarchy from late 1973 until the purge of the Gang of Four in 1976.

The latter view – that of the right-moderate political group – is much better documented than the former. The right-moderates around Deng have generally favoured the publication of Chinese economic statistics – which was banned almost completely by the left-radicals when they were in power. But even today the statistical information on more than one fifth of mankind is grossly inadequate. Foreign trade statistics have to be laboriously pieced together from the customs returns of China's trading partners, and the annual grain harvest is given in vague terms which do not even specify what crops account for how much of the total.

Until recently, statistics were released in an unbelievably niggardly fashion, and even then usually in the almost meaningless terms of percentage increase over another year for which no figure was given. In this way, authorities in the central China province of Hubei disclosed that steel output in 1978 was '10,264.67 times as high as in 1949'! The tiniest inaccuracy in the 1949 figure – were it even stated – would produce a gross distortion.

As the ultimate absurdity, a group of foreign correspondents in Peking once visited a new industrial town in Henan province, where they were welcomed by a team of municipal Party administrators who informed them that 'before Liberation [1949] there was no industry here; now it has increased by over a hundred times'.

Happily, the Chinese authorities are nowadays releasing more and more concrete statistics on their economy and society. While these must be treated with caution – because of the difficulties of collecting and checking them – they are at least something to work on.

China's worst single industrial problem is the in-built fault of all State planning: it tends to produce a vertically organized economy, in which the Party sets targets and makes demands and the government ministries attempt to formulate them as detailed plans and impose them on the industrial sector. In such systems, the producers receive their orders from above, do their work, and turn their products over to the State. The instructions from on high reach the various industries through a complex chain of command, passing down through the provincial and local levels. In the Chinese phrase, the factory becomes 'a bead on the abacus, to be moved up or down'.

In the case of light industrial consumer goods, the factories sell them at fixed prices to commercial bureaus, which in turn distribute them to retail outlets. Products of national strategic importance – such as armaments, special steels, turbines, aircraft and ships – are handed over to the ministry concerned. The wage bill is paid either out of the price obtained from the commercial bureau or from funds supplied by the ministry. A factory making millions of yuan worth of ball bearings each year is allowed to retain a cash emergency fund of no more than 50 yuan (US$28) because it is expected to apply to the State for any funds and investments it needs! To work in such an industry conveys a feeling similar to that of people working in a government ministry in any country: profit and loss are unimportant – indeed, to operate at a loss may be considered 'glorious', because it shows that the managers and workers are unconcerned with cash, in the 'higher interests' of serving the State.

In this type of system – which is now undergoing rapid modification in China – market pressures were non-existent. The industrial managers were almost as unconscious of profit as army officers. They had a task, and they carried it out. The ministries had to worry about a shortage of goods here, a surplus of substandard or unwanted products there. Mountains of forms in triplicate documented the industry's docile acceptance of its task. Meanwhile other industries and export corporations were clamouring for its products, the armed forces commanders were grumbling about their obsolescent or inadequate equipment, and – on the lowest rung of the ladder – the patient consumers lined up to buy goods often shoddy and faulty.

Below Politburo level, the highest decision-making bodies for industry are nowadays the specialized bureaus of the Party Central Committee, revived in 1980, and below them the various ministries, including those of the seven machine-building industries, divided up in their functions according to the type of military and civilian goods they produce.

Until recently, the big industries turned all their profits over to the State, after deductions had been made for welfare funds, improvements in workers' housing, and so on. The individual state-owned enterprise had to apply to the higher authorities if it wanted new equipment or more factory buildings, and these would then be supplied by the State. There was no obvious link between the profitability of an enterprise, the wage level for workers and administrative staff, and the funds available for expansion or modernization. In addition, equipment was depreciated at an extremely slow rate – about twenty-five years, in most cases – which worked strongly against technical innovation and the streamlining of productivity.

An enterprise's financial affairs have been handled through the state banks and their branches, which are still in most places run with the wooden abacus and handwritten accounts. The banks' functions have been mainly mechanical: transferring, depositing, and paying out funds for routine expenditures such as wages and for purchase of raw materials. Loans from the banks to aid expansion, or to finance extra purchase of materials, have usually been given on the instructions of the higher authorities, not on the initiative of the local bank managers.

The argument today is that the enterprises must be forced to link up horizontally – for instance, a timber mill should have its own paper plant and furniture-making workshop, and spinners of synthetic yarns should belong to the same enterprise as the refinery and the chemical plant which supply their materials. Depreciation rates are to be slashed to ten years, even five in some cases. The banks are to take a more active role in aiding and supervising industry.

Chinese economists and management specialists – having been given their head to find the flaws in the system – have concluded that the vertical arrangement of management must be changed. Industries must market their own products and, if they cannot sell them, reform themselves so that they can show profits. Nothing short of an armaments factory will be expected to show a loss, and the income of workers and managers alike will be directly affected by the factory's level of profit.

The mechanism being introduced for this purpose is the bonus system: workers are paid an extra sum every month if they are conscientious and productive. But obviously the management must also have greater freedom to fix its wage rates, purchase raw materials where it can get them at the best price, and market its products wherever there is the best market – without the interference or *diktat* of the ministry concerned.

Six basic rules have been worked out for the running of new-style

Chinese industrial concerns, aimed at increasing profits and, there-fore, the incomes of the workers and staff.

Factories and other state-owned industrial enterprises should draw up their own production plans and enter into contracts for the supply of goods to the State or other bodies.

They should have the right to sell their own products to whom-ever they please, when these exceed the amount needed to fulfill valid contracts with ministries or commerce bureaux.

They should control their own funds. After payment of tax and interest on bank loans, the enterprises should make their own decisions about replacement of plant, leasing or sale of surplus equipment, establishment of welfare facilities for workers and staff, and payment of bonuses.

Enterprises should have the right to adjust the wages they pay and the size of their labour force. They should be able to advertise vacancies, instead of relying solely on the state-run employment bureaux.

With the exception of certain important products whose price is controlled by the State, the enterprises should be able to set their own prices for their products.

They should have the right to defy state organs which want to appropriate their funds, labour force, materials, equipment, or products.

If fully implemented, these six points should give Chinese indus-trial concerns almost as much freedom to manage their own affairs as is enjoyed by any business in the capitalist world. The only big difference will be that the enterprises are still publicly or collectively owned, so there are no shareholders or dividend payments (though in the case of frequent bonus payments, the workers themselves gain something close to the status of shareholders). It is arguably no longer possible to call such enterprises state-owned, in view of the power to resist state commands which the reform calls for.

The bonus system is more difficult to operate than it would seem. To pay all workers a bonus of the same amount – simply because they come to work on time and are not notorious malingerers – negates the whole purpose of the scheme. Instead of just penalizing a very few of the worst workers by stripping them of their bonus, the industrial manager needs to pick out the hardest-working and most innovative workers and reward them more for their pains. There have been so many reports of managers failing to do this, since the bonus system was made nationwide in the late 1970s, that there is obviously passive resistance to the scheme.

Throughout the Eleven Years, the Party clung doggedly to the idea that offering extra pay for extra work was 'economism', or 'sugar-coated bullets for the workers', or 'putting cash in command'. Leftist theorists Zhang Chunqiao and Yao Wenyuan (both members of the Gang of Four) argued in the media in 1975 that differentials in wage rates for different workers were a form of outdated 'bourgeois' privilege which should be abolished as soon as possible, but even they admitted that the time was not yet ripe to do so.

During this period, the official criteria for a raise were seniority, years of service, and 'attitude' (both political and professional). On the whole, the older workers got more pay than the younger ones – which in the case of an industry like coal-mining meant that some people were being paid more for less work, the younger men being stronger.

After Mao's death, the Party plunged headlong into the new bonus-incentives scheme which, by rights, should have made the old Chairman turn in his crystal sarcophagus. Money once again became the carrot by which the workers were motivated; the big problem was that the industrial managers and responsible Party cadres in factories feared the grumbling or open revolt of workers who did not receive bonuses, so that the money was just shared equally, exceptions being made mainly for those who had a bad attendance record. This was called 'crew-cut' or 'eating out of one pot'. It made a nonsense of the whole idea of bonuses for harder work or greater productivity, and by the end of the 1970s it was clear that the bonus system would have to be seriously overhauled if it was to contribute at all to rapid growth.

The abuse of bonuses, and their conversion into nothing more than extra wages, is scathingly dismissed by current-day Chinese economists as the 'iron rice-bowl' system. This is a metaphor for total job security, since an iron bowl, unlike a porcelain one, cannot be broken. It is seen as the main hindrance to the rationalization of wages and bonuses in industry.

Nor have ultra-left-wing Maoist ideas about economics completely disappeared from the debate. Economist Liu Zizhen has risked the wrath of the Deng leadership by arguing in favour of the 'iron rice-bowl' concept, calling it 'the very manifestation of the superiority of the socialist system'. Liu has also criticized the cutting down of excess manpower in industry, which he sees as synonymous with creating unemployment. Instead, he puts forward the highly advanced idea of a four-hour working day, leading to 'an increasingly comfortable and beautiful life'. He sees low wages and a high employment rate as preferable to the Deng group's method of forcibly raising wages and productivity even if it means creating (or admitting the existence of) quite widespread unemployment. Liu even holds that, if necessary, China should accept a situation in which five people do the work of three, and five people eat rations designed for only three. 'Everyone must have food and work,' he polemicizes. 'What is wrong with this?'

Besides the low productivity of the work force, however, one of the biggest problems of socialist economies is the fact that they often do not calculate their performance in terms of value as defined by free-market forces. Useless goods for which there is virtually no market are included in the output figures for a factory and, ultimately, in the figure for the country's GNP. At the most ludicrous extreme, a factory might even claim double figures for the production of a faulty metal part which had to be recast!

No capitalist economy would produce figures for the production of, say, pairs of shoes and judge that if more shoes were produced this year than last year, economic growth has taken place. The achievement of the shoe industry would be measured in pairs sold and in their price.

The problems caused by overemphasis on volume of production are long familiar in the East European socialist states as well as China. If a metal-goods factory is trying to turn out so-and-so-many tons of product to fulfil the annual plan, it will certainly favour heavy saucepans over light teapots: the input of labour and capital per ton will be much less in the case of the saucepans, and the output will be higher. But if no other factory in the region is specifically programmed to make teapots, there will be no teapots on the market.

The solution, obviously, is to price teapots in such a way that their cost to the consumer allows for the extra labour involved in making them in large numbers, not just the amount of metal in them. However simple this may seem to the Western economic mind, it is a big stumbling block to the rationalization of consumer-goods production in socialist economies, which tend, in differing degrees, to mistrust money values as the yardstick of performance.

One reason for the relatively low esteem in which money is held in China and other socialist countries is the fact that it may not in itself be the means of purchasing wanted goods. If supplies are rationed, no amount of money (short of a bribe to the sales clerk) will buy more grain or cooking oil or cotton cloth. A person who has saved the cost of a bicycle will not be able to buy it until his or her turn comes on the waiting list. And in times of left-wing political ferment, many consumer goods just disappear from the shops or people will be afraid to buy them for fear of being labelled 'bourgeois'.

Because output is not basically planned in accordance with market demand – but in accordance with available supplies and an arbitrary set of instructions from the State – there are huge discrepancies between what the consumers want and what industries produce. Some of the most serious shortages are found in the building materials sector. Numerous applications for supplies of cement – for uses varying from the lining of pits to produce methane gas out of sewage and compost to the casting of concrete hulls for boats and even ships – are held back by shortages. In the advanced industrial countries, cement production has been one of the fastest-growing sectors, and so it will have to be in China if she is even to think of catching up with the developed world. Other important building materials in short supply today are asbestos, glass, bricks, timbers, tiles, sand and stone. Without a big increase in production of these materials, the industrial construction industry cannot be expanded as is needed.

Shortage of electric power is one of the most pressing problems facing Chinese industry and, to a lesser extent, agriculture. Most power in China is generated from coal, though the amount generated by small and medium hydroelectric stations has been growing. In some big industrial centres, whole factories have to be shut down for hours at a time in order to boost power supply to those industrial plants considered more important. Private consumption of electricity is very restricted: there are few electrical home appliances on the market, cooking with electricity is discouraged, heating is mostly by coal or vegetable matter, and lighting is held down through the rationing of light bulbs and their restriction to a low wattage.

Until recently, Chinese state-owned industries have not normally marketed their own products; this has been the responsibility of the commerce bureaux which act as wholesale distributors, crude market researchers, and sometimes as watchdogs for fulfilment of the production plan. Relations between the industrial managers and the commerce department heads are not always harmonious; as was noted at a conference of commerce bureau directors in Guangdong province, 'They tend to grumble at each other.'

Causes of friction are many. A factory is badly organized or cannot get enough raw materials and parts for assembly, so it fails to meet its agreed supply quota to the commerce bureau. The latter is then in trouble with the department stores or export corporations which have been counting on it to deliver the goods on time. The factory manager has his instructions as to the number of workers he can employ, the basic wage they are to receive, the raw materials and parts he can requisition for, the selling price of his product, and a number of other indicators. If someone else lets him down, or he is hamstrung by his instructions, he has to let the commerce bureau down.

The commerce bureau, by contrast, has to react to market pressures – which, in the absence of flexible pricing, must be determined by simple observation or by wrangles with other official bodies trying to obtain supplies of manufactures. Even if the commerce bureau accepts the criticisms or demands of its customers, it still has to find ways of twisting the factory manager's arm (or, more likely, bribing him with gifts and banquets) in order to get the goods out of him.

As in the Soviet Union, this situation had given rise to a class of semi-official wheeler-dealers – once called 'fixers' in Russia and styled 'purchasing agents' in China. These astute characters flit around from factory to raw-material supplier to commercial bureau, buying up a consignment of raw cotton here, a warehouseful of tin trays there, a ton of metal scrap somewhere else. Inevitably, they often become corrupt, but they are essential to the most elementary functioning of the system, because without them it would bog down in a sea of useless inventories and disregarded purchase orders.

The Party has in the past few years recognized that, in order to speed up the sluggish turnover of goods, the commerce bureaux must act to some extent like business firms in the West: they must go out and push products which are not selling well and find out more accurately what changes will make future lines of merchandise sell better. If they do well in selling, they will almost certainly receive some 'token of appreciation' from the factory manager, and if they can browbeat or cajole the factory manager into meeting the needs of the end users or retail outlets more closely, there may be something in it for them at that end of the deal too.

Favourite kickbacks are perishable foodstuffs, which the recipient can enjoy without leaving any traces. Fish, vegetables, melons, tobacco, wines, restorative cordials and herbal tonics – these are all excellent coinage on the bribe market. Since the opening of China to luxury products from abroad from 1978 on, foreign-made watches, cassette recorders, colour TV sets and other such items have also entered the corruption grid. Graft has increased particularly in those activities concerned with contacts with the outside world: foreign trade, issue of travel permits and exit visas and provision of special facilities and luxury goods for returned overseas Chinese or overseas Chinese dependants in China.

Hand in hand with China's modernization drive goes the expansion of foreign trade. With a *per capita* trade volume of only about US$40 per annum, the country is 'self-sufficient' in oil, coal, non-grain foodstuffs, basic consumer goods, 1950s-level industrial equipment, and some important metal ores. But the term 'self-sufficient' must be seen as meaning 'only just self-sufficient' or 'on a very tight rein'. Actually, self-sufficiency in China usually means a top-level decision not to import, rather than an abundance of the product concerned.

Goods which are very scarce and have to be imported are grains – mainly wheat and maize – soybeans, copper, aluminium, special alloys, TV sets, pulp, sugar, lorries, cars, airliners, freighters, offshore oil exploration and drilling equipment, modern mining equipment, cocoa, rubber, up-to-date medical instruments, and advanced equipment such as electronic gear, computers and automated plant. The government's shopping list is as long as a man's arm, but the country's foreign exchange resources – unfortunately – are not. Until recently Peking pursued an ultra-cautious line in foreign trade, rejecting commercial credits and long-term loans, foreign aid or imports of consumer goods and, with the exception of some very big deals, paying on the nail for everything and keeping respectable reserves of foreign exchange and gold.

This policy was quite sensible as long as China's leaders were content to see her develop at a slow but reasonably steady pace, avoiding international financial entanglements or overdependence on any one source of supply. But China has to coexist and compete with other nations and cannot opt for a slow pace of development without running the risk of losing her national power and even her sovereignty. The weaker her armed forces are – and their strength depends on the country's economic and technological performance – the stronger will be the temptation for the Soviet Union to invade her. And the ordinary people of China will not forever put up with being so obviously poor and disadvantaged by comparison even with their relatives in Hong Kong, let alone the rich countries of the world. The post-Mao leadership has frankly acknowledged that it must produce more, or it will fail in its entire mission.

The solution chosen is the throwing open of the Chinese economy to many foreign influences which can help enrich it, on a basis of mutual advantage. Foreign businessmen are now welcome to set up garment factories, dig mines, build and operate hotels – on the understanding that once they have made a healthy profit and passed on their knowledge and experience to the Chinese side, they will either make a fresh investment or pack up and go home, leaving China to operate the facility concerned. Judging from the response in the developed world, this 'joint venture' policy is seen by Western and Japanese businessmen as the answer to the old question, 'Who will light the lamps of China?' – the lure of the billion-strong market, where it only needs each person to drink one can of soft drink in a year to make the manufacturer rich. Still, even the most enthusiastic exporters have had to acknowledge that a national *per capita* purchasing power of less than US$300 per annum – of which only 12 per cent is accounted for by foreign trade – hardly justifies such grand hopes, and to grow rich by selling to China is to be a long-term process, in which the enrichment of the Chinese people themselves will be the prerequisite for big profits for China's trading partners.

Despite the long haul ahead, it is astounding how many foreign business firms have been permitted already to open branches and agencies in China – so that the big modern Peking Hotel has practically turned into an office building. Others brave the astronomical rents in British-ruled Hong Kong and set up there in order to take advantage of its 140-year-long expertise in trading with China.

An outline code for foreign investment in China has been published, under which business firms from Western countries and Japan or overseas Chinese businesses can enter joint ventures with the Chinese state-owned enterprises, many of which are already being given some autonomy over their foreign currency earnings, a thing which would have been unheard of a few years ago. Under the new code, each joint venture will have a chairman appointed by the Chinese side, and vice-chairmen or vice-presidents mutually agreed upon. The foreign businessman will be expected to open an account with the Bank of China or some other approved bank, train Chinese personnel to take over the operation in due course, give priority to Chinese sources of supply of materials or parts, and not back out without the agreement of the Chinese side. In exchange, China will supply land – at a rental of between US$4 and US$8 per annum per square metre, as well as facilities such as electric power, water and roads. China will provide commercial insurance for the investor, including even 'political risk' – such as expropriation or change of government policy. And, of course, most or all of the work force will be Chinese.

Despite the relatively high land rent, the proposition is attractive to many manufacturers who have previously had low-cost, labour-intensive operations such as transistor assembly and garment-making in Hong Kong, Taiwan, South Korea or Singapore, as well as to big industrial concerns such as oil companies. The average Chinese industrial wage of less than US$50 a month is still tiny compared with the minimum $250 which an employer would have to pay in Hong Kong in 1982.

Just as important as the boost in earnings for China is the social and educational effect of sending thousands of technicians and workers to be trained in foreign technologies, some of them going abroad to study the manufacturing or servicing process at source. Knowledge of foreign languages and foreign cultures will mushroom, while familiarity with China's institutions and the attitudes and customs of Chinese people will become more widespread in Western countries.

The former left-radicals would have condemned this policy as 'semi-colonial', but that is an oversimplification. Foreign businessmen in China will have to obey Chinese laws and treat their Chinese workers and technicians with respect. It is an exciting experiment in mutual tolerance and education, as well as profit, and probably in future centuries it may be seen as the measure which contributed most to bringing China and the Western world together after two centuries of mutual suspicion and conflict.

14. *The Wider Chinese World*

People have long been – and still are – among the most important of China's exports. In addition to those who settled in South-east Asia both before and after the arrival of the European colonial powers in the nineteenth century and the creation of new business opportunities in commerce, mining and plantations, there are by now Chinese people in almost every country of the globe. The great majority – estimated at a total of about twenty-two million – are in Malaysia, Singapore, Indonesia, the Philippines and Thailand.

Chinese emigration to those countries has virtually ceased since the Second World War. But during the late 1970s, a quarter of a million people – a staggering figure – were leaving the People's Republic each year. Most were illegal border-crossers who slipped into neighbouring Hong Kong, often at a rate in excess of *one thousand a day*.

Immigration from the mainland used to induce a kind of resigned desperation among British authorities in the 400-square-mile territory at the east side of the Pearl River estuary. Unlike the so-called 'boat people' – ethnic Chinese and Vietnamese refugees from Vietnam, most of whom will eventually be resettled in the United States and elsewhere – the 'illegals' from China usually have to stay on in Hong Kong, whose estimated six million population already poses near-intractable problems of housing, education, hospitals and welfare.

Hong Kong has been absorbing people from China ever since it was seized by the British in the early 1840s as a prize of the First Opium War. Between then and the turn of the century, the colony was enlarged through acquisition of the Kowloon Peninsula, on the mainland opposite Hong Kong Island, and later the rural New Territories, which include over two hundred islands, mostly small and uninhabited. (In the local parlance, the People's Republic is still called 'the mainland'.)

Miraculously, the booming industry and commerce of Hong Kong in the post-war period have succeeded in absorbing almost all comers. Though even today many have to take jobs paying no more than US$250 a month, still they keep on arriving from neighbouring Guangdong and occasionally from other Chinese provinces, where their total incomes as peasants or fishermen would mostly have been about US$20 to $30 a month. Even with the low cost of living in China, their lives there are hard, poor and unpromising, and many continue trying to slip into Hong Kong, even after being caught and sent back more than once.

The Hong Kong police, the British Army, and – on the other side of the border – the Chinese People's Liberation Army (PLA) proved incapable of stopping this flood of discontented people who hoped to find a better life in Hong Kong. Some top Hong Kong officials even wondered aloud whether the Peking and Canton authorities really tried very hard to stop illegal exit. After all, it relieved the pressure on jobs in southern China; it generated foreign currency earnings, by creating new mouths who must pay in Hong Kong dollars for the food shipped in daily from the mainland; and it ensured that cash remittances sent back to relatives in China continued to grow. It was, in brief, a profitable export. However, the Chinese authorities did seen genuinely anxious to stop the flow of people; their failure to do so was apparently due mainly to bad organization.

Tourists who are shocked by the slum conditions in some parts of Hong Kong wonder why anyone would want to leave the relative security of a socialist country to risk exploitation, destitution, prostitution and drug addiction in a foreign-ruled colony. The question is best answered by encouraging overseas visitors to take the one-day tours which allow them to enter China for a little sightseeing, with minimal formalities. Having walked around the near-medieval back streets of the border town of Shenzhen (or Shumchun, as the Cantonese call it) and seen the ragged clothing of the people on a mainland fishing commune, they can look at the poorer parts of Hong Kong in a new light – as relatively affluent communities, in fact.

Even if a tourist in Hong Kong and southern China should feel that, all in all, the austerity of the latter is better than the squalor of parts of the former, the people who count – the Chinese people of all ages who make the dangerous crossing to Hong Kong – still are apparently convinced that they will be better off in the British-ruled territory.

The risks are considerable. Those who take their chance in the coastal waters off Hong Kong are sometimes prey to sharks, while others die of exhaustion or are simply swept out into the ocean. Boats are hard to come by, so the more ingenious make rafts of plastic bags, rubber tyres, even inflated condoms (issued free in China) – anything that will float. Despite the constant patrolling of the coastal waters by Hong Kong police, British naval vessels, and small fast boats loaded with Gurkha soldiers, many of the 'swimmers' – as they are known – have made it to shore in some remote part of the colony.

Operators in Hong Kong, Macau and Guangdong province have made big business out of organizing mass escapes in the so-called 'snake boats' (immigrant smuggling vessels), some of which have powerful engines enabling them to outrun the Hong Kong Marine Police. The racketeers in 1980 were actually offering numbered tickets to their illegal passengers, who had to pay the equivalent of US$600 to $1,200 for the risky trip, a small fortune by mainland standards. There have inevitably been tragic accidents, such as when a 'snake boat' capsized while being taken in tow by the Hong Kong police and more than thirty people – mostly women and children – were drowned.

Once in the city, the newcomers used to be immune from deportation back to China. The Hong Kong government made this rule because, officials said, it would be too difficult and costly and would create an underground of fugitives – easy meat for criminal gangs, Triad-type secret societies, or stingy employers who would pay them well below the legal minimum wage. So the British authorities permitted them to obtain identity cards and become Hong Kong residents. They used to line up in their hundreds to register, already smartly dressed and looking no different from longer-term residents of Hong Kong.

Sheer weight of numbers forced the Hong Kong government in 1981 to abandon this humane and sensible policy. Tossing aside the former argument in favour of the so-called 'touch-base policy', it announced that in future no illegal immigrants (known locally as 'eye-eyes') would be given identity cards or permitted to remain if caught. The totally predictable result was a massive increase in armed robberies at goldsmiths' shops, jewellers' and banks. Not all the culprits were 'eye-eyes', of course. But quite a few were believed to be desperate youths who could see no other way to survive once they reached Hong Kong and went underground.

The pressure on the government was admittedly heavy. With the world recession and slacker demand for Hong Kong manufacturers, unemployment became a problem for the first time since the 1950s. However, the government itself was to some extent responsible for the economic downturn because of its policy of permitting astronomical rents (all land in Hong Kong is owned by the British Crown, and can only be leased up till 1997). By releasing land for development too slowly, in the interests of gaining the maximum revenue from it, the government fuelled the activities of land speculators and big real-estate firms, which by 1981 were charging up to and over the equivalent of US$6,000 a month for a three-bedroomed apartment of about 2,500 square feet. These rents, reflected all the way down the economic ladder, produced heavy inflation and discouraged non-property investment in Hong Kong. And at the bottom of the pile were the wretched 'eye-eyes' with their forged identity cards, or none at all.

The clamp-down on illegal immigrants, which required heavy expenditures on police and troops, could mainly be justified by the strain they put on Hong Kong's housing, medical and schooling amenities, and social welfare. The outflow of people from China will always exist, though in reduced numbers, unless the Chinese People's Liberation Army positions one man every five yards along the twenty-five-mile border, on the other side of the high fence which has been scaled or crushed down innumerable times by fugitives. There is both a push factor – the low standards of living in Guangdong province and elsewhere in China – and a pull factor, the relative prosperity of Hong Kong, Vice-chairman Deng Xiaoping himself said as much to Hong Kong's governor, Sir Murray Maclehose, when the latter paid the first official visit of a Hong Kong governor to Peking in 1979.

Such 'eye-eyes' as do still come across may swim – using crude rafts or plastic bags for flotation. In winter the overland route is more practical. Some risk freezing to death after smuggling themselves into the refrigerated cars of freight trains crossing the border with food supplies for Hong Kong, or are mangled beyond recognition when they fall or jump after hiding or clinging to the underside of the waggons as far as the last tunnel leading to downtown Kowloon. Others use the cross-country route, over the rugged hills and scrubby undergrowth of the New Territories.

All captured illegals – with the exception of a very few who can convince the police that they have a claim as political refugees – are driven back to China in police trucks the next day. Throughout the 1970s, no persistent reports from Guangdong suggested that the returnees were seriously ill-treated by the Chinese authorities, who regard running off to Hong Kong as a misdemeanour rather than a crime. They were put in uncomfortable detention centres for anything up to a fortnight and then returned to the towns or communes where they came from and forced to work under supervision, with docked wages, for a while. Their families would have mixed feelings about seeing them return. To balance the remittances which many successful escapers sent back to their relatives once they had secured jobs in Hong Kong, the State often imposed socio-economic penalties on the families. They could be ordered to write to the runaway and urge him or her to send money back only through the official banking system, thus imposing a kind of 'refugee tax'. The ones believed to be imprisoned or executed on their return to China were those who were accused of having organized mass escapes, stolen state or commune property such as a boat, or killed someone – say, a member of a border patrol on the Chinese side.

Some Hong Kong residents living near the border area have preyed on the illegals by offering them a place to hide and a chance to get in touch with their relatives – who will usually be prepared to pay several thousand Hong Kong dollars (HK$5.60 = US$1) to help their family members sneaking down from Guangdong. The British authorities have imposed very stiff penalties – up to eighteen months in jail – for people aiding illegals. This is fair enough for those who prey on the fugitives' desperation, but it is rather rough on a soft-hearted person who has simply taken pity on an escaper and given him or her a little food or cash.

The task of tracking down border-crossers in the frontier zone is a dreary one. 'A lot of the men don't like catching people to be sent back,' a senior British officer said. 'The younger officers are unhappy about it too.' The troops on the British side are mostly unarmed, though they carry stout sticks, and some have been wounded when fugitives tried to knife them and escape.

The situation is not without its humorous side. Hong Kong police at one post near the border awarded a 'special certificate' to a young Chinese woman who, they said, was the 10,000th person they had caught. A press photograph showed her obviously enjoying the joke – and probably intending to slip back across the border again at the first opportunity, after she was sent back and completed her period of detention.

A British television crew, who came to Hong Kong to investigate the problem of refugees from Vietnam as well as illegals from China, filmed a young Cantonese man who had been caught and was waiting disconsolately to be returned to the mainland. 'Ask him why he came to Hong Kong,' the interviewer told the Chinese interpreter. Back came the reply: 'To find a job.' Interviewer: 'What kind of job would you like?' Answer: 'I wouldn't mind a job like yours.'

The other big category of immigrants from China to Hong Kong are the so-called 'overstayers', people who arrive with legal Chinese exit visas, and then just go to ground. The police have little chance of tracking them down when their visas expire (and an estimated 98 per cent of people leaving China with visas for 'temporary visits' to Hong Kong become 'overstayers'). They become virtually stateless, though the Hong Kong government may issue them with travel permits if they wish to go abroad.

Most of these people – who include former cadres, professors, engineers, musicians and journalists – are leaving China either to be united with relatives or because they simply cannot fit into mainland society. Most of them retain a strong patriotic affection for China, and quite a few have left-radical political views – now discredited in the PRC. They see nothing anomalous in praising socialism while choosing to live under capitalism.

These 'legal' immigrants are in many ways a bigger headache for the Hong Kong authorities than the 'illegals'. They are often too old to find jobs or unwilling to work in factories, where the demand for labour is still strong. They drift into the ranks of underemployed intellectuals, giving language lessons or clerking and every so often trudging up to the huge United States consulate, to join the long line of people applying to emigrate.

British officials feel let down over the understanding they reached with China in 1973 – to the effect that British troops and Hong Kong police would send back 'illegals' caught in the border area, if China would restrict the growing number of 'legals' entering Hong Kong through normal channels to fifty a day. British immigration officials at the main border crossing point, the railway bridge across the Shenzhen River, are not empowered to turn away people with valid Chinese exit visas unless they are on the blacklist of undesirables.

China has consistently flouted the terms of this undertaking, granting exit visas to several times as many people as Hong Kong feels it can cope with. But in January 1980, the Guangdong provincial authorities did announce tough new measures to discourage illegal border crossing to Hong Kong and Macau under the new criminal code.

The regulations disclose just how serious a problem of public order has been caused in Guangdong, with its population of roughly sixty million people, through the constant flood of people running away to Hong Kong. They single out for special condemnation people who play on 'feudal superstitions' to instigate illegal emigration – fortune-tellers who choose auspicious days for people to make the attempt, in accordance with their sign of the zodiac; people who forge documents, assault border guards, intimidate those who try to prevent illegal emigration, build boats and sell them to would-be runaways, storm detention centres to free people who have been caught trying to get out, accept bribes to turn a blind eye, or are caught with guns or secret documents. (Some disillusioned Chinese cadres who cross illegally into Hong Kong bring government or Party documents as an offering to the intelligence services on the British side, in the hope that they will not be sent back.)

The double standard involved for the British is painful, if perhaps unavoidable. While any British government would support the right of Jews or Lithuanians to emigrate from the Soviet Union – and even let them settle in Britain in modest numbers – a British administration in Hong Kong is collaborating as vigorously as it possibly can with the authorities of a Communist country, where living conditions are much tougher then they are in Kiev or Vilnus, to *prevent* free emigration.

The message is plain enough: the West welcomes the exiled intellectuals of Russia and East Europe but is desperately anxious to keep out Chinese, especially Chinese peasants. It is glib and easy to say that this is a racist policy, but that is not the real story. The policy of free emigration – which Senator Henry Jackson and former President Jimmy Carter, for instance, espoused with regard to the Soviet Union – is possible precisely because the numbers leaving there will probably never be very high. The idea of coping with a massive Chinese emigration – even more massive than the present one – is a nightmare to any government interested in a high employment rate and avoidance of racial tensions. Australia wants people with skills, not just farmhands. Britain's quotas are filled mainly by young people from the semi-rural New Territories of Hong Kong, who go to work in the Chinese restaurants which are now to be found in almost every sizeable British town. France has already resettled scores of thousands of Indochinese – Khmer, Lao, and Vietnamese, as well as ethnic Chinese – and Holland has absorbed Indonesians from its former East Indies empire. West Germany and Scandinavia have no recent colonial tradition and will accept only relatively small numbers of Asians, since the lower-paid jobs in those countries are already filled by Turks, Yugoslavs and workers from North Africa.

On top of that, Chinese people in Hong Kong are choosy about the country to which they would like to emigrate. The overwhelming majority want to go to the United States, but quotas there have been affected by the need to resettle Indochinese refugees (many of whom are of Chinese origin). Others would be content with Canada, Britain or Australia, but very few want to go to countries with a low standard of living or severe unemployment problems. I talked once to a Bolivian government official who said Bolivia, needing labour for development, 'would be glad to take Indochinese refugees' – of Chinese origin or whatever. He seemed astonished when I pointed out that some of the 'boat people' who had made it from Vietnam to Hong Kong had refused to be sent even to Ireland – where living standards are much higher than in Bolivia – because they had never heard of the place and wanted to go where more of their kind had gone before.

Most Chinese people in Hong Kong, whether they were born there or not, feel insecure about the future. The 99-year-lease on the New Territories, which Britain obtained from the Chinese imperial government in 1898, expires in 1997. It is hardly a lease at all, in fact, since Britain has never paid any rent for the New Territories. But in the course of a couple of decades the area has been transformed from a rural backwater into the site of the colony's most dynamic industrial development, with new towns, high-rise buildings and roads spreading across the landscape like a rash. Hong Kong Island, Kowloon Peninsula and the New Territories are an indivisible economic unit. If the New Territories revert to China in 1997, Kowloon and the Island must almost certainly revert too. So a Chinese person in Hong Kong sees precisely seventeen years – from 1980 – in which to accumulate some savings, rear a family, and make plans to get out before the expected crunch.

Suggestions that the People's Republic may want to keep some special status for a Hong Kong still under British administration, well into the twenty-first century, are perhaps plausible when one takes into account the pump-priming effect of Hong Kong on China's modernization drive. But this does not greatly impress a Chinese resident of Hong Kong who knows from experience how unpredictable the Chinese Communist Party leadership has been in the past and how seemingly immutable policies can be thrown out of the window almost overnight when the balance of power in Peking changes.

The Soviet Union has often taunted China about its unwillingness to do away with the 'colonial remnants' on its doorstep. But for China, the reasons to leave Hong Kong in its present status seem overwhelming. Peking earns some US$3 billion annually from Hong Kong in sales of foodstuffs, medicines, consumer goods and fresh water. Hong Kong has been buying piped water from the mainland since the early 1960s, to augment the inadequate supply from its own reservoirs. In 1979 the colony paid HK$100 million (US$55 million) for this extra water. China's earnings through thirteen directly or indirectly controlled banks in Hong Kong – including a huge branch of the Bank of China – and through dealings in shipping, real estate, insurance, warehousing, advertising, cold storage, oil supply and cigarette manufacturing, may nearly double this figure. Earnings from Hong Kong help cover China's huge deficit with its biggest trading partner, Japan.

But money is not the whole story, especially since Mao's successors have adopted a new and outward-looking policy in their modernization drive. Hong Kong is a sophisticated, modern, industrial and commercial community which has huge reserves of know-how and expertise in business management, insurance, building, design, engineering, tourism, advertising, finance, technical education, publishing, port-handling methods and air freight. China needs advice and help in all these spheres; where better to get it than in Hong Kong, where there is no language barrier, where cultural values and customs are similar, and communications are easy and cheap?

To help absorb the many forms of expertise which are lying around in Hong Kong almost begging to be used, the authorities in Guangdong and other mainland provinces have since 1979 begun a series of developments involving export-processing zones which will provide cheap Chinese labour to process or finish goods made in Hong Kong, or made with materials supplied through Hong Kong. Industrial wage rates in China are about a fifth of those in Hong Kong, and although the productivity of the mainland work force is poor, a result of years of overmanning and underemployment, it still promises a big saving to the Hong Kong manufacturer – Chinese, European, American, or Japanese – faced with rising costs for land and labour. Marxist purists would denounce this as a new form of colonial or semi-colonial exploitation, making profits for foreign businessmen at the expense of the working people of China. But the present Chinese leadership would turn the argument upside down, saying this is the fastest and surest means of earning enough capital to raise living standards in China, and therefore highly important to the attainment of socialism.

Hong Kong, which is the communications hub of East Asia, is also of great value to China in gathering both public and secret information about conditions in the whole region. It can act as an easy channel for clandestine agents working abroad, who infiltrate the overseas Chinese communities of South-east Asia, where the best and most reliable information on the society and economies of those countries is often available.

On top of all these advantages of the present set-up in Hong Kong, China must take into account the enormous problems which would be created by the injudicious re-absorption of the territory. Food would have to be supplied to some six million people, who would no longer be earning foreign currency to pay for it. Huge numbers would be thrown out of work – for Britain, the United States and other importing countries would probably scratch Hong Kong off the list of places from which they accept textile imports under quotas designed to minimize damage to their domestic industries. In slump conditions, Chinese people would start drifting from Hong Kong back into the hinterland, where they or their parents or grandparents came from in the first place – but they would be people with a taste for the 'bourgeois' life-style, unamenable to socialist discipline and cynical about official propaganda. Some would have criminal backgrounds, and the disruption of law and order in parts of southern China could be quite serious. There would also be many well-educated and Westernized young people, who might begin to question the socialist order in China, form dissident groups, circulate underground journals, and so on.

The maintenance of Hong Kong's bristling high-rise buildings, with their complex air-conditioning and elevator systems, would become increasingly difficult and unacceptably wasteful of energy. Girls and women who persisted in wearing make-up and fancy clothes would exercise an 'unhealthy' influence on their plain-Jane cousins across the former border, and to 'reform their morals' would be a lengthy and not always successful process. Many of the people from Hong Kong would not know how to speak Mandarin.

If these problems seem exaggerated, it should be recalled that Shanghai, which the Communists took over in 1949, was still a political thorn in their flesh right up till 1976, spawning as it did the left-radical movement which supported the clique around Mao, while paradoxically revelling in quasi-'bourgeois' ways of life and attitudes and exercising a bad influence in the surrounding provinces. Hong Kong reabsorbed in the wrong conditions could be a second Shanghai.

So what future is there for this thriving Chinese community, in a Chinese socialist state which until recently has placed political ideals above prosperity and could do so again in some future leftist convulsion? The answer may lie in a convergence between the two societies – just as it does in the case of Taiwan, the island province which, in Peking dogma, must be 'liberated' and reintegrated into the People's Republic as soon as is practicable.

There is little chance of Hong Kong's becoming more socialistic, though the British-controlled government is being forced progressively into providing better social services. The other solution is for China itself to become more free-enterprise minded, more orientated towards material incentives and the profit motive, more adept at using modern technology, more tolerant of divergent intellectual views, less puritanical about morals. And fortunately – from the point of view of most of the people of Hong Kong – this is exactly what has begun happening and seems likely to go on throughout the 1980s.

As though to emphasize the natural convergence in relations between Hong Kong and the People's Republic of China, many ambitious schemes for economic and technological cooperation are under way or being considered, from the setting up of tariff-free industrial processing zones to the likely construction of a nuclear power plant with British aid to feed the energy hunger of the entire Pearl River basin and Canton city.

There are now one-day tours across the border for foreign visitors without burdensome visa procedures; pay-bed medical facilities in Canton for Hong Kong patients, who may prefer the mixed modern–traditional style of medical treatment used in China but not in the hospitals of Hong Kong; excursions into the rural areas of Guangdong province to eat lychees, or even to city restaurants to eat dog meat (banned by the British in Hong Kong); and burgeoning holiday resorts on the relatively clean beaches of the mainland. Border-crossing points have multiplied, with the opening of a surface-skimmer service up the Pearl River to Canton, direct flights from Hong Kong's Kai Tak Airport, and a fast new through-train service connecting with rail and air routes to Peking and other parts of China.

This new 'porous' border may create problems for the security forces on both sides who are trying to prevent illegal border crossings, but it is creating a new economic entity in south China which might be aptly dubbed 'Hong Kong & Hinterland, Inc.'. Given a few more years, this may turn into the boldest experiment in mixed socialist–capitalist enterprise in any country of the world. People-to-people contacts are increasing at a rapid pace, as the two administrative systems coexist and learn from one another. With such a development, the prospect of a political changeover, in which Britain will resign from its position as the administrator of Hong Kong and turn it over to a relatively sophisticated and experienced Guangdong provincial government – with special transitional arrangements to smooth the way and prevent undue disruption of people's lives – will no longer seem impossible.

The fortunes of tiny Macau, which has been under Portuguese rule since the mid 1500s, are inextricably bound up with those of Hong Kong. The post-Salazar government of Lisbon inquired in 1977 whether China would like to take Macau back – and China refused, knowing that a change in the enclave's status would cause grave loss of confidence among the investors of Hong Kong and at least a temporary slump in business. Macau, which depends mainly on income from tourists, gamblers and dog-racing fans who make the forty-mile crossing from Hong Kong, would probably have no economic future once the British territory was reabsorbed.

One cloud on the horizon is that Hong Kong is so valuable – some would say vital – to China's economic and technological progress that in any possible war between China and the Soviet Union the temptation for the Russians to neutralize or isolate the colony would be almost irresistible. Assuming that no British government would be likely to risk an all-out war with Russia in order to protect the interests of Hong Kong and its 98 per cent Chinese people, it is easy enough to imagine a Soviet naval blockade of the territory – for instance if the state of tension between Vietnam and China exploded into a war more drastic than the limited Chinese invasion of Vietnam in February–March 1979.

Conflicting Chinese and Vietnamese claims to the Paracel and Spratly island groups in the South China Sea also threaten to block Hong Kong's air and maritime lines of communication. However, the prospect of Sino-Soviet war is so fraught with implications for the entire East Asian region that there is little point in trying to construct a detailed scenario for Hong Kong alone.

An important development in 'Hong Kong & Hinterland, Inc.' has been the search for oil deposits in the South China Sea off the coast of Guangdong. As long as the oil does not become the subject of a still more violent conflict with Vietnam, it may mean a significant boost for the economies of both Hong Kong and the adjacent mainland areas. China is ill-adapted to servicing offshore oil rigs, whereas Hong Kong business firms could do so easily and profitably, perhaps in partnership with mainland organizations.

For admirers of Chinese culture, Hong Kong is surpassed only by Taiwan as a community where traditional values have been upheld and developed, instead of being violently shaken and twisted by the rigours of revolution. Chinese painting and calligraphy – both traditional and experimental – thrive quietly in the British-ruled territory, as do scholarly studies of classical Chinese literature, history, and philosophy, which have been badly disrupted in the People's Republic for political reasons. There are parts of Hong Kong – the busy 'ladder streets' with their multifarious hawkers and markets, and quiet corners with old temples where incense still rises to the Buddha – in which a romantic can feel transported back to the old China of the nineteenth-century Treaty Ports and earlier.

An important fact about Chinese attitudes to history and to their own culture is that there is very little 'national' feeling among the native Cantonese – although their spoken language, much more than a mere dialect, is as different from northern Mandarin as French is from Italian, or German from Swedish, and, contrary to a widely held belief, they *do* have a workable written language of their own (but used mainly for language study, comic strips and pornographic books). The Cantonese take a cheerfully practical attitude towards their own language and cultural patterns, willingly conceding that Mandarin is the true national language of China and heir to the nation's culture – although in fact Cantonese is much closer to ancient and classical Chinese than Mandarin is. The northerners, meanwhile, tend to view the Cantonese as vulgar, materialistic and grasping, and make jokes about their eating habits. ('If it's got four legs and isn't a chair, if it swims underwater and isn't a submarine, if it flies and isn't an aeroplane – the Cantonese will eat it!' they say.)

Hong Kong also has a sizeable minority of Shanghai Chinese, speaking the ugly, sibilant dialect of the former 'paradise of adventurers' and controlling many businesses – especially in the textile industry, which was to a large extent imported to Hong Kong from Shanghai after the Second World War. They coexist reasonably well with the local Cantonese, though some of the older Shanghai exiles have resolutely never learned more than a few words of the Cantonese dialect.

Among the other socio-ethnic groups in Hong Kong are the Chiu Chow (Teochew, Chaozhou), from the Shantou (Swatow) area in the northeast tip of Guangdong province, speaking a dialect closer to that of Fujian (Fukien) province than to Cantonese. Then there are the Hakka (meaning 'strangers'), mainly rural people descended from wandering clans who left northern China centuries ago when famine overtook their homelands. Their women, clad in black pyjamas, with enormous lampshade-like hats, take on the heaviest, dirtiest, and worst-paid jobs in market gardening and the construction industry.

The island of Taiwan (Formosa) is a Fujian-dialect area, though it also has aboriginal hill tribes related to the Polynesians. The Nationalist troops and government officials who followed Chiang Kai-shek to Taiwan in 1949 quickly made themselves hated by their high-handed attitude and the oppressive regime they imposed – which, as a former British naval intelligence officer with a good knowledge of the region put it, 'convinced the people of Taiwan that no good can ever come out of the mainland'.

The future of Taiwan is one of the really big question marks over the Chinese world. Its seventeen million people – roughly divided into mainland-born overlords and locally born working and middle classes – have four principal options, none of which is very attractive or very practicable. They can resign themselves to being reintegrated – whether peacefully or by force – into the People's Republic, in which case their best hope is that Peking will do as it has intimated it may and let them keep their economic and social structure for as long as it is not naturally transformed into a socialist mould. Or they can go for an independent Taiwan under the economic umbrella of Japan, a former colonial power which many of the older people born in Taiwan think of nostalgically. Or – in the event of a Sino-Soviet war – they might seek the protection of the Soviet fleet, in exchange for granting of naval facilities. Partly because President Chiang Ching-kuo has a Russian wife, and because the island has been visited by a notorious KGB and Soviet Communist Party propagandist, this option has been quite actively discussed from time to time. But that would be a desperate move, which the United States would oppose almost as strongly as China would.

The only other option is war. The Taiwan armed forces would take a heavy toll on amphibious landings and parachute drops by mainland troops, but they would almost certainly succumb in the end to sheer weight of numbers. Happily, this option now seems the least likely, the Peking leaders having indicated they they are impressed by Taiwan's American-primed economic success and would rather join peacefully with its people in some arrangement that would be mutually beneficial. Unfortunately, nobody can decide on the formula, and it seems likely that Taiwan will continue in its present twilight status until the end of the twentieth century, or even beyond. Peking has often linked the outstanding problem of Taiwan with that of Macau and Hong Kong, but there is no overriding reason why reabsorption of Hong Kong or Macau should automatically mean reintegration of Taiwan, or vice versa.

It is often discussed whether the twenty-two million or so Chinese people spread out over South-east Asia – called *huaqiao*, 'Chinese sojourners', in Mandarin – are an asset or a liability to the People's Republic. They have carved out economic empires for themselves which in many places have aroused the resentment and sometimes the fury of the indigenous people. Only in Singapore is the Chinese population in the majority. In Malaysia, the Chinese dominate the economic life of the cities, and special legislation has been enforced by the predominantly Malay government to ensure opportunities for *bumiputras* ('sons of the soil' – Malays and aboriginal peoples) and gradually shift the weight of economic control from the hands of the Chinese, who are mainly of Fujian origin. As in Malaysia, there have been violent anti-Chinese riots in Indonesia, where the position of the local *huaqiao* was made still more precarious by the failure of a Peking-backed coup attempt in 1965. Huge numbers of anxious Indonesian Chinese returned to the 'homeland' in the late 1950s and early 1960s, but many of them have since left China again in disillusionment.

  In Indochina, the Chinese settlers who mostly came in the wake of the nineteenth-century French colonial regime were predominantly Cantonese. They coexisted well enough with the Vietnamese, whose language and customs are quite closely related to those of China. It was widely assumed during the Vietnam war that the merchants of Cholon – the Chinese city adjacent to Saigon – bought protection for their trading firms by paying off the Vietcong and supplying them with information. So it was doubly ironic that when Hanoi won the war in 1975, one of its first acts was to make life so difficult for the ethnic Chinese in both North and South Vietnam that they fled in huge numbers. Those living in the north – who included technicians, administrators, factory workers and peasants – trudged painfully across the so-called 'Friendship Bridge' into China, where some 200,000 of them were resettled on state farms in the southern provinces in 1978, putting a considerable strain on the local economy. Others – especially merchants and traders from Cholon and their families – climbed in their thousands aboard often unseaworthy boats, having paid off Vietnamese officials in gold, and headed for anywhere the shifting monsoons took them. The lucky ones reached Hong Kong, where the British authorities accommodated some 100,000 in make-shift camps and shelters, while the United Nations High Commissioner for Refugees and US officials set about finding places for them to settle. Most wanted to go to the United States, either to join relatives, or because they had American friends from the war days, or simply because they felt they had the best chance of building a new life there.

  Nobody knows how many thousands drowned or were murdered

by Thai pirates, who normally raped the women and girls before allowing their boats to proceed. Thousands of 'boat people' landed on the poverty-striken east coast of Malaysia, where there were barely any facilities to house and feed them, and were mercilessly exploited by Malay policemen and officials who exchanged their gold or US dollars at extortionate rates for food and daily necessities. Singapore, a mainly Chinese community, simply closed its gates and refused to accept any refugees over an arbitrary limit of 1,000 awaiting resettlement. Other 'boat people' fetched up on the coasts of Indonesia and the Philippines – both of them countries with histories of hostility to Chinese settlers and various degrees of persecution or disadvantaging of people of that race. A few actually made it to the north coast of Australia.

The Vietnam refugee problem has seriously disturbed many of the South-east Asian governments, because it has highlighted the latent sources of conflict in Peking's desire to extend help and protection to its kinsfolk living in other countries where they may be subject to per-secution. Any serious political conflicts between China and the govern-ments of South-east Asian countries could result in anti-Chinese pogroms, while the quite widespread hatred of Chinese in several of those countries threatens to cause incidents which could spoil government-to-government relations.

The problem has not been made any easier by China's changing attitude toward the *huaqiao*. Having inherited the former imperial government's *jus sanguinis* policy of regarding all people of Chinese race – no matter where they were born – as Chinese citizens, the Communists amended this in the 1950s to a policy of *jus soli* – the determination of nationality by place of birth. The new policy was unsatisfactory, however, because South-east Asian countries dragged their feet over granting citizenship to their Chinese minorities, and the Chinese settlers themselves often failed to register for naturalization, for fear that they would fail and merely draw attention to their presence. Throughout the 1970s, China from time to time urged the *huaqiao* to adopt the nationality of their places of birth and be good citizens of those nations. But it made plain that those who did so would forfeit all claim to Peking's protection and would be regarded as foreigners (although special amenities are still reserved by the China Travel Service, and other official bodies, for people of Chinese descent who wish to visit China).

The example of Vietnam showed that such a simplistic approach could not handle the problem of overseas Chinese communities in conflict with their host governments. Hostility towards the *huaqiao* is quite likely to arise precisely because of vagueness in the definition of their status, and attempts to redefine it. Hanoi and Peking could not even agree on the basic status of *huaqiao* in South Vietnam, and Peking found itself in the strange position of defending a decree of the defunct pro-American Republic of Vietnam, bestowing Vietnamese citizenship on the ethnic Chinese.

Some thoughtful overseas Chinese were worried by the policy, evolved by Peking in 1977–80, of inviting *huaqiao* business people to invest in new industries on the mainland, a policy which could be seen as encouraging a drain of capital from the struggling economies of South-east Asia. Similarly, China has risked upsetting its relations with those countries by offering to provide higher education for overseas Chinese students, a move that could cast an aura of suspicion around students who return to their countries of residence – most of which are desperately anxious to exclude any Communist influence from their society. The situation has not been helped by the memory in some countries – especially Burma – of local Chinese residents and Chinese diplomats trying to spread the Cultural Revolution in 1966–8 and entering into violent conflicts with the host government by flaunting Mao badges and copies of the *Little Red Book* or staging provocative demonstrations.

The places worst affected by the spillover from the Cultural Revolution were Hong Kong and Macau (where the people are not called *huaqiao* by Peking but *tongbao*, or 'compatriots'). Inexperienced Portuguese troops in Macau shot dead several Chinese rioters in December 1966, resulting in the virtual takeover of the administration by the powerful pro-Peking Chinese business community, acting on instructions from Canton or Peking.

In Hong Kong, the authorities behaved more flexibly and resolutely in the riots of 1967, fighting the pro-Communist trade unions, left-wing workers and students with an astute blend of propaganda and strong-arm methods. Though there were riots, disturbances and bomb attacks throughout most of 1967 – and the Canton authorities caused some discomfort by not turning on the piped water supply when they would normally have done so at the height of the summer – the Hong Kong leftists were eventually discouraged by Peking's obvious lack of anything more than verbal support, and the disorders petered out. A number of policemen, rioters and civilians were killed and hurt, but significantly no European was badly injured, until the undiscriminating bombs took their toll of courageous disposal experts. While British colonialism and exploitation of the Chinese people were held up as the big bogey for the rioters, at bottom it was a fight between Chinese and Chinese, related principally to the political turmoil on the mainland. Colonialists or no, the British must not be prevented from continuing to feed Peking's coffers with foreign exchange – which was all the more badly needed because of the damage the Cultural Revolution wrought on China's foreign trade.

Hong Kong and Macau are in a special position, which Peking has long ago learned to live with and exploit. But on the whole, the overseas Chinese of South-east Asia have proved a political liability to China, which may not have been entirely offset by their economic contribution through cash remittances to relatives and – subsequently – direct investment in China. Ironically, the liberalization of Chinese society and the opening of diplomatic relations with most of the South-east Asian countries (Indonesia and Singapore still hung fire in 1981) has increased the pride of the *huaqiao* in their ethnic identity, and this has made tensions and conflicts between them and the indigenous peoples if anything more likely than before.

The overseas Chinese problem is by no means just one of foreign policy. The presence of millions of returned overseas Chinese or dependants of overseas Chinese in the People's Republic has caused difficult social dilemmas for the authorities. On the one hand, many of these people could not adjust easily to the austere brand of socialism practised under Mao and could often afford to pay in foreign currency for luxuries such as extra food rations and apartments roomier than those allocated to ordinary citizens. On the other hand, privileged treatment for them could lead to social tensions and resentments. One solution found was to settle the overseas Chinese in apartment complexes or villages where they would be surrounded by their own kind, hived off from the population at large. But inevitably many just took up residence among the citizenry, so that the material privileges they enjoyed may have seemed to be being flaunted.

The overseas Chinese paid dearly in the Cultural Revolution for their little extra comforts. They were abused and denounced for having 'overseas connections' – virtually an accusation of treason at that time.

Entry into the Party, good jobs, college educations, and service in the armed forces were mostly denied them. They were watched suspiciously and their homes were targets of raiding Red Guards, who confiscated property on the excuse of searching for proofs of subversion. To receive foreign currency from abroad became proof of a 'bourgeois' world outlook, and the envy of people who had no such sources of income added to the fury of the onslaught on overseas Chinese privileges. Many of them were afraid to collect their foreign currency remittances from relatives abroad, who in many cases stopped sending them. The best chance of survival for overseas Chinese and their dependants in China was to dress in their oldest clothes, hide any valuables they had, and chant the praises of Chairman Mao louder than anyone else.

From 1972 on, allegedly at the behest of Mao, overseas Chinese who could no longer stand life on the mainland were permitted to emigrate again – mostly to Hong Kong. Mao was reported to have said that, far from looking down on people who re-emigrated, the local authorities should give them a farewell dinner.

This was an astute policy, for it got rid of malcontents who might have a bad influence on other people, and it created goodwill among the overseas Chinese abroad. Seeing that to visit China need not mean being forced to settle there for life, overseas Chinese visitors streamed in throughout the seventies, spending freely, bringing gifts to their relatives, and fixing up business deals with the mainland trading corporations. Most of them left China again fired with sentimental and patriotic enthusiasm – even though they chose not to take up residence there.

15. Words at Work

The reverence of the Chinese for the written word is proverbial. Their script is not only the most complex but also the most ancient system of writing still in use in the world today. Encyclopedias, dictionaries, paper and printing were all Chinese inventions. More people can communicate with each other in written Chinese than in any other language. And yet in the 1980s – more than three decades since the founding of the most powerful Chinese state in history – the prestige of the written language is only just recovering from its lowest-ever ebb.

The crisis is both technical and spiritual. Sweeping changes in the Chinese script, aimed at making it easier to learn, have altered the face of the language more than at any time in the past two thousand years. Chinese people living outside the People's Republic are finding it more and more difficult to read things printed there, while people educated in China have been increasingly alienated from their own historical culture and from the various forms of Chinese being written in Hong Kong, Taiwan, South-east Asia, and other places where Chinese people have settled.

Most of the promising left-wing writers of the early revolutionary period have seen their works denounced, banned, or burned at one time or another. Well-known authors are only now taking up the pen again, after enforced or voluntary silences of twenty years and more. Libraries in China have been subject to severe restrictions, bookshops denuded of all but the most banal books.

The press has emerged from a period of more than a decade during which it became so devious, obscure, and repetitive that only skilled reading between the lines could make any sense of it at all. Playwrights and actors have been forced either to stick to a tiny range of approved themes or give up their careers – sometimes their liberty or their lives. Poetry was reduced to mere declamation in the Eleven Years, and literary criticism became an exercise in political survival.

The promises of change and renewal in the post-Mao period have still to be substantially fulfilled: so far, the press and the publishing houses have been kept busy pouring out explanations of what has gone wrong in the past. The Chinese 'new writing' is still largely a thing of the future.

But the picture is not wholly gloomy. A generation of young writers is bursting with things to say, even if they too often lack the skill to say them well. Once-famous authors and stage performers have been plucked out of their obscurity in remote country villages, where they were exiled, or released from jails and labour camps. The press, though still stodgy and skimpy, is showing encouraging signs of an attempt at honest and interesting reporting. Dozens of journals and periodicals, both literary and scientific, are sprouting on the book-stands again. Classic European authors can once more be bought in the shops, and China's own cultural legacy is being studied with the respect which it deserves – and not just to find ways of scoring cheap political points.

To understand how exciting the new intellectual atmosphere is for people in China, one need only compare the situation of the daily press there in 1980 with its situation in 1975.

A casual glance would reveal little difference in the soberly arranged columns of the *People's Daily*, the main Party organ. It consists of two big sheets of newsprint, each folded once to make a total of eight pages. Comparing it to the obese wad of reports, features, advertisements and pictures which lands on a European or American doorstep every morning, it hardly rates the use of the word 'newspaper'. But over the years it has been carefully read by hundreds of millions of Chinese people seeking to understand the mysteries of their own country's government and society – to say nothing of thousands of foreign specialists, to whom it has been an obscure but always authoritative guide to what is going on in China.

The big change today lies in the content of the *People's Daily*, and all the other national and local newspapers which more or less follow its style. Where previously there were acres of sterile polemics and abstruse political theory, there are now facts and statistics, serious discussion of social problems, humour and satire and sports news. Editors occasionally own up to errors of judgement or reporting, print critical letters, and actually air differing viewpoints on controversial matters. To people in China, the press is now a real source of information and food for thought, rather than a quasi-astrological guide to the political currents swirling through the halls of power, as it was in the decade before Mao's death.

This new approach – unthinkable still in 1978 – has awakened a lively response from the readers. According to officials at the *People's Daily*, letters from readers rose from about 1,200 a month to some 2,000 a *day* – a fifty-fold increase – in the late 1970s. One explanation for this is the tremendous social ferment in China which has greeted the post-Mao leadership's announcement of new, more liberal policies. Another has been the growing confidence, on the part of the general public, that one may write to a national newspaper without fear of being arrested and jailed without trial if one voices the wrong sentiments. Previously, any letters which seemed seriously 'deviant' in political terms were referred for investigation to the local police in the sender's place of residence. Despite post-1976 efforts to locate such cases and provide amnesty for the victims, the inadequate records kept at the time mean that many cannot be traced until friends or relatives come forward to demand redress.

In the latter part of the Eleven Years, the *People's Daily* was edited by one Lu Ying, an obscure journalist from Shanghai who had evidently caught the eye of radical propaganda boss and Gang of Four member Yao Wenyuan. (When, after Yao's disgrace in 1976, Lu was replaced by a Deng supporter, Hu Jiwei, newspaper staff members said they had privately nicknamed their former editor 'Loony Lu'.)

Mao himself, at different times in his career, stood out for frank and honest reporting in the press, but, with that peculiar ambivalence which marked most things he said, he also warned about its dangers, supposedly having proclaimed in the 1960s: 'If a newspaper reports only about failings, when every commune has its own point of view, the paper won't be able to print them all.' Mao's supporters took this to mean that critical reporting should be suppressed, except when the leadership itself felt like criticizing someone or some institution. It became near treasonable to dwell in print on 'the dark side of society' – that is, social abuses or oppressive practices, poverty or disorganization. A journalist was supposed to be 'positive', reporting only things which reflected well on the leadership's management of affairs. Even an article criticizing something as trivial as rude service in a shop had to be balanced by another article, pointing out how conscientious the sales clerks were in some *other* shop.

This drum-beating, gong-clanging style of coverage joyously hailed every real or reputed success in economic and scientific work, every good deed performed by a selfless soldier, every increase in grain yields – but fell silent when things went badly wrong, as though acknowledging a flaw in the social system would bring disgrace and doom on the leadership. Just about any piece of reporting – from commune, factory, or army unit – was peppered with such phrases as 'The masses were all filled with enthusiasm' or 'Everybody said: This is a brilliant victory for the line of the great leader Chairman Mao'.

To preserve the mystic dignity of the press, there were no cartoons, no columns on leisure activities, no law reports, no profiles of important people in the news, no birth or marriage announcements – or any of the things which people in most countries expect to find at their breakfast table. Subjects such as sports, theatre reviews and details of serious accidents or natural catastrophes were fitted in only when they could be written up with some inspirational political message.

There was, however, abundant political theorizing and severe denunciation of people – usually unnamed – who were considered to be opposing the Maoist line. Sometimes these polemics were fairly direct, as when Yao Wenyuan and Zhang Chunqiao in 1975 published their thoughts on the growth of a new 'bourgeoisie' within the Party; or in the succeeding year, when Deng Xiaoping was for the second time in his career denounced and singled out as the most dangerous political deviant in the country. At other times, top-level power struggle was reflected in lengthy and almost totally unreadable discussion of classical works of literature and philosophy, from the *Analects* of Confucius to the great eighteenth-century novel *Dream of the Red Chamber* (translated as *The Story of the Stone*, Penguin Books), and the writings of the influential author and critic of the 1920s and 1930s, Lu Xun.

A favourite trick of the press under Mao was to give unjustifiably glowing accounts of construction projects which were actually facing severe difficulties, as though the written word could somehow conjure away the problems and bring the project to completion. Little care was taken to check the impressive 'production figures' cited by steel mills or communes, whose top officials had every reason to want to inflate their achievements. The result was that anybody who read Chinese newspapers every day (and believed what he or she read) would soon be living in a dream world of gleaming socialist construction, where willpower alone could surmount all obstacles.

The accounts of foreign students who attended Chinese universities at the time report something similar in the attitudes of their Chinese room-mates: everything in China was done right, because the leaders said it was, and almost everything done in foreign countries not allied with China was fatally flawed and decadent, doomed to failure.

This attitude helps to account for the amazing lack of curiosity about the outside world shown by Chinese intellectuals and officials in the late-Mao period. Industrial workers, who have less time to read the *People's Daily* and who know from direct experience how inflated its claims have been, showed lively interest in conditions in foreign countries and cheerfully cross-examined foreign students about them when they came to do a spell of labour in a factory. But the depressing lack of curiosity noted among intellectuals and officials in the 1970s was not natural, and when the liberalization was begun after Mao's death, they too started to show an intense desire for knowledge about foreign countries.

A commentator in the *People's Daily* complained in 1979 that boastful and systematic falsification of news reports was still going on:

> There are cases of increases or decreases in production, but the [newspaper] report has it that all communes and brigades have increased their production. The market has a greater supply of vegetables occasionally for a few days, maybe for the purpose of greeting an 'investigation group' and a 'visiting group', or the vegetables are displayed for a short while for a visiting reporter. But the report describes this in an exaggerated way, such as: 'There is an ample supply of vegetables in the off-season', and 'There is a flourishing market'. Some work is being carried out in a few spots, but some comrades write in their reports that this work is being carried out in the whole county and even the whole province.

When Deng Xiaoping's appointee, Hu Jiwei, took over the editorial chair at the *People's Daily* in 1977, there was an almost audible sigh of relief from veteran Party workers and intellectuals. Hu is a highly experienced journalist and propagandist with long experience in

Deng's native region, the former 'grain bowl' of Sichuan province which was reduced to poverty through the inept economic policies pursued in the Eleven Years, and had done a stint on the country's most prestigious paper as long ago as the mid 1950s, when he was already a deputy editor in chief. Under Hu, the Party organ's reporting became markedly more factual.

Today, an intelligent person reading nothing but the *People's Daily* for six months would have at least a smattering of knowledge about events in the world outside China, a fairly realistic picture of the main economic and political trends inside China – and virtually no knowledge at all about big international controversies over culture, religion, education, the arts, environmental protection or sex. But reasonably well-educated Chinese people are not wholly dependent on their own press to get knowledge about the outside world. They can listen (nowadays) to major international broadcasting stations such as the BBC or the Voice of America, in both English and Chinese. (This was not always so. In past years, 'listening to enemy broadcasts' was a serious crime. These days the only habit which might earn someone a reprimand would be listening regularly to Radio Moscow or to the other Soviet propaganda station, 'Radio Peace and Progress'. Moscow broadcasts regularly in Chinese – but it is unknown how many in China tune in to the Soviet wavelengths.)

People can also read *Cankao Xiaoxi* ('Reference News'), a daily compendium of translated reports from foreign news media which are thought to be of legitimate interest to Chinese readers. Sometimes, news about events in China may be first broken to the general public through the reproduction of a report on it in a foreign press organ. Foreigners, however, are *not* supposed to read *Cankao Xiaoxi* – so that a foreign correspondent in Peking may be banned from reading one of his own articles in Chinese translation.

This extraordinary sensitivity of the authorities is apparently caused by their desire to conceal from foreigners the degree of interest they are showing in any particular issue in the news, which would be reflected by the amount of treatment it received in the *Cankao Xiaoxi*. In any case, foreigners living in Peking often see copies of it, filched by foreign students at the university or picked up somewhere by chance. Many Chinese intellectuals find it humiliating that they must rely on reproductions of foreign news media to learn about events which their own newspapers are too coy to report. As a writer styling himself Xu Wei complained in the 1979 unofficial journal *Beijing Qiu-shi* ('Beijing Fruit'), 'People want to read the foreign accounts of major events at home and abroad, because the foreign reports tally with the facts, or because foreign reports are sometimes the only source of news.'

With a daily print order of about ten million, the *People's Daily* cannot reach every reader in the country, and in the provinces it is often on sale a day after the Peking edition comes out, despite the jetting and facsimile transmission of the matrix to provincial centres for local printing. Every province and large city has its own newspaper, similar in format to the *People's Daily* and carrying a good deal of identical material. These local newspapers are not freely available outside China – or even in provinces other than the one in which they are printed – though this may change as the national leadership becomes more self-confident and allows a greater degree of public criticism of official policy. But some of their content is broadcast over provincial radio stations and picked up by American monitoring services in Hong Kong and South Korea. From this monitoring, and from provincial newspapers which filter out of the country, it is clear that there is little difference in approach between them and the national media, only more information about local conditions and a somewhat less formal style.

The basic building blocks of Chinese are monosyllables such as *wa*, *gu*, *min*, *wang*. The principal northern dialect – called Mandarin or *putonghua* ('ordinary speech') – counts 410 of these syllables, or a little over 1,000 if one takes into account the different pitches of the voice, or tones, which distinguish the meaning of otherwise identical syllables. Mandarin has four tones, but not all four of them are used on every one of the 410 syllables. The southern dialects – especially Cantonese, which is widely spoken in Hong Kong, South-east Asia and overseas Chinese settlements in the United States and Europe – have a greater range of syllable and tone, but *putonghua* is recognized as standard Chinese everywhere in the world.

Over the centuries, the range of sounds in the Chinese language has shrunk, especially in the northern dialects. As this process went on, the language tended to compensate for it by combining words of similar or related meaning in pairs, thus creating words of two or more syllables: e.g., *kanjian*, 'to see', made up of *kan* (to look) and *jian* (to see) – thus, pidgin English 'looksee'. Or words of quite different meanings were combined to form new concepts: e.g., *maodun*, from *mao* (spear) and *dun* (shield), meaning 'contradictory'. Or two words which go logically together, such as *nian* (to chant) with *shu* (book or writing), to make *nianshu*, 'to read'.

The Chinese language has also taken to stringing words and phrases together to express new or foreign concepts which did not exist in traditional Chinese thinking: e.g., *gongchanzhuyi*, meaning 'communism', from *gong* (common, collective), *chan* (product or property), *zhu* (master or dominant), and *yi* (ethics) – or, in combination, 'the dominant ethic of sharing property and products'.

The narrow range of syllables in modern Chinese makes it impractical to spell the language phonetically, except for the most basic purposes, such as elementary language training or the romanization of names of people and places. For one thing, each word would need a tone mark, which it is somewhat troublesome to write in (though it can be done, as in Vietnamese). And even with the tones, there would be numerous ambiguities, especially in the more literary or technical styles of writing. For instance, *jing ji*, or 'manager', would be spelled the same way as *jingji* meaning 'economy' or 'economic'. And *tian* (sky) could be confused with *tian* (to add). *Tiao* (a strip) could be confused with *tiao* (to adjust), and so on. In writing, the difference is perfectly plain, because the Chinese script shows ideas as well as sounds.

The script originated some three thousand years ago as a system of simple drawings – the most natural way for any early society to express thoughts in writing. But it soon became necessary to supplement this purely pictographic script with some means of indicating the sounds of words too; otherwise the language would only be able to express quite simple concepts and could not develop as flexibly as the spoken language did.

Take the symbol *mu* 木, meaning 'tree'. It is recognizably a picture of a tree, but to know that the concept 'tree' is pronounced *mu* one must either have been brought up speaking Chinese or have learned it laboriously. Put two trees together, thus 林, and they symbolize a forest, which is pronounced *lin* (again the pronunciation is not indicated by the symbol). But there are several other words in Chinese pronounced *lin*, including one meaning 'drizzle'. Rather than compose a whole new character for 'drizzle', the Chinese took the picture symbol for 'rain', 雨, and joined it up with the 'forest' symbol to make 霖 – a word which the reader knows is pronounced *lin* and has something to do with rain.

That provides the necessary data for identifying the word. (However, the word for rain, pronounced *yü*, is used as a symbol of meaning, and its own sound does not enter into the eventual character. So when learning Chinese it is often hard to decide which part of a character is the meaning sign, or 'radical' as it is called in English, and which part is the sound sign, or 'phonetic'.)

There are 214 of the signs called radicals, most of them existing as words in their own right: e.g., 手 *shou* (hand); 馬 *ma* (horse); 人 *ren* (man). And there are a large number of characters frequently used as phonetics bereft of their original meaning, e.g., 包 *bao* (enfold); 巨 *jü* (big); 奴 *nu* (slave). When used for this purpose, they lose their original meaning and serve merely as a form of spelling. Since many of them have changed their sound value over the centuries, learning to use a Chinese dictionary is a complex and baffling task and is nearly half the battle of learning written Chinese.

The picture has been further complicated by the 'simplification' of the script which was decreed by the Communists in the 1950s, in an attempt to aid literacy programmes. The reasoning was that many characters had unnecessarily large numbers of strokes (the record is thirty-eight strokes in one character) and could be trimmed down in a systematic manner. Thus the ten-stroke 馬 *ma* (horse) became 马 (four strokes), while 龍 *long* (dragon) was abbreviated from sixteen strokes to five 龙.

Since many of the abbreviated characters are radicals or phonetics in their own right, the trimming process has had a multiplier effect, and the script has been transformed to a point where it cannot be easily read by someone who has learned only the traditional, more complex forms. And schoolchildren in China are unable to write the traditional forms still generally used in Chinese-speaking communities outside the People's Republic.

A further drastic series of over eight hundred simplifications, introduced in 1978, were never put permanently into effect, because they caused too many ambiguities. (As in the case of Western shorthand, many abbreviations make a script difficult or impossible to read back, defeating the purpose.)

Language reform in China is aimed at three main targets. The first is teaching everyone at least to understand *putonghua*, as opposed to the native dialect they may speak at home. Most young people in China can now understand *putonghua*, though they may speak it very imperfectly. The second aim is to consolidate, and if possible continue, the simplification of the written characters. And the third aim is to make everyone familiar with a single systematic form of romanized Chinese, called pinyin (the system used for most Chinese words and names in this book), in preparation for an eventual move to full romanization, and abandonment of the ideographic characters which make Chinese so difficult to learn. But this in itself will require further standardization and simplification of the spoken language, to get away from the old literary forms – which cannot be comprehensibly written without their ancient symbols. On present showing, romanization is decades away.

The Chinese typewriter – so slow that it is used mainly for cutting stencils – has a tray of 1,000 to 2,000 characters which are picked up by a small mechanical grab and slammed against the paper when the operator pushes the control levers. Since the indexing of Chinese characters is a complex matter, much time is wasted in hunting down the right one, and characters not in the tray will have to be written in by hand. New electronic systems will make the Chinese typewriter easier to use, but it will still be a laborious process.

Telecommunications are also hampered by the complex writing system. Each of the 9,999 most frequently used Chinese characters has a four-digit code number, which enables a skilled operator (with a good memory) to transmit cables quite effectively – though they have to be re-translated into characters at the other end. A Chinese teleprinter has been devised on the principle of facsimile writing, and full-page electronic facsimile transmission will probably be widely used in the future.

The problems of writing and reading Chinese have been multiplied by the language's adaptation of thousands of Western terms over the past century and more. These include the vocabulary of modern commerce; the chemical elements and their combinations; mechanical, electrical, electronic, and modern medical terms; mathematical concepts; political vocabulary; names of places previously unknown to the Chinese; names of great historical figures and events in the non-Sinic world; and many other areas of knowledge.

This does not mean that the Chinese had no commerce, medicine, or mathematics before their contacts with the West. On the contrary, until about the sixteenth century their science and their economic system were in many ways more advanced than those of Europe. The question is not why China progressed little in knowledge, in what we regard as the 'modern' period of history; it had all the knowledge which its scholars considered necessary until the late nineteenth century. The real question is why the West suddenly soared off into such a steep curve of knowledge, experiment, technology, observation and more knowledge, to the point where catching up with it meant not just a spurt of effort by the Chinese but a leap into an entirely new way of viewing and treating the physical world.

The first big wave of Western-originated vocabulary reached China via Japan. Quicker to adjust themselves to Western knowledge and influence than the Chinese, the Japanese invented many new expressions – built up from the Chinese characters, which they had for centuries used to write their own language with nothing more than the addition of a few dozen phonetic signs. Among the new Sinic words coined in Japan in the nineteenth century are those for 'society', 'revolution', 'philosophy', 'economics', 'production', 'trade' and 'sanitation'.

These new terms were relatively easily absorbed back into Chinese, which had known some of them in now obsolete usages. By the end of the last century, considerable numbers of Chinese had studied modern Western learning in Japan, which it was easier for them to adapt to, culturally and socially, then Europe or America. However, the Chinese language did not have the great advantage of Japanese – a simple, ready-made phonetic system capable of transliterating foreign words which were too cumbersome or too difficult to translate. For instance, the Japanese took the English word 'engine' and wrote it as *enjin* in their native syllabary, which had previously been used mainly to intersperse Chinese written symbols and thus indicate the pattern of their own language's grammar (quite different from that of Chinese).

The Chinese could arguably have done the same thing, taking for instance the word *en*, meaning 'grace' or 'favour', and combining it with any number of words pronounced *jin* and meaning variously 'near', 'enter', 'pound', 'gold', 'ford', etc. – all written differently from one another. And in the case of a small number of foreign words, Chinese has done precisely that. 'Logic', for instance, is written with two characters, pronounced *luoji* and meaning respectively 'to patrol' (*luo*) and 'to edit' (*ji*). There is no attempt to link the meanings of these two words in Chinese; they are used simply for their phonetic value.

The problem with this method of absorbing foreign words is that it uses a string of characters purely for their sounds and without their original meaning, which is confusing to the reader, lengthy and cumbersome to write, and a perversion of the true nature of the Chinese written language. China did in fact try this road once, in the transliteration of Buddhist terms from Indian languages, but it resulted in the creation of an ugly jargon which only adepts could understand.

With most foreign words, the Chinese have chosen to protect the integrity of their own script and use conceptual translations instead of phonetic renderings. Thus 'engine' in Chinese has been rendered as *jiqi* – a combination of two native words, meaning 'mechanical implement'. The main disadvantage of this method is that both Chinese and foreigners have to learn completely new words when they want to say 'engine' in each other's language – whereas the Japanese just use the English word, and English-speaking people can easily recognize it in Japanese.

In chemistry, the problem was solved by putting together the meaning symbols for 'metal', 'stone' or 'gas' with other Chinese characters having a pronunciation at least vaguely similar to the first syllable of the European words. This is a rare example of the creative development of Chinese characters to suit modern purposes; in general, the coining of new characters is not acceptable, except for abbreviation or the rendering of dialect words.

A further problem is the break with the past made in this century, through the movement to write in *baihua* – colloquial rather than literary Chinese – which means, quite simply, writing down in Chinese characters exactly what people say.

This may seem common sense to the Westerner, but in China it has been a revolution. The written style used by educated people, up till quite recently, was an elaborate and stilted language, based on a wide knowledge of the classics and drawing its wealth and diversity from many different periods of Chinese writing. The abstruseness of this literary language, and the richness of the country's literature, meant that until our century few people could become fully literate unless they were rich enough or dedicated enough to invest the necessary effort in study. At the civil service examinations – an important feature of the imperial system – it was not uncommon for middle-aged men to sit alongside precocious youths, and there are famous stories of grey beards who passed the exam only when they were quite old, and after taking it many times.

The use of *baihua* has greatly reduced this barrier to literacy; now one need only learn some 2,000 to 3,000 characters to read most things in print – and that, astonishingly, is a task which schoolchildren are quite able to take in their stride, owing to the great adaptability and flexibility of the young mind. But a well-educated Chinese person should really know upwards of 5,000 characters, out of a recorded total of some 45,000 excluding ones only ever used once.

The impact of foreign political ideas and technologies on the Chinese language has brought about important structural changes in it. Traditionally, the Chinese sentence is arranged *subject-verb-object*, as in English. But the need to translate complex prose – from Japanese and German, in particular – has resulted in the much wider use of the form *subject-object-verb*, and in the insertion of enormously long subordinate clauses, in lieu of the relative clause. This has made much modern Chinese writing on politics, economics and philosophy almost unbearably turgid, enlivened only by graphic or earthy phrases such as Mao liked to use.

The *baihua* writing of the twentieth century can hardly be held up as one of the most distinguished episodes in the long history of Chinese literature. The *baihua* movement tended to be connected with political and educational reforms – and championed by writers who stood for such reforms – so that much of it was preachy or else pursued a Zola type of realism-with-a-moral which often took the place of first-rate writing.

From the 1930s on, Chinese writers were increasingly split between those who supported or accepted Chiang Kai-shek's Kuomintang (Nationalist) regime and those who rebelled against it and supported the Communists. Many of the latter found their way to Mao's head-quarters at Yan'an in the late 1930s and early 1940s, and it was there that a coherent strain of proto-Communist writing was bred. In 1942 Mao delivered his 'Yan'an Talks on Literature and Art', laying down the principle that writers should serve the great political cause rather than seek self-gratification or fame through literary merit.

Some of the writers who had come to Yan'an stood out against this view of literature and its purpose. Among them was the popular woman novelist Ding Ling, who was to fluctuate in her political attitudes until 1957, when she was denounced as a 'rightist' and sent successively to labour camp, to manual labour in the countryside, and to prison. (In 1979 she was released and admitted to the best hospital in Peking, where she began writing a sequel to the novel that had got her into trouble over twenty years previously. Other famous writers of the period from the 1930s until the 1960s – for instance, the veteran novelist Ba Jin – also reappeared at this time.)

The modern movement in literature did produce some works of universally recognized quality, especially short stories of the gloomy and sceptical Lu Xun, who became the *only* pre-Cultural Revolution twentieth-century Chinese writer (other than Mao) whose works were published during the Eleven Years.

With its best writers consigned to disgrace and obscurity in the purges of 1957 and 1966–7, it is not surprising that China has failed to produce much modern literature of anything more than academic interest to people in other countries. The translation of this literature into European languages has been hesitant and patchy, and much of it was done before the Cultural Revolution under the aegis of the Chinese authorities themselves. Figures for sales of these translations abroad are not available; most of them were withdrawn from sale after 1966, gradually finding their way back into the bookshops in the 1970s. Few people in the West who otherwise might count themselves well educated have so much as heard of Ba Jin, Mao Dun, Ding Ling, Hu Feng, Wu Han or Hao Ran, around whom the political–literary debates of recent times have raged in China.

The published word has tremendous importance in Chinese ideas of government, partly because of the subtlety and ambiguity of the Chinese language and its ability to praise or blame the country's rulers through allegory or obscure allusion. Even today, a minute change in the phrasing of a political slogan can signify a difference of up to 180 degrees in the policy being pushed. Fiction and journalism are closely scrutinized by the censors, to see whether the author has slipped in any oblique comment on current-day politics. Sometimes such meanings have been deliberately read into works whose authors may never have intended them – if it was thought expedient to silence a particular writer by holding his or her works up as 'poisonous weeds'.

The use of literature as a vehicle for political instruction reached its climax in the Eleven Years, when the works of most of the distinguished writers of the day were banned. The permitted novels, stories and dramas of this period mostly followed a set pattern:

A young worker or peasant, heart glowing red for love of Chairman

Mao, encounters serious difficulties at work. A sinister older person – a former landlord, rich peasant, or 'revisionist' – takes advantage of the gullibility of the masses to sabotage some important collective project, either for gain or out of sheer malice (usually the latter). The villain is smooth-tongued and hypocritical and succeeds for a while in bribing or hoodwinking people who lack a sufficiently high level of class consciousness. But the hero catches the villain out and leads the masses in a valiant struggle to unmask him. It is discovered that the villain has been putting fibreglass in grain sacks, or rigging up a roadside tree to startle horses and cause accidents, or trying to kill brave young children who see through his game. The masses' anger is turned to joy as their beloved work project is brought to fulfilment and the villain is handed over to the police.

This banal plot – repeated again and again in various guises – was the one considered most suitable for the novels and dramas put out during the period when Jiang Qing held sway over China's cultural and literary life. In the cases of some dramas, the overall tedium was relieved by exciting dancing and acrobats, and sometimes the 'class struggle' theme was disguised in a historical plot about the civil war against the Nationalists and the Japanese. Action movies such as *Taking Tiger Mountain by Strategy* and *The White-Haired Girl* – adapted from stage productions – were entertaining enough in small doses, and they were certainly preferable to an item such as *On the Docks*, in which stevedores stood around endlessly singing arias about 'class struggle'.

The crude theory behind the literary productions of the Eleven Years was that characters must be depicted in black-and-white terms: heroes and heroines must be perfect in ideology, motive and action, wholly courageous, and never deceived; villains, by contrast must be wholly bad, with a suspect or disgraceful class background, moved by sentiments of revenge and envy. There could be no 'in-between' characters, who might show the subtle interplay of socialist morality and individual self-interest. People's actions had to be determined by their class origins, and downright villains be incapable of reform – doomed in advance to execution or imprisonment for life. War was always portrayed as dashing and romantic, and heroes scored one victory after another. The enemy could never be shown to be impressive or intimidating, but always as ridiculous and loathsome. The only moral wavering permitted was that of some members of the 'masses', or some inexperienced young people, who might be temporarily hood-winked by the villain. But as genuine 'masses', they were easy to awaken to righteousness, and the hero or heroine could always count on their support at vital moments. The 'masses' could never be wrong – only a little misled, and that not for long.

The best-known exponent of this type of literature was Hao Ran, the literary name of Liang Jinguang, who was born into a peasant family in 1932, joined the Communists at the age of fourteen, and was largely left-taught. After publishing some short stories and working on the staff of a propaganda magazine destined for readers in the Soviet Union, he was employed by the official Party journal *Red Flag* to study Marxist ideas on literature. He enjoyed considerable protection in the Cultural Revolution and in 1972 published his first novel, *The Broad Road in Golden Light*, which was claimed to have sold four million copies. He prided himself on taking into account criticisms of his work made by peasants and workers and tried to depict his heroes as heroically as possible. His second novel, *Bright Sunny Sky*, which was also made into a film, sold three million copies. Its appeal, to a reading public starved of most other forms of fiction, probably lay in its detailed portrayal of the habits and speech of the peasantry rather than in its political message.

From 1978 on, a fascinating and hopeful new trend appeared in Chinese literature. Younger writers began publishing a spate of new short novels and plays, describing with great frankness – though still encumbered with political jargon – the tragedies which struck countless people in the Cultural Revolution. In a development similar to the publication in 1962 of Aleksandr Solzhenitsyn's *One Day in the Life of Ivan Denisovich*, a Chinese author named Cong Weixi published a work of fiction entitled *The Red Magnolia by the Main Wall*, a hair-raising account of conditions in a 'reform-through-labour' camp set as recently as 1976.

It tells of the high-principled commandant of a camp who somehow falls foul of the Party authorities and is himself sent as a convict to another camp. He is mistreated by a brutal guard and a fellow prisoner and is eventually shot dead while climbing the compound wall to pick a magnolia flower in memory of the recently deceased Zhou Enlai. His blood stains the flower red – hence the title of the novel.

This is strong stuff. Few people would be naive enough to believe that conditions in Chinese labour camps have changed greatly since

1976 – even if many of the inmates are different, now that the inquisition into the crimes and violations of human rights committed in the Cultural Revolution has been rolling on for several years. So the novel may be seen as a criticism of the entire system of coercion which has been built up since 1949, and which will probably continue to exist, even if those coerced are now 'leftists' rather than 'rightists'. If author Cong Weixi continues to attack social and political conditions in the China of the Eleven Years, there will come a time when such exposés begin to sound eerily familiar to people living in the post-Mao period.

As a parallel, Solzhenitsyn's writing became increasingly intolerable to the Soviet authorities as he moved relentlessly on with the allegory-studded novels *Cancer Ward* and *The First Circle*, and the documentary *chef d'oeuvre Gulag Archipelago*. Writing what he saw as the truth became a mission so sacred to Solzhenitsyn that he became impervious to threats and eventually was expelled from the Soviet Union because he was uncontrollable. There is no obvious reason why something similar should not happen in China – the rise of a great humanitarian author who becomes well known in the outside world and who pursues, through his writing on the past, themes which are still valid in the present but are increasingly unwelcome to the authorities.

The first collection of English translations of the new literature is a slim volume of short stories called *The Wounded*, chosen by Geremie Barmé and Bennett Lee, a young Australian and a Canadian who have both studied in Peking. For all the naivety and crudity of much of the writing, this is an impressive selection of work by new authors aged between twenty-two and forty. One of the best and most revealing stories, called 'Ah, Books!', describes a change of attitude on the part of a former Red Guard who has always despised reading and book-learning. During a spell in the hospital a young nurse persuades him to read *Les Misérables* by Victor Hugo, and his appetite for literature is awakened. He joins the huge crowds thronging around the city bookstores to buy newly reissued works by Chinese and foreign authors. (The big liberalization of the publishing industry in China in 1977–9 brought back to the bookshops authors such as Hugo, Shakespeare, Balzac, Cervantes and Tolstoy, together with many of the more prominent twentieth-century Chinese authors whose works had been banned since 1966.)

To a Western mind, this might not seem great progress; many

Europeans would scoff at Victor Hugo nowadays. But the fact that – at least in a story – Hugo could transform a hardened young Chinese philistine into a book-lover is evidence of the extreme literary starvation which people have had to put up with and which has created in them a fierce hunger for strong and moving writing. The story ends: 'We squeezed through the endless sea of people lined up to buy books. As I walked I looked at them contentedly and they looked at my pile of books admiringly.'

One of the most interesting writers to have surfaced since Mao's death is Liu Xinwu, a Peking schoolteacher who has given outspoken interviews to Hong Kong-based journalists. Liu, a stocky, plainly dressed man with a wiry crew cut, about forty years old, won a national commendation in 1978 for his story 'The Teacher in Charge' (translated by Barmé and Lee as 'The Class Counsellor'). This little work deals with the problem of juvenile delinquency – a taboo subject until only recently, because it is partly the result of the social upheavals and disruption of the educational system caused by the Cultural Revolution.

Liu has long experience of the difficulties of being a writer in China. He chose short stories as his medium because they go through fewer censorship organs than – say – a film script and can be published more quickly. But he, and younger writers like him, share the risk of being denounced in some future swing back to the left in literary politics – or simply an authoritarian clamp-down by the Party authorities. Even though a book is printed and well received, it may later be criticized for paying too much attention to 'the dark side of society', or any accusation designed to stifle writing that tries to come to grips with the problems of modern life.

The future probably holds fewer perils for Chinese writers than the past did. In the early stages of the Cultural Revolution, Liu only narrowly escaped persecution because an article he had written was printed in the same issue of a newspaper as something which was later denounced as 'revisionist'. He says he decided then never to write anything again – and though he probably wrote secretly 'for the bottom drawer', he looked on silently as Hao Ran and other ultra-left writers dominated the bookstores, regarding their work as 'false and unreal'. When at last the political atmosphere loosened up from 1972 on, he began to think of writing for publication again – over the strong opposition of his wife!

One of Liu's most telling short stories, called 'Wake Up, Brother', tells of a young worker who, as a boy, tried to show his enthusiasm for the Red Guard movement by pinning a Mao badge to the bare flesh of his chest. But by 1976 he is so disillusioned with the twists and turns of top-level politics, and the deception and abuse practised by officials at his factory, that he has withdrawn completely and just sits at home, drinking and strumming a guitar. Finally, a new Party Secretary at his factory awakens in him the desire to participate again, by moving decisively against inefficiency and abuses.

Despite what Liu says about the difficulty of writing for the stage, some of the most fascinating new literature coming out today is in dramatic form. The dilemmas of modern Chinese writers are illustrated by the debate in Shanghai in 1979 about a short play called *The Artillery Commander's Son*. This one-act comedy, written by three students at the Fudan University Chinese Literature Faculty, aroused a storm among writers and critics because of its head-on attack on the snobbery and 'back-doorism' of middle-aged cadres. The story line is as follows: Sun Jie, the daughter of a factory manager, wants to marry Fang Hua, an upright young worker from a working-class family. But her father, Manager Sun, violently objects, wanting her to marry another young man, Chen, who is the son of an industrial bureau director. Manager Sun is portrayed as dishonest, hypochondriac, self-indulgent and stupid. But he is able to invoke parental veto against the marriage of his daughter and Fang Hua. Chen, who is not in love with the girl, persuades Fang Hua to dress up in army uniform and introduces him to the short-sighted Manager Sun as 'the son of a senior artillery commander'. Sun is delighted at the prospect of his daughter's marrying the offspring of anyone in such an exalted position and treats the disguised Fang Hua with elaborate respect. But Fang Hua can stand the pretence no longer and confesses that his father is just a plain worker. Sun insists on believing that he is just being tested for his views on class and holds forth on the worth of the individual and the dignity of labour. Trapped by his own hypocrisy, he eventually has to accept the marriage of his daughter to Fang Hua – whose father, it turns out, is an old craftsman in Sun's own factory.

This simple little farce – reminiscent of Molière and Gogol – became highly controversial because it portrayed no redeeming features in the cadre, Sun, and gave the impression that cadres as a class were typified by him. This went against the doctrine that 'the great majority' of Chinese cadres are 'good or fairly good'. Sun was not considered to be a typical model, so the play could be criticized for a 'negative' approach. (This was a sort of reverse side of the very bitter debate – revived in the late 1970s – about the portrayal of some former imperial officials as wholly or partly good. The Cultural Revolution in 1965–6 chose for one of its opening salvos an attack on a play by Wu Han, then Deputy Mayor of Peking, about an honest mandarin, since leftist doctrine held that all mandarins had been corrupt and oppressive.)

One of the most outstanding satires of the new writing is the one-act play *Pavilion of the Wind and Waves*, which was written by hitherto little-known dramatists Sha Yexin, Li Shoucheng and Yao Mingde. This brilliant little work – which can be performed in not much over an hour – encapsulates not only the problems of actors and theatrical writers and producers but also launches a devastating broadside against the built-in cowardice and lack of decision-making among senior and middle-level officials in modern China.

The plot is deceptively simple. A provincial theatrical group has produced a traditional-style Chinese opera about the Song (Sung) dynasty hero Yue Fei, long celebrated as one of the Chinese nation's most valiant protectors, in the period when the country was split in two through the occupation of the northern part by the Jin Tartars. The troupe faces the fundamental problem in putting on any traditional Chinese opera: can any aristocrat, official, or military officer of the imperial period be regarded as a hero? Chinese traditional opera deals primarily with such characters, but radical Marxism condemns them all as oppressors of the 'masses'. In Yue Fei's case, there was the saving grace of his Chinese patriotism and his defence of the nation. But he is still regarded as 'blindly loyal' to the emperor, to the point where a forged order sent to him by disloyal courtiers in the emperor's name commands his total obedience, even against his own better judgement – a point which has obvious contemporary significance.

Officialdom in the play is satirized in the person of the director of the local Bureau of Culture and Education, a dull and philistine, elderly man, whose speech is riddled with platitudes and who goes to sleep in the auditorium while supposedly vetting the play for political accepta- bility. The producer and the performers want the play to be shown to the public the next night, and much of the farce revolves around the posting of the playbill outside the theatre. The Bureau Director is unwilling to give any decision too quickly, especially when he learns the play has not yet been shown in Peking and so could be politically suspect. When he is prevailed on to make a decision, the youngest actress takes out a notebook to record it. 'Don't take notes!' exclaims the official. 'In the Cultural Revolution I had too much trouble from other people taking down what I said!' To which the actress retorts, 'I had too much trouble from *not* taking down what other people said! There used to be plays which the leadership clearly ordered me to perform in, but when the wall posters went up, I took all the blame!'

The producer demands that the Bureau Director give a verdict on the play's acceptability, asking him, 'Just tell us if this type of content involves any big questions of principle.'

'That's hard to say too,' replies the Bureau Director. 'It might not seem to have any problems like that now, but in a few years' time, perhaps it will! And you still want me to make a cut-and-dried decision?'

The Bureau Director decides not to let the play be shown to the public, when a note suddenly arrives from the Deputy Director of the Propaganda Department, congratulating the cast on their play and telling them to put it on immediately. The Bureau Director instantly changes his mind and assents, and the young actress notes down the exact date and time of his decision, 'in case there's another Cultural Revolution in a few years' time'.

Then the telephone rings, and the Director of the Propaganda Department tells the Bureau Director that the play may contain some dangerous implications in its critique of 'blind loyalty'. The provincial Party Committee has not yet 'taken a stand' on the political issue of the day, Deng Xiaoping's declaration that 'reality is the only criterion of truth'.

The farce becomes predictable from here on. The playbill, only a few minutes ago proudly displayed outside the theatre, is whipped down. Then someone still more senior rings up and asks for tickets, so the playbill goes up again – until a notice arrives from the provincial Party First Secretary (to all intents governor of the province) saying the play is *not* suitable!

The ludicrous situation is finally resolved when someone finds a newspaper photograph of one of the Peking leaders congratulating the cast of another provincial troupe which has put the play on. All that is known of this leader's reaction is that he said, 'Good!' (Surely this is a satirization of Mao's lapidary comments, such as 'The comrades are good', or 'The people's communes are good', which in their day were elevated to the status of divine pronouncements.)

Absolved at last of the bothersome responsibility of making a decision, the Bureau Director settles down on the sofa and falls asleep.

The controversy about the role of literature in China has not been solved once and for all by the disgrace of Jiang Qing and her radical theorists. In at least two important cities the new view of literature as the craft of realism has been openly challenged: Peking authorities have had to intervene in support of the modernist faction seeking to get away from the old political clichés of the Maoist period, and in Canton a bitter quarrel raged in 1979 through the pages of the provincial press about whether literature should 'look forward' or 'look back'.

A Western critic would probably see nothing mutually exclusive in these two functions, but in China they are seen as warring opposites. 'Looking back' is the phrase used by left-inclined critics to condemn the kind of writing which is surfacing more and more often now: the dissection of the excesses and evils of the Cultural Revolution and the portrayal of the human misery caused by them to countless people. 'Looking forward' is the euphemism for the type of literature favoured during the Eleven Years: cheery, confident stuff about dedicated Party members building a bright new future for China.

When this set of definitions surfaced in the Guangdong provincial newspaper – in a series of articles by a critic named Huang Ansi – critics in Peking promptly denounced it as 'ultra-leftist' and claimed that the future could not be planned properly without a true and factual reflection of the recent past in literature. In the big central-China city of Wuhan, meanwhile, another leftist critic published a demand for more new literature 'praising virtue' – by which he meant extolling socialism and keeping silent about its failures and abuses. He too was taken to task by influential critics in Peking. Soon the brickbats were flying between the rival schools, with the leftists calling their opponents 'animals who like to smell stinking things in the dark and damp blood and sludge' and 'only fit to be maggots in the corpses of their revisionist masters cast on the garbage dump of history'. The defenders of the new style of writing retaliated by proclaiming that 'the pernicious influence of the ultra-leftist line is very far from being eradicated'. The leftists returned to the charge, denouncing the new writings as 'the literature of scars and tears' and saying it had no relevance to the real aspirations of the 'masses'.

In this case, the top Party leadership stood on the side of the new writing and against the leftist critics. But the relationship between the Party and the writers has always been a delicate one, in which mutual dependence is offset by in-built causes of mutual hostility.

The Party needs good writers to propagate and popularize its policies. But writers need the freedom to describe situations and emotions realistically, which is often seen by the Party as a kind of opposition – and a dangerous one – which at some stage it must suppress. This deadens the interest of the general public in what is being published and creates scepticism and a credibility gap, defeating the Party's purpose.

The Party also needs writers to keep the bureaucracy on its toes, by writing about abuses and inefficiency and the overbearing attitudes of officialdom which are holding up economic development and social progress. But unless the writers enjoy top-level protection, they may call down on their heads the wrath of the officials whom they have satirized or attacked and who may be in a position to do them harm: ban publication of their books, have them locked up, or even kill them. And the top leadership of the Party will never give absolute or unconditional protection to writers who attack the bureaucracy, because the leadership itself is the apex of the bureaucracy, and failings in the administrative machine farther down can easily be seen as a reflection on Party policy as a whole.

So the relationship tends to be cyclic: in periods of relative liberalization, writers are welcome to attack areas of the bureaucracy which seem to be impeding progress. But when the Party cracks the whip and calls for more discipline, the writers are the first to feel the icy wind of official displeasure.

Perhaps this cycle has been broken, and Chinese writers will at last be able to write frankly and critically about what is wrong with the country's social order – tempering their criticism, of course, with a judicious amount of loyal praise. But the crackdown on dissidents and authors of non-official political journals in 1979 was not an encouraging sign. It indicated that whatever faults the leaders may find in their own past performance – or that of their administrative machine, or their predecessors – they will not for long tolerate writers who are too keen to tell the general public all about those failings.

As has ever been the case in China, literature and literary criticism are tightly bound up with politics. When the commanders of the People's Liberation Army began to feel uneasy about Deng Xiaoping's partial liberalization of cultural affairs in the late seventies and early eighties, they chose modern literature as one way of making their views known. The armed forces newspaper bitterly attacked a serving officer who had written a film scenario which was considered unpatriotic and anti-socialist. The Party was less than enthusiastic about this attack on the writer Bai Hua, and after formally endorsing the armed forces' view of his work, ordered a halt to the campaign. Bai Hua himself published a self-criticism, but came to no harm as far as is known. No sooner was this issue shelved than the army commanders lunged out at another of their own serving writers, Ye Wenfu, who had bitterly satirized a general for building a private bathroom for himself. 'Have a good wash, General,' Ye's poem said, 'then at least when you die your corpse won't be dirty.' As long as this kind of outspoken criticism of the establishment is able to surface, it is impossible to talk about a totally controlled literary scene in China.

16.   *The Talking Walls*

The fifteen years 1966–80 may go down in Chinese history as the age of the wall poster – a uniquely Chinese contribution to the process of political communication. The decision of the Deng-Hua leadership to abolish it seems to spell the end of an era, albeit a brief one.

Wall posters are called in Chinese either *dazibao* ('big-character notices') or *xiaozibao* ('small-character notices'). Of these, the *dazibao* are by far the more important; they have spearheaded scores of important political movements in Peking and the provinces, openly challenging established office-bearers and power-holders and frequently bringing them down, either directly – by instigating mass demonstrations, riots and sit-ins – or indirectly, by convincing an official's superiors that he was intolerably unpopular with the common people. Posters have also been used as weapons in devious political intrigues, slyly discrediting unnamed people and casting dirt on the reputation of political rivals.

The origins of the *dazibao* are somewhat obscure. It was customary in traditional China for a person who felt himself or his family or community to be grievously wronged to post up a big protest notice on the wall of the local prefecture. This, however, was a risky business which could well result in arrest, beating, torture and execution for the person responsible.

During the Communist Party's sojourn in Yan'an from 1935 to 1945, Party members and adherents of the movement were encouraged to post suggestions or criticisms of the way affairs were being handled, but there is no record of their being used as major weapons in any top-level power struggle.

Posters as a serious political institution in China date from 1966, when they were used to criticize and bring down Peking's mayor, Peng Zhen, followed by scores of other national and provincial leaders. With the growth of factional fighting among different activist groups of the Red Guard type, the posters became vehicles for polemics, accusations, mob-rousing, self-justification and the voicing of grievances.

Sometimes a poster campaign was mounted at the instigation of a powerful or dominant faction in the leadership, with scores, hundreds, or even thousands of individual posters appearing, all following the same line dictated from above: for example, the campaign against Deng Xiaoping carried out at the campuses of Peking's two main universities in the winter of 1975–6. More often, posters were the work of groups or individuals, possibly put up by one leadership faction trying to under-mine the positions of another, or simply expressing the woes of the man in the street. Posters which originated behind the scenes were often put up by the offspring of highly placed cadres.

The merits of the poster as a means of political expression are that it is cheap and easy to produce (only one copy is needed), attracts attention immediately from passers-by, and assembles dozens or hundreds of people in one spot, where they can debate or at least ponder the issues raised.

Until 1980, there was a moral onus on the authorities and the police not to destroy or remove posters, for their use was sanctioned in the 1975 State Constitution and reaffirmed in the 1978 revised Constitu-tion, as one of the four 'big freedoms' which Mao considered essential to keep in touch with the pulse of the masses. (The other three were called 'big debates, blooming, and contending', named after the short-lived policy of letting 'a hundred flowers bloom and a hundred schools of thought contend' in 1957.) But in January 1980, Deng said in an important speech that the 'four big freedoms' would be removed from the Constitution at the next session of the National People's Congress. Until 1980, people who removed posters could be denounced and attacked in fresh posters – on account of that very act. And the appearance of posters on the streets usually excited passers-by and attracted comment in a way newspapers and political pamphlets could not.

The wall poster was a sort of moral and political shock tactic. The bright reds, pinks, greens, and yellows of the writing paper, and the black brush strokes marching boldly across it with their message, created a tingling excitement and a hollow apprehension in the pit of the stomach. Things which people would not dare to say openly could be voiced in posters, if not always with impunity.

The mere act of reading posters was a form of mute communication among Chinese people. By standing together and fixing their concentration on the writing, they proclaimed the poster's validity and relevance to their own lives. Here, the crowd on the pavement silently asserted, is a daring statement. The person who wrote it may be a fool to expose himself in this way. But what he says is worth thinking about.

Sometimes a member of the crowd would get excited and in a hysterically rising tone denounce the poster as the work of counter-revolutionaries, traitors, revisionists, and 'rotten eggs'. A few of the more cautious souls among the readers would drift unobtrusively away as they sensed the approach of trouble. Someone might reply to the objector, who by this time would be in a highly lathered emotional state. If tempers got short, there would be a shouting-and-pushing match and the police would eventually intervene, if only to try to stop the protagonists from coming to blows. Police or soldiers would also tear down posters thought too seditious or extreme.

After the fall of Defence Minister Lin Biao in 1971, poster-writing stopped in most parts of the country as people attempted to line up behind Premier Zhou Enlai's policy of bringing about stability and tranquillity in the interests of production and social order. But with the onset of the 'Criticize Lin Biao and Confucius' campaign in late 1973, reports from provincial cities told of rashes of posters on railway stations and streets calling for the overthrow of local Party and military bosses.

In the summer of 1974, an extraordinary outbreak of poster fever hit Peking – at first mainly directed at the municipal committee, later taking in protests and complaints from workers as far away as the city of Nanchang in Jiangxi province – telling of strikes and bloody riots and calling on the Peking leadership to put things straight. There were individual petitions – for instance, accusing a local official of rape and intimidation – and such cries for justice were frequently addressed to 'Chairman Mao, old gentleman!' (*lao renjia*). Even Hua Guofeng, at the time active not only in Peking but also in Hunan province, where he headed the local administration and Party apparatus, was criticized in a large series of posters referring to local conditions in Hunan – which were, however, quickly torn down.

The 1974 posters petered out after a few weeks, and the wall where they had been stuck was scrubbed clean again. The campaign seemed to have achieved nothing except the airing of a few personal and local grievances. From then on Peking was virtually poster-free until the Qing Ming Festival of the Dead on 4 April 1976, when the Martyrs' Monument on Tiananmen Square was plastered all over with small-character posters and poems, declarations of loyalty to Zhou and his legacy. These were removed, an act which provoked the riots of 5 April. From then on, poster campaigns were of only small importance in national affairs for over two years. The fall of the Gang of Four, the return of Deng Xiaoping and other important events called forth reams of satirical cartoons denigrating Jiang Qing and her associates – often extremely witty and extremely cruel. In provincial cities there were occasional outbursts of poster-sticking. But it was not until November 1978 that the movement came back into its own again as an important tool of political change.

For the past year and half, Deng had been locked in confrontation with General Wang Dongxing, the inner Party security chief who regarded himself as one of the custodians of Mao's political legacy and had boasted in the media of their former close links. To oppose Deng's aim of discarding most of Mao's policies of the Eleven Years, Wang and his supporters proclaimed that whatever Mao had said was right and must be followed to the letter. This earned them the nickname of *fanshipai* – the 'Whateverist' faction.

Almost certainly at the instigation of members of Deng's group, young and sometimes not-so-young people went out on the streets, putting up posters calling for greater democratization and discussing critically some fundamental problems of socialism. The call for greater democracy suited the Deng group's purpose well, as their platform at the time was to denounce the policies of the Eleven Years as having suppressed mass opinion and resulted in dictatorial, autocratic behaviour by the Gang and their adherents. This helped discredit Wang, as well as Peking's Mayor Wu De, around whose neck hung like an albatross the fact that he had been the first to denounce the 1976 riot, now seen as pro-Deng and anti-leftist. Wu had lost the post of mayor in 1978 but still sat on the Politburo (until sacked from all his posts in February 1980).

Hand in hand with the new rash of wall posters went the appearance of several home-printed political journals which discussed matters of human rights, democratic freedoms, and cultural liberty in a forth-right way not seen since the 'Hundred Flowers' campaign of more than two decades previously. The stretch of wall on the north side of Changan Boulevard (often misleadingly referred to as Xidan, the name of a nearby street), where posters went up, became known as 'Democracy Wall' and was also used as a handy site for selling unofficial journals. Crowds at the wall stood around for hours on end debating with each other – and even with foreigners – the merits of the socialist system. Some of the bolder spirits began going to restaurants with foreigners, inviting them to their homes and doing what only a few months before was unthinkable: visiting foreigners in their guarded compounds. As long as they were accompanied by the foreigner or brought in his or her car, it seemed the military guards at the gates of the compound did not think it wise to interfere or demand to see the Chinese guests' testimonials – as was the usual practice until then. Some foreigners were even able to visit and photograph the apartments where the unofficial journals were edited and duplicated on primitive inking machines.

Evidently Deng gained tremendous popularity from this experi-me..t with free speech – enough to permit him decisively to confront the Wang group at the Third Plenum of the Eleventh Central Committee in December 1978, winning a hands-down victory which isolated the Politburo leftists and marked them for demotion. In February 1980, at the Fifth Plenum, Wang and Wu De were dismissed, together with two other prominent opponents of Deng, Peking Mili-tary Region Commander General Chen Xilian and Party apparatchik and agriculture specialist Ji Dengkui.

After his victory at the Third Plenum, Deng turned against the Democracy Wall movement, calling it anarchistic, counter-revolutionary and reactionary. Several noted polemicists were ar-rested, and in 1979 the best known of them, a young electrician named Wei Jingsheng, was put on trial as an object lesson to all others. The posters and unofficial journals continued to be pasted up and cir-culated, but in December of 1979 it was announced that Democracy Wall was being closed down. In future, anyone who wanted to put up posters could do so with official sanction only at the Altar of the Moon

Park – located far away in western Peking. Few of the activists took up the invitation to put their posters there, and the movement withered and died. Deng had announced in an important speech to high-level cadres on 16 January that not only were the posters and journals to be completely banned, but the freedom to use posters would be written out of the Constitution as soon as possible.

The short-lived dissident movement in China in 1978–9 provokes some eerily reminiscent comparisons with the more robust and tenacious movement which has held its own in the Soviet Union since the mid 1960s. The grim, glum knots of people outside the courtroom, the lying of court officials, the packing of the court with stooges called 'members of the public', refusal to admit friends of the accused, perfunctory proceedings with only a nod in the direction of legality or the accused's right to defence – these hardly seem worthy of a country which has come through one of the worst periods of political persecution in history, has repudiated and condemned it, and has vowed to follow to the letter a new, just and fair legal code.

The ease with which the Chinese dissident movement was suppressed – which Leonid Brezhnev must doubtless have envied his Chinese counterparts – seems to speak for the position taken by many students of China, that demonstrative intellectual dissidence is a specifically Western and Russian phenomenon unsuited to the traditionally 'despotic' societies of Asia.

Such a generalization is obviously absurd, however, if one only glances at the tenacious dissident movements of India, Japan, South Korea, Taiwan and most other places in Asia. One can certainly make a case (as I have done in Chapter 7) for the idea that the Chinese lack of institutionalized opposition in imperial times has carried over into the modern period, making political conformism unchallengeably strong as the dominant social attitude. But the 1978–9 'Peking Spring' demonstrated how attractive the plain ideals of human rights and freedom of expression are, even in a country which has had little experience of what Westerners regard as essential political liberties.

There is no question of the Chinese dissidents copying their poses from those of dissidents in Russia or any other country; they have had far too little information on such places. What comes through astonishingly clearly is the similarity of the dilemmas and challenges which dissidents face in any centrally controlled socialist society. What the

Chinese dissidents said during their short heyday could have been transferred almost word for word into the Soviet underground journal *Chronicle of Current Events* and accepted as Russian dissidence in the classic mould.

The big difference between the Chinese and East European types of dissident movement seems to lie mainly in the ease with which the Chinese one was put down. Here perhaps is the most telling evidence that the Chinese political world by nature is conformist. The bold young dissidents who hung around with Western journalists and diplomats in Peking for a few months in 1978–9 have mostly melted into the background again, whereas in Moscow nothing seems capable of preventing ever new nests of them from sending their messengers out to keep in contact with the world at large. This indicates that the influence of West European and American liberal ideas has been more profound in semi-European Russia than in China.

The other important distinguishing feature of the Chinese dissident movement is that it has been manipulated with great skill in the interests of factional power struggle in the Politburo. Nobody has yet plausibly suggested that Russia's dissidents are covertly encouraged by any particular leadership group, in the interests of embarrassing or even bringing down a rival group. The most that can be said is that Nikita Khrushchev did once use the popularity of culture heroes such as the poet Yevtushenko to push his own rather primitive ideas about the need for a bit more intellectual freedom.

As the Soviet protest movement grew in depth and scope, it attracted some prominent authors – Aleksandr Solzhenitsyn being the best known – and scientists, especially Academician Andrei Sakharov, designer of the Soviet H-bomb. Although much of the contact work with foreign journalists – essential for knowledge of the movement in the outside world – was done by quite obscure and even dubious people, it has continued to attract prominent culture heroes, such as the cellist Mstislav Rostropovich.

None of the people actively involved in the Chinese dissident movement appeared to be culture heroes, or even slightly known to the general public. They became known mainly through attacks on their activity in the national press, which accused them of anarchism, counter-revolution, and slander of the socialist order. Ordinary, uninvolved people who had never in their lives seen Wei Jingsheng felt obliged to applaud when the fifteen-year jail sentence on the young dissident was announced on Radio Peking and factory loudspeaker systems.

The Wei trial was a landmark in the leadership's policies towards dissidents, for it made a martyr of him in the eyes of other relatively free-thinking people but frightened most of them into silence. The only one bold enough to stand up for him publicly in Peking – another dissident publisher named Liu Ching – was himself arrested. In Zhengzhou, capital of Henan province, a man drew an eight-year jail term for putting up a *dazibao* defending Wei. There may have been other such cases in the provinces.

Wei, a native of Anhui province, was born in 1950. After he began publishing his unofficial journal *Tansuo* ('Exploration') in 1978, he became known to a number of foreign correspondents and diplomats in Peking. Because of these contacts, the public prosecutor accused him of treason in allegedly passing military secrets to a Western correspondent. However, it was clear that the real reason for his prosecution was his free-and-easy mixing with foreigners, discussing politics in an uninhibited manner, and writing critically about the socialist system in his journal. According to another journal which was still being published after Wei's trial, the indictment (never published in full in the Chinese official press) ran as follows:

Defendant Wei Jingsheng, alias Jing Sheng, male, aged 29, is a native of Chao County, Anhui province. He is a worker of the Peking Municipal Park Services Management Office and a resident of No. 2, Unit 6, North 4th Lane, Western City District, Peking. He was arrested on 29 March 1979 by the Peking Public Security Bureau with the permission of the Peking People's Procuratorate for Counter-Revolutionary Charges. He is now under custody. Investigation of the counter-revolutionary case of defendant Wei Jingsheng has been concluded by the Peking Municipal Public Security Bureau and transferred to this procuratorate for examination and prosecution. After examination, a conclusion was reached that defendant Wei Jingsheng be prosecuted under the following charges:

Supplying military intelligence on our country to a foreigner. On February 1979, during our country's self-defensive counterattack against Vietnam, defendant Wei Jingsheng furnished a foreigner with the names of our commanding officers and the strength of the troops we employed. He also supplied the foreigner with military intelligence on the progress and number of casualties in the war. All these are counter-revolutionary crimes violating Article 6 of the Penal Code Against Counter-Revolutionaries [a set of regulations promulgated in the early 1950s].

Carrying out counter-revolutionary propaganda and agitation. The defendant used the writing of reactionary articles and the editing of the reactionary journal *Tansuo* as a means to achieve his counter-revolutionary aims. During the period from December 1978 to March 1979, he wrote several articles ... aimed at propagating and agitating for the overthrow of the regime of the dictatorship of the proletariat and the socialist system. These articles were widely circulated in Peking and Tientsin. Article 2 of the Constitution stipulates that Marxism and Mao Zedong Thought are the guiding ideologies of the People's Republic of China. However, Wei Jingsheng slandered Marxism and Mao Zedong Thought as a prescription only slightly better than the medicine peddled by charlatans. Article 1 of the Constitution stipulates that the People's Republic of China is a socialist country of the dictatorship of the proletariat led by the working class and based on the worker–peasant alliance. Article 56 of the Constitution stipulates that citizens of the Republic should support the leadership of the Chinese Communist Party, the socialist system, the unity of the motherland, and the unity of all nationalities. The citizen should also adhere to the constitution and the law. However, Wei Jingsheng vilified our state system of dictatorship of the proletariat as a feudalistic monarchy under the cloak of socialism. Thus, he tried to incite the masses not to believe in 'the stability and unity advocated by dictators', to refrain from becoming 'the modern tools of expansionism of dictatorial rulers', and to 'give up their illusions'. He urged the people to focus their rage on 'the sinister system which has brought a tragic fate to the people'. He also advocated the seizure of power from the hands of overlords ... in violation of Article 10 of the Penal Code Against Counter-Revolutionaries ... It is the view of this procuratorate that defendant Wei Jingsheng has betrayed his motherland by supplying military information to a foreigner, thus endangering the People's Republic of China. He has violated the constitution of the National People's Congress by writing reactionary articles agitating for the overthrow of the dictatorship of the proletariat and the socialist system. All these make up the charges of counter-revolutionary crimes against him. For the sake of safe-guarding the socialist system, strengthening the people's democratic dictatorship, maintaining stability and unity, ensuring the smooth progress of socialist modernized construction, and supression of counter-revolutionary sabotage, the defendant should be publicly prosecuted according to Article 2, Item One, of Article 6 and Item Two of Article 10 of the People's Republic of China's Penal Code Against Counter-Revolutionaries. It is hoped that the defendant will be punished according to law.

Wei, refusing the court's offer of counsel, defended himself boldly and intelligently – which probably helped account for the stiff sentence. His defence is a detailed critique of the confusion existing in the Chinese judicial apparatus as late as 1979, before the introduction of the new criminal law and procedural codes.

Wei claimed to have been exercising his rights under Article 45 of the Constitution, which specifies that Chinese citizens have 'freedom of speech, correspondence, assembly, publication, association, parade, demonstration and strike, as well as the freedom to air their views freely, write big-character posters, and hold big debates'. (Significantly, the last two of these freedoms – writing big-character posters and holding big debates – are among the four guarantees of free opinion which Deng has proposed be expunged from the Constitution.)

Answering the charge of passing on military secrets concerning the Chinese invasion of Vietnam in February 1979, Wei said, 'The words "military intelligence" are a very broad concept. Citizens have the duty to keep secrets, but the premise is that citizens know what secrets are to be kept. In other words, these secrets must be made clear to them beforehand and indicated as military secrets before people have the duty to keep them. Only such matters can be called secrets or military secrets in the legal sense. I was never told of the secrets I must keep.'

Wei went on to claim that he had a perfect right to talk to foreigners about such an important event as the China–Vietnam war. 'I am an ordinary man in the street and my source of information was hearsay and not any official government documents. I had no way of knowing whether my news coincided with documents marked confidential because I did not read any confidential government documents. The news I talked about could not cause any harm to the situation on our front. This was what I took into account beforehand. For instance, I mentioned the name of the commander-in-chief at the front. Who has ever heard that one side ever lost a battle because the other side knows the name of its commander? How could mentioning the name of the front commander be detrimental to the situation on the front? It has never been heard since ancient times that the name of a commander would become a decisive factor in war. This argument is untenable. Of course the procurator might say that according to our country's law it is a military secret. But during the time of the Gang of Four, the practice of isolation could arbitrarily take anything as secret and could regard any random talk with foreigners as collusion with foreign countries.'

Turning to the charge of counter-revolutionary propaganda and agitation, Wei said, 'Owing to the influence of cultural autocracy and the policy of hoodwinking the people adopted by the Gang of Four for many years, some people now hold the following view: it is revolutionary if we act in accordance with the will of the leaders in power and counter-revolutionary to oppose the will of the people in power. I cannot agree with this debasing of the concept of revolution.'

In a cleverly reasoned argument, Wei picked up the post-Mao leadership's line that Marxism is not a rigid or fossilized system of ideas but must be modified in the light of changing social conditions and needs to be constantly debated, not just by the leaders but by the people as a whole, in order to make sure it keeps up with the times. He concluded with two points which were really the core of his defence:

'First, the Constitution gives the people the right to criticize leaders, because they are human beings and not deities. Only through criticism and supervision by the people can they reduce their errors, avoid becoming overlords who ride roughshod over the people, and really make the people feel at ease.

'Second, to carry out reforms of the socialist system in our country it is necessary to rely on the people of the whole country to discover the shortcomings in the present system through criticism and discussion. Otherwise the reforms cannot be successfully carried out. Therefore it is the right of every citizen to criticize any unreasonable people or things that he sees. This is also a responsibility which he cannot shift. No person or organization has the right to interfere with this sovereign right. Criticism cannot possibly be nice and appealing to the ear, or all correct. To require criticism to be entirely correct, and to inflict punishment if it is not, is the same as prohibiting criticism and reforms and elevating the leaders to the position of deities.'

Wei's ability to compose such a defence – quixotic and entirely counterproductive though it proved to be from his own point of view – is highly impressive in a country where access to liberal political opinion had been tightly restricted, if not made completely impossible, for all his adult life. It is hard not to feel that a young man of such intelligence and spirit would have been better co-opted into the national leadership then sent to jail.

But there is one bright side to the Wei case: if it happened under Mao, the world would probably never have heard of it, and the most likely judgement would have been sentence of death.

17. *Allies and Adversaries*

The friendship with the United States and other capitalist countries which China pursued doggedly throughout the 1970s and into the 1980s has been perhaps the most important single factor in the long-term development of global relations for the rest of the twentieth century.

Often obscured by more immediate areas of international concern and crisis, especially in the Middle East, China's pro-Western stance has been one of the few really stable elements in the international politics of the seventies. There seems little reason to believe it will be changed drastically in the foreseeable future.

The factors which impeded close Chinese–American relations in the 1950s and 1960s were the American fear of all Communist regimes, the Korean War, support for Chiang Kai-shek's Nationalist regime on Taiwan, and the Vietnam War. All of these were seen by China as threats to her own security. So it was the more extraordinary that Mao could receive and welcome President Richard Nixon while American troops were still in Indochina and were confronting China's ally, Kim Il Sung, in Korea; and while Washington still had its defence agreement with Taipei.

Mao's sudden decision to seek security and alliance in partnership with 'imperialist' America was typical enough of his mercurial political mind and his ability to switch tactics while making out that his line had all along been consistent. So it is not surprising that many Europeans and Americans have been unable to adjust mentally to a situation where their government is even prepared to sell arms to a Communist country which just over a decade ago was one of the most fiercely anti-Western powers in the world.

Probably two main factors influenced Mao and the other top leaders to seek closer relations with the United States. One was their disillusionment with the Third World and the non-aligned movement, which they had once seen as a global force capable of confronting and containing the two superpowers. The other was the increasingly dangerous state of relations with the Soviet Union, which had shed the blood of Chinese soldiers on the northern river frontier in 1969.

The importance given to close links with the Third World – a policy associated with the name of the late Premier Zhou Enlai – seemed based on a certain degree of naivety in Peking. Following Marxist generalizations about the nature of imperialism and colonialism, they assumed that the newly emerging nations would be motivated by a standard set of anti-imperialist impulses and would forge national and international unity out of their common desire for freedom and prosperity.

Religion, race, caste, and colour were not factors which the Chinese took seriously enough in assessing the behaviour of the Third World countries. In Marxist–Leninist theory, conflicts over such issues are simply the outgrowth and reflection of underlying economic contradictions which are relatively simple to analyse. Nor did the Chinese take fully into acount either the border quarrels and border wars which would set so many Third World countries at each other's throats, within a few years of independence from the colonial powers, or the continuing attraction of affluent Western civilization for the ruling elites in those countries.

The Chinese encountered their first big setback in their Third World policy when their newly forged friendship with India was wrecked by the 1962 border conflict. Three years later, in Indonesia, which they regarded as a close ally, they were witnesses to the savage power of regional and communal rivalries fired by religious fervour. When the Cultural Revolution began in 1966, Peking simply threw its foreign policy out of the window, withdrawing all its top envoys (except the ambassador to Egypt) and harassing foreign nationals in China.

For the next few years, China had barely a friend in the world except tiny Albania. Even her relations with neighbouring allies North Korea and North Vietnam were strained. The few foreigners who visited China emerged with baffling tales of a society seemingly gone mad.

The Kissinger–Nixon thaw in relations with Peking in 1971–2 resulted in a sudden scramble by other countries to recognize the People's Republic and withdraw recognition from the 'Republic of China' on Taiwan. European countries, Australia, New Zealand and Japan, and countries of the Third World which had previously shunned Peking out of deference to America's pro-Taiwan policy, sent their diplomats pouring into Peking to open spanking new embassy buildings. A Chinese delegation assumed its seats at the General Assembly of the United Nations and on the Security Council. China became madly fashionable – with journalists and editors, film-makers, politicians, bankers and jet-setters clamouring for visas to admire the Great Wall, talk to Premier Zhou and even Chairman Mao, eat Peking duck, and enthuse over hospitals and day nurseries and communes. The Chinese encouraged this upbeat mood, discreetly repudiating the ultra-leftist and anti-foreign antics of the Cultural Revolution, and blaming it all on the late Defence Minister Marshal Lin Biao, who was said to have been burned to death in the crash of a British-made Trident jet airliner over the People's Republic of Mongolia. (Later versions said the Chinese Air Force had shot him and his family and friends down as they attempted to flee to the Soviet Union after the failure of a coup attempt.)

More substantively, the US administration hoped that friendly relations with China – which could still be only semi-official because of the continued American presence in Taiwan – would help it to extricate itself from the Vietnam War without too much loss of honour or credibility. Signs are that Peking did encourage the Americans to believe this and were angry with Hanoi for its blitzkrieg victory over South Vietnam which sent the last Americans scrambling humiliatingly aboard helicopters on the roof of the US embassy in Saigon in 1975. Arguably, Peking's inability to deliver Hanoi to any agreement about peace with the Thieu regime in the South delayed American full diplomatic recognition of the People's Republic of China until 1 January 1979 – nearly seven years after Nixon's first visit to Peking. But in the meantime trade and cultural and scientific contacts went ahead, laying a firm basis for the new Chinese–American relationship.

The temporary absence of fully fledged embassies in each other's countries did not deter either the Chinese or the Americans from speculating on the prospects of their relations in the future. While the Americans steadfastly proclaimed that their friendship with China 'was not aimed at any third party', it was perfectly obvious that the Soviet Union must consider itself threatened by a possible future alliance between the world's most advanced country and the world's most populous nation, with which they shared some seven thousand kilometres of potentially explosive frontier.

The Chinese, for their part, were less coy about the prospects of their new American connection, for they were not committed to any détente programme with the Soviet Union and insisted that, as its former close allies, they had a unique insight into its dangerous and aggressive nature, its duplicity and its ruthlessness. From 1973, the Chinese Communist Party, Foreign Ministry, and official media daily proclaimed the new theory of 'the three worlds': the first made up of the two superpowers, Russia and America; the second world taking in the non-superpower advanced countries (Western Europe, Japan, Canada, Australia and New Zealand); and the Third World consisting of all the poor and underdeveloped nations, many of them post-colonial, with which China was said to have a community of interest, counting herself as one of them. The advanced countries of Eastern Europe were not assigned any particular role in this global *dramatis personae*, being viewed in Peking as unhappy victims of Russian expansionism and helpless tools of its worldwide espionage and subversion programme. Only Yugoslavia – once the whipping-boy for Russia in China's denunciation of 'revisionism' in the 1960s – and Romania – with its deliberately even-handed foreign policy – were lined up in an ill-assorted pro-China Balkan block which until 1978 also included Albania. (The Albanians finally broke with China because – it is speculated – party chief Enver Hoxha did not like the Chinese friendship with the West and the debunking of Mao.)

The improvement of relations with Washington was Peking's long-term priority. But while it was impeded by the Taiwan problem and some less important issues such as expropriated property and frozen assets, the Chinese pushed ahead with a vigorous programme of friendly relations with the 'Second World'. Especially favourable to Britain because of its strong opposition to Soviet expansionism, the Chinese also cultivated closer trade and scientific relations with Western Europe, Japan, and the other advanced countries. Through exchanges of traders and specialist delegations, China formed a picture of the extent of her own backwardness and her desperate need to drop the most counterproductive of Mao's economic and educational policies. But Mao was still mentally alert, if not active, in the mid 1970s, and his desire to fence China off from all 'unhealthy' influences of the capitalist world put a heavy handicap on the efforts of more outward-looking officials, such as Premier Zhou Enlai and Vice-Premier Deng Xiaoping, to face up to the failure of extreme-left policies and swallow their national pride in the interests of getting maximum help to modernize the economy.

At the same time, a strange paradox became apparent in the form of China's friendly attitude towards entrenched right-wing politicians abroad. Among their favourites were Britain's Edward Heath, West Germany's Franz-Josef Strauss, and the Shah of Iran – to say nothing of Richard Nixon. The criterion for judging foreign leaders and governments was: how do they behave towards the Russians? China's intense desire to isolate the Soviet Union in world political opinion became so obsessive that one could predict Chinese reactions to emerging foreign-policy situations with almost complete accuracy: what was bad for Russia was good for China, and vice versa. At the same time the Chinese let it be discreetly known that they considered social-democratic politicians in the West to be dangerously woolly-minded in their tolerant attitude towards the Soviet Union and their desire to see the success of détente and arms-control measures. But in 1980 they modified this stance, evidently realizing the importance of European social democracy and Euro-Communism.

For most of the 1970s, the one sure way for a European politician to be banned from visiting China had been to be a card-carrying member of one of the mainstream communist parties. The small Maoist splinter groups in Western left-wing parties were still welcomed and honoured in Peking, but China made it perfectly plain that it was pinning its real hopes on the big ruling parties – preferably right-wing ones. An essential feature of the 'three worlds' theory was that it proclaimed war was inevitable unless world revolution forestalled it, and considered that World War Three was most likely to break out in Europe, whereas political commentators and strategic analysts in the West tended to believe there was an odds-on chance of the next big war being touched off by a fresh Sino-Soviet border conflict. Western leaders visiting Peking nearly all reported that, however interesting they found the Chinese world view, they could not go along with the dogmatic Chinese opposition to détente or the harping on the theme of war.

Ironically, the theory of 'people's war' elaborated by Mao, and by Lin Biao before his death, was now being turned against the East European socialist block, in partnership with the massive technological and strategic armed might of the West: a military doctrine originally aimed at the overthrow of capitalism and imperialism became aimed at the countries of the Moscow-led Warsaw Pact. The general idea of 'people's war' is that people, not machines, determine the outcome; will and fighting spirit are stronger than nuclear weapons; and the global 'countryside' – the Third World – can encircle and destroy the 'cities' – the capitalist world.

Though seemingly proven successful in Vietnam, 'people's war' is fraught with problems as a strategy for defending a country of China's size against an attack by a country as powerful as the Soviet Union. China was well aware that America's hands were tied in Vietnam, and that invasion of the north and perhaps bombing of southern China could have tipped the war the other way. There is no reason for China to suppose that Russia would similarly fight with one hand behind her back. The importance of possessing advanced weapons has been highlighted by China's series of nuclear weapons and missiles tests and by approaches made to the United States and West European countries about the possibilities of Chinese purchases of up-to-date arms.

Though arms sales to China have not materialized at time of writing, they seem likely in the future, though they will arouse fierce opposition on the part of the Soviet Union. Russia's only means of attack against China's important north-eastern industrial zone, or on Peking itself, is by way of her Far East territories or Mongolia, both of which have only a tenuous rail link with Western Russia. Airlifting all the supplies and men needed for a major offensive could be cripplingly expensive in the likely event that China knocked out the Trans-Siberian railway in the first few days of hostilities. For the Russians to take on the Chinese Army on Chinese soil would be altogether a different matter from imposing military occupation on Afghanistan.

By the late 1970s, China's military strength consisted of a standing army of 3.6 million, mainly infantry, with armoured divisions including some 8,000 to 9,000 tanks of obsolete Soviet design and about 22,000 artillery pieces and heavy mortars. Her navy has 23 capital ships, nearly 100 submarines, and a large fleet of small vessels for coastal defence. The air force counts some 10,000 pilots out of a total strength of 400,000; over 90 medium bombers and 500 light bombers, all of originally Soviet design; over 2,000 jet fighters, mostly based on the Soviet Mig-19; 400 military transports and perhaps 400 helicopters; and surface-to-air missiles. In addition there are some 7 million trained militia capable of bearing arms in the event of war, while most able-bodied people in China have enough rudimentary training and organization to enable them to act as an important support force for the front-line troops: carrying stretchers, supplying ammunition and rations, and carrying out emergency repairs and civil defence.

In any prolonged war of attrition, the Chinese – with their shorter lines of communication and their almost unlimited manpower – would take a heavy toll of the Soviet Red Army. But it is doubtful whether they could put up meaningful resistance if the Russians took the lid off and destroyed their major cities with nuclear missiles.

China has the capacity to destroy several Soviet cities with its own nuclear weapons, whether missile-delivered or carried by bomber. But the consequences of all-out nuclear war for China are too horrible to contemplate.

Mao sought to provide adequate civil defence against nuclear attack by ordering the people to build a massive network of tunnels and underground installations beneath every significant town and city in China. Many Western military specialists believe that these tunnels would be little more than mass graves in the event of a nuclear blast. They were never, in any case, designed as long-term shelters, but only as a means of evacuating the surviving population to the rural areas as quickly as possible. (Perhaps recognizing that the tunnels are a white elephant, the post-Mao leaders have begun converting them into factories and hotels.)

Both China and Russia fear the outbreak of war between them, yet both seem to see it as inevitable in the long run. In 1980 Vice-Chairman Deng said in an important policy speech that world peace was essential to China's carrying out the Four Modernizations programme – a significant shift of policy from the Maoist position that China could and must be prepared to fight and survive a war with anyone at any time. Nonetheless, China has persistently refused to get seriously involved in such important measures as arms control, nuclear test bans, prevention of nuclear proliferation, and conventional force reductions. Since the 1969 clash, negotiations to rationalize the Sino-Soviet border have been held intermittently in Peking without any apparent progress. Further negotiations – thought to be aimed at winding down some aspects of the political conflict with the Soviet Union – were begun in Moscow in late 1979, but the Soviet intervention in Afghanistan resulted in their break-up *sine die*.

The NATO powers have been understandably disturbed by the possibility that the death of Mao and rejection of his domestic policies might be accompanied by a Peking–Moscow rapprochement, especially since the restoration of late Stalinist-type political and social institutions in China has been accompanied by a Chinese decision to stop criticizing the Russians for 'revisionism' in their internal policies. A fresh Sino-Soviet alliance would seriously upset the world balance of forces, so that the Afghanistan affair may be seen by some Western statesmen as a disguised blessing. At the very least, it has served to remind people of the nature of Soviet expansionism – all the more menacing to China, which is one of Afghanistan's neighbours.

A major problem which faces China in her defence planning to counter the threat of a Soviet attack is the fact that most of her borderlands are in wild terrain and partially inhabited by people who are not Hans (ethnic Chinese). Ethnic minorities account for perhaps five per cent of China's population (there are no recent census figures), living on about two-thirds of the land area. The principal minorities are the Zhuang, a people related to the Thais, in south-west China (numbering about 8 million); the Uighurs of Xinjiang, a Turkic people related to the Kazakhs, who are also represented in Xinjiang (a total of about 5 million); the Hui, a largely assimilated Chinese-speaking group who retain certain Islamic customs, such as a ban on pork (4 million); the Yi, related to the Tibetans (about 4 million); Tibetans (3 to 4 million); Miaos, hill tribes of the south-west (3 million); and Mongols (upwards of 2 million). The total 55 different ethnic minorities also include Koreans, Puyi, Tadjiks, Dai, and Shans.

The biggest problems are posed by the Mongols and the Uighurs. The 'Autonomous Region' of Inner Mongolia, which is ruled by China, contains twice as many Mongols as the Soviet-dominated puppet state of the Mongolian People's Republic (Outer Mongolia) just across the border. In a war with China, it would be simple for Soviet and Mongol troops to drive across the rolling grasslands in armoured strength and claim to have liberated the people of Inner

Mongolia from 'Chinese oppression'. The several million Chinese who have settled in the region could be expelled to China proper – those who survived the invasion, that is. Similarly, an armoured assault into Xinjiang from Soviet Kazakhstan could be followed by the declaration of an 'independent' Republic of East Turkestan – under Soviet domination and merged to all intents and purposes with the Turkic-speaking areas of Soviet Asia. If this scenario should seem alarmist, it has been confirmed quite blatantly by a Soviet KGB propagandist, Victor Louis, who in 1979 published in English a book entitled *The Coming Decline of the Chinese Empire*, which proposed precisely this 'solution' to the problem of China's minorities.

Tibet poses a lesser problem of security because of its remoteness and isolation. India seems in no mood for another border war with China, and though they have failed to modernize and sinicize the Tibetan people, the Chinese overlords have long since put down armed resistance to their rule. Nonetheless, Chinese administrative policies in Tibet were excoriated publicly in 1980 by a senior secretary of the regional Party committee, who said the basic needs of the Tibetan people – such as saddles, milk bowls, churns and barley – had been neglected in favour of inappropriate crops and new industries. More consideration for the culture and beliefs of the Tibetans has been promised by Peking, perhaps with an eye to persuading the Dalai Lama and as many of his followers as possible to return from exile in India and elsewhere.

The Zhuangs of Guangxi province, though numerous, pose little security threat, since they are quite closely integrated with the Hans and have apparently rejected attempts to write their language down phonetically, preferring instead to use the Chinese script. However, there are problems associated with the many different minorities who span the mountainous borders between China, Laos, Vietnam and Burma (the notorious 'Golden Triangle'). Showing scant regard for international frontiers, these hill people mingle freely with their kin in the neighbouring countries and in the event of continuing hostilities between China and Vietnam might be used by the Soviet-backed Vietnamese to carry out harassing operations behind Chinese lines. This cuts both ways, however, for China could quite seriously destabilize Vietnam by arming the minority peoples on the Vietnamese side – as the Americans did in the case of the South Vietnamese Montagnards during the Indochina war.

China now admits that the policies she pursued towards her ethnic minorities during the Eleven Years were arrogant, oppressive and counterproductive. Following an ancient Chinese tradition of looking down on all non-Han ethnic groups in the borderlands, Chinese officials attempted during the Cultural Revolution to reduce the use of minority languages, abolish their 'feudal customs', prevent casual border crossings, and make the minorities regard themselves as 'younger brothers' of the infinitely more 'civilized and enlightened' Hans – Mao cult and all. Post-1976 pronouncements on the minorities problem suggest that the Party and government will now take a much more gradualist approach to the absorption of these fringe cultures into China's own, instead of trying to force the pace.

China has certain cultural and ideological difficulties in its relations with minority peoples, which the Russians have managed to avoid to some extent. The Chinese diet is very largely grain-based, and most Chinese people dislike the taste of dairy products and mutton, the main types of food on the grasslands of Mongolia and the semi-deserts of Xinjiang. The history of China's relations with nomadic and semi-nomadic peoples is one of encroachment, settlement, and the turning over of pastureland to grain by the Hans. In 1979–80, the leadership in Peking has admitted that this was not the best policy, either economically or politically. The Mongols especially are very attached to their free-and-easy life-style and resent the loss of their grasslands to low-yielding grain crops. In a move to appease Mongol feeling – as well as to rationalize administrative procedures and military regions – Peking in 1979 reunited the main Mongol-speaking areas which had been split up among different provinces.

The Russians have on the whole shown a greater respect for the cultural traditions of racial minorities, and studies in Uzbek, Tadjik, Georgian and Armenian subjects, for instance, are pursued vigorously in the various Union Republics. Moscow's attitude towards its minorities is to let them have whatever native cultural freedoms they want, provided they are not disruptive to the stability of the State. China still has to learn this lesson and put it into practice if it is to keep or restore the goodwill of its ethnic minorities. Major concessions which Peking *has* made to the minorities are the granting of extra grain and cloth rations and freedom from birth-control measures.

China's handling of its minorities is a microcosm of some of the problems it has encountered in constructing a workable foreign policy.

Failing to appreciate the complexity of politics in Third World countries, the Chinese have suffered setbacks through faulty analysis of the situation on the ground. They backed the losing sides in the struggles for control of Angola and East Timor and lost respect in Iran for their close relations with the Shah. In the Arab world, they discovered through hard experience that it is impossible to be backing everybody at the same time. And the late Zhou Enlai's call to Kenyans to go all out for revolution in the 1960s was deeply resented by the newly independent black Kenyan government.

Though China still ascribes importance to the Third World – if only to make it difficult for the Soviet Union to dominate it – she is most of all interested in uniting with the Second World (a term which has already gone out of fashion in Peking, though the concept remains valid) and with the United States, to control Soviet adventurism. It becomes increasingly apparent that Peking sees the United States as the only force capable of exercising such control and has shown disappointment at the relative weakness of the American response to Soviet expansion in Africa and the Persian Gulf region. Peking was among the first governments to back the US boycott of the 1980 Moscow Olympics, after the Soviet intervention in Afghanistan, and in general is more hawkish about American strategy and global postures than even the most hawkish generals in the Pentagon. The near collapse of détente and the Strategic Arms Limitation Treaty (SALT) talks were welcomed with almost overt glee in Peking.

What disturbs the Chinese is the relative success of the Russians in recruiting client states to do the heavy work for them in parts of the world where they are inexperienced or unwilling to commit their own troops other than as military advisers. The Vietnamese expulsion of some 250,000 ethnic Chinese from Vietnam in 1978, and the subsequent China–Vietnam war in 1979, were seen in Peking as direct and inevitable results of Hanoi's following the Soviet line in foreign policy. The Chinese media made Vietnam out to be the 'Asian Cuba' – after the use of Cuban troops in Angola and Ethiopia in the interests of Soviet strategy.

The 1979 Vietnam crisis was a heavy blow to any lingering Chinese ideas of socialist or Third World solidarity, and it marked a new stage in the development of an essentially nationalistic Chinese foreign policy. China had already declared that there was no longer any 'world socialist camp', because most of the socialist nations were dominated by

Moscow. She had had differences with Hanoi for years – over the amount of aid Vietnam needed in the war and the postwar reconstruction period and over Hanoi's support for the Soviet line on world affairs. But actually to go to war with once 'fraternal' Vietnam – and with a 20,000-strong casualty list at the end of a mere two weeks' fighting to show for it – was a big step for China, and one which showed that whatever may happen elsewhere in the world, she will not tolerate Soviet interference in what she regards as her rightful sphere of influence in Indochina.

This approach to the Vietnam problem both alarmed and gratified other nations in South-east Asia, which were becoming increasingly apprehensive about the aggressive posture taken by Hanoi in the postwar period, and irritated by the constant arrival of seaborne refugees whom they were ill-equipped to shelter or feed. Leaders in Bangkok, Manila, Djakarta, Singapore and Kuala Lumpur were alarmed at the matter-of-fact way in which China launched her 'self-defensive counterattack' against Vietnam – but at the same time gratified that at last here was a regional power willing and able to act positively to restrain the Vietnamese and their Soviet patrons. Thailand especially has looked towards a closer link with China in order to protect its own border areas from Vietnamese incursions. The more aid Peking sends to the Khmer Rouge remnants in Kampuchea to fight the Vietnam-backed puppet government of Heng Samrin, the less pressure there will be on Thailand, for whom the presence of scores of thousands of Kampuchean refugees has become a chronic and insoluble problem. But in international terms, China has gained no kudos for winking at the appalling atrocities of the Khmer Rouge which have turned that once lovely and peaceable country into a vast mass grave.

This is an indication of the essence of China's new foreign policy: in the 1980s, the Chinese leaders plan to relate to all countries purely on the basis of their international behaviour, especially their attitude towards the Soviet Union. Their internal social and political conditions will be considered their own affair, since Peking no longer claims the right to pronounce on the 'class struggle' in other countries at a time when it is doing its best to tone down and, if possible, eliminate such struggle at home. Almost any national leader, however oppressive or cruel, will be welcomed in Peking if his or her attitude towards the Soviet Union is sufficiently hostile.

In this China differs little from the other great powers, which maintain 'correct' relations with most countries regardless of their internal policies. Indeed, if governments were choosier about the people they maintain relations with, the global diplomatic system would break down altogether. China, which not so long ago looked down on the United Nations and other world bodies as irrelevant because she was not a member of them, has found that the membership she now enjoys can be put to all sorts of purposes – from tongue-lashing the Soviet Union to soliciting aid and loans. It is in everyone's interest that she should become progressively more deeply involved in the activities of all international bodies of a non-political nature, for out of mutual ties grow mutual cooperation and mutual dependence – the best guarantors of peace.

Epilogue

China – once thought of as a timeless civilization – nowadays shows keen awareness of the pressure of time, as the twentieth century heads into its last two decades. 'Only twenty years left!' proclaim the propaganda messages, as though the age were to be crowned in the year 2000 by some cosmic settling of accounts.

In fact, A. D. 2000 is just a convenient benchmark which the ageing leaders in Peking use to spur their people on to a fulfilment few of them will witness. 'Chinese-style modernization' is the catchword for the aims of the post-Mao leaders, and the truly awesome modesty of its definition can be glimpsed in Deng Xiaoping's forecast that things will have gone pretty well if, by the end of the century, average *per capita* incomes in China are almost quadrupled from their present level to about US$1,000 a year at current prices.

Deng, nevertheless, has pointed out that this $1,000 per annum does not represent the abject poverty it would spell in the developed world. As free and subsidized services continue to grow and be improved, a person's cash income is of less account in defining living standards. In real terms, China is coming through a sticky patch in her development, in which the rising expectations of the people – urged on by the new advertising craze and greater knowledge of conditions in the outside world – are threatening to outstrip the State's ability to meet them, while some basic supplies (vegetables, for instance) are becoming scarcer or dearer. China, all in all, will have done well if, in A. D. 2000, her people enjoy a standard of living roughly equivalent to that of, say, South Korea today.

In the meantime, the Chinese are beginning to enjoy a richer and more satisfying cultural life, greater political freedom, and the prospect of an easier, more comfortable existence. The country's international prestige has never been highter, and the rich nations are all keen to lend China money for development, now that she has dropped her pose as the champion of worldwide revolution.

The big question is whether this period of relative calm and moderation can be maintained, while the country draws breath for another stab at the huge tasks ahead.

Somewhere along the road from cultural and economic dictatorship to liberalization there is a halfway house, where a feeling of compromise may be enjoyed for a while. This is where the Soviet Union had arrived by the late 1960s and where it still is – a society ruled by dogma and coercion but providing just enough in terms of new clothing, cars, books, art, music, TV, and the other 'good things of life' to make the majority of the population, if not favourable to their rulers, at least quiescent. It would seem that China is groping her way towards a similar compromise in the 1980s. On paper, it should be easier in China, the historic home of consensus politics and social stability. In practice, the attempt at a halfway house between liberalization and discipline is raising thorny issues which are exacerbated by the deadly seriousness of the leadership's attention to them – right down to such trivia as popular music and the cut of a blouse (it should not, the Communist Youth League's organ warns its female readers, show either the collarbone or the hairs under the arms).

The pop-music craze has acquired a symbolic significance far beyond its real importance. The sudden availability of imported cassette recorders has brought in disco music, Beatles songs, sentimental ballads from Hong Kong, and even numbers by crooners in Taiwan – anything that can be copied from a friend's tape or recorded from a shortwave radio. Pop music, already becoming a national fad among young people, has caused much soul-searching by those who like to concern themselves with the morals of youth. Frivolity, decadence, immorality, and doom are predicted by solemn editorials in the press and in lectures by Party activists. Love songs especially have been criticized, for love is not considered suitable subject matter for teenagers or people in their early twenties; it detracts, so the prudish official line claims, from young people's concentration on their studies and makes them pariahs among their more virtuous classmates.

Comic though it may seem, this flurry of concern about the moral ill effects of 'frivolous' music represents a deep-down anxiety among older people – a concern that their children and grandchildren may not follow the austere conventions which they themselves have had to follow. Older people in the Soviet Union and the West have often taken exactly the same attitude: 'Why can't young people be glad just to have jobs, as we were, instead of wasting money on such rubbish?' The older generation feels not only affronted but – what is perhaps worse – left out of a form of fun and excitement which it cannot even understand.

Stirred to action, the Party has hit back at the pop-music craze with TV programmes and concerts devoted to 'healthy' music, including such foot-tappers as 'The [People's Liberation Army's] Three Main Rules of Discipline and Eight Points for Attention'. (Mercifully, the higher-ups have at least seen the folly of trying to popularize songs with names like 'The Nightsoil Collectors Are Coming Down the Mountain'.)

The attempt to construct a new Chinese-style culture has been a failure, though there are hopeful signs for the future. Jiang Qing's exclusion of traditional Chinese story lines from drama and opera – while retaining the musical conventions and the old dance styles – did not, as it was supposed to, focus people's minds on what was essential for their socialist consciousness but just bored them instead. The exuberance with which actors, writers, producers and stage designers have launched themselves into the relative freedom of the post-Mao era bears witness to the tremendous creativity bottled up for over a decade.

One of the new dance dramas, *Flight to the Moon*, suggests a rich future for the artistic imagination in China. Based on an ancient myth, it tells how the legendary archer Yi shot down nine suns which were scorching the earth and fell in love with the beautiful maiden Chang E, saving her from sacrifice by the tribal chief. Later, in a jealous rage, Yi forces her to take poison, and her soul flies to the moon – where Chinese tradition locates her to this day.

The ballet's invocation of prehistoric China – its brutal landscape marked by totem poles and huge beasts, and its human beings ruled by dark and untamable psychological forces – would have been as inimical to Maoist critics as to the Confucianists. This Shanghai production would arouse interest in New York or Paris. It speaks volumes about the richer vision of human nature that was brewing all along in the minds of Chinese artists and intellectuals, throughout the period when art and drama had been reduced to crude pastiches of political creeds.

The creative arts have a long way to go to make up the time lost and the opportunities missed in the search for a truly modern idiom. Much skill and talent is being squandered still on sterile reproduction of traditional art forms – huge and hideous vases and simpering embroideries in the style of the late Qing dynasty (roughly the Victorian era), which connoisseurs consider to have been the most vulgar and decadent period in the whole history of Chinese art, but which is being perpetuated because tourists and foreign art-goods dealers buy it.

Other artists have gone the way of the 'official' modern Soviet style – either 'socialist realist' oil paintings in the nineteenth-century manner or woodblocks, enamels, tiles and ceramics with a tentatively symbolic content, actually very weak and conventional. Aged painters in the traditional Chinese style – and some of their now elderly pupils, selling off the pavement – are offering their work again, but so far there is little to excite critics or collectors in the West.

The striking thing about intellectual life in China today is the immense proliferation of journals and periodicals dealing with the most disparate subjects. During the Eleven Years, almost the only periodicals were political and technical ones, and there were not many of them. The determination of the left-radicals to cling to power under Mao's protection was reflected in their banning of any printed matter which did not eulogize the Cultural Revolution and the Great Leader. The local press – including Peking's daily newspaper – was banned to foreigners, and it was an offence to try to take copies out of the country. (Censorship went to ludicrous lengths. When our boxes were being inspected by the Peking Railway Customs prior to our departure for Hong Kong in 1976, the customs officers prised one open, found an almost complete four-year run of the English-language propaganda magazine *Peking Review*, and began leafing through it, removing any issues that had pictures of the recently disgraced Deng Xiaoping. This was so ludicrous – thousands of copies of the same issues had been mailed to overseas subscribers – that we burst out laughing. The customs people became embarrassed and stuffed the magazines back into the box, which they then had to have nailed up again for their pains. A couple of ordinary Chinese workers, standing nearby, smirked.)

Nowadays, relatively speaking, Peking's newspaper booths are a feast for the mind. There are journals on zoology, wireless, modern literature, economics, philately, Peking opera – almost any sphere of interest or activity relevant to modern Chinese life. Local and provincial newspapers, as in the Soviet Union, are again being freely sold or can be bought by subscription. The press has become so much livelier that to read the local *Peking Daily* over breakfast has become an entertainment rather than a chore. There are now columns about problems of love in adolescence, fashion, popular music, pollution, crime on the streets, and dozens of other topics similar to those handled by the daily press in the West, though the Chinese treatment of them is more staid, and of course there in no cheesecake.

Conditions have certainly improved for those foreigners in China – diplomats, journalists, or visiting academics – who are in search of factual data. It is both easier to contact knowledgeable people, and to get them to speak their mind, than it was in the late Mao period, when such contacts were all but impossible. A journalist with experience of the earlier periods finds it downright flabbergasting to be rung up casually at his hotel by a Chinese journalist, whom he met while on a trip to Europe, and be able to invite that person round for lunch – without the hotel staff's either preventing him from coming in the door or making the occasion so embarrassing, with constant surveillance and eavesdropping, that neither party would want to repeat the experience. And the talk has become so much more direct: 'I see the Party is worried about unemployment,' says the foreigner tentatively, expecting a rebuff or noncommittal answer. 'Oh, that!' says his Chinese acquaintance contemptuously. 'That's been a problem for twenty years.'

Fine: at least once can nowadays discuss it. But the foreigner with experience of pre-1979 China will also feel tempted to ask, somewhat sardonically: 'And what would you have said if I had asked you about it three years ago?' Of course, five years ago the Chinese would have dismissed such a suggestion as a bourgeois fiction.

Nobody, however, should judge too harshly the millions of officials in China who until recently would have run a mile rather than admit there was a chronic problem of unemployment – or of juvenile delinquency, black-marketeering, or any number of other quite normal social phenomena. What does a small fib to a foreigner matter, if the price of frankness is investigation by the Party or the police, rebuke, enforced self-criticism, possibly demotion, and all the attendant misery suffered by one's dependants?

Foreigners interested in finding out what makes China tick had a heady period of frank exchanges with political dissidents and ordinary citizens during the 'Democracy Wall' period in 1978–9. By 1980, the wall had been banned to poster-stickers and covered up with smart new glass-fronted display cases explaining points of popular science. Nonetheless, the chances to make meaningful contacts with Chinese people – not necessarily dissidents – are much better now than at any time since the period before the Cultural Revolution began in 1966. Indeed, once the veil of reserve which inevitably separates foreigners from Chinese is penetrated, conversations can come closer to the truth and be more enlightening than a talk with someone in an equivalent position in the Soviet Union would be. In Russia, lying to foreigners has become a kind of national sport which only hard-core dissidents reject completely, and then at the risk of their liberty.

One of the least helpful aspects of the Chinese approach to living in society is their compulsion to paper over and pretend to ignore past failings, especially if they have involved the explicit or tacit assent of the top leaders now in power or now back in power. The assumption that the whole nation will equally forgive and forget is truly blithe. If millions of people were made destitute or physically persecuted, lost their jobs or died unjust deaths in some great political movement, there are investigations and nowadays many reversals; but the original victims receive no substantial compensation, only a meeting at which they are officially rehabilitated; their confiscated property may be returned to them if it can still be found, and they will be authorized to reclaim their former house or apartment – if the present tenants can be persuaded to leave. Thereafter they are expected to return to the role of loyal citizens and enthusiasts of the Party. It is small consolation for the common man that the leaders also periodically throw each other out of power, with or without giving reasons, but all too noticeable that the leaders thus disgraced, unless they die in the meantime, are quite likely to turn up hale and hearty again at the next turn of the political wheel. And the nation will once more be whipped up into a fervour of denunciation of the recently overthrown faction.

In the face of this clubbish, mutual leniency among the feuding leadership groups in China, it would be astonishing if cynicism and passivity had not become common among the ordinary people. It was they, after all, who sacrificed limbs, health, and life to build grandiose industrial projects which are now castigated as uneconomic (or who even – as in a recently exposed case – tunnelled with picks and spades through a mountain to try to divert a river), and are now told by the leaders that it was just a stupid waste of time. Likely as not, the officials responsible will still be living in comfort, with no more than a verbal rebuke for their 'mistake'.

The Russians have learned to bear their leaders' incompetence by making jokes about it. Laugh, and the experience was not wasted, they seem to feel. The Chinese view it differently: if wronged by the leaders, hope for redress, be happy if you get it, and do not be foolish enough to stick your neck out again. Chinese tradition warns the common man against contact with officialdom, so that when the highter-ups come on inspection tours, it is thought wisest in most cases to give them a rosy picture and send them packing again as soon as possible. This, of course, makes it doubly difficult for the officials – many of whom are well-meaning – to identify problem areas and do something about them.

An important new reform is the campaign to retire cadres at a specified age, sixty-five for men and sixty for women. Until recently, an official post was considered an 'iron rice-bowl', and people clung to their desk jobs even when chronically ill, rather than let someone younger step in and take over. The Party leaders – who themselves have a high average age – have at last laid it down that officials below Politburo level should be prepared to retire gracefully when their age dictates it. This not only creates much-needed jobs at the base of the administrative pyramid but may also stimulate new ideas and the vigour of youth to carry them out. China's youth, unfortunately, has recently come through a severe social and psychological crisis, with lingering effects, and is still unsure of its own power and opportunities. But barring another political upheaval, this situation should right itself in time.

While the new social atmosphere in China is welcome to most people, one can sense a certain creakiness in the joints, a feeling of 'Haven't we been here before?' Socialism is becoming middle-aged, as it already is in Russia, and instead of throwing out exciting new challenges to be solved with Marxist dialectics, is tending to reiterate old, tired problems, which in other Marxist states have shown themselves more persistent than either Marx or Lenin would have thought possible. The growth of individualism and pleasure-seeking, corruption, careerism, and even emigration in search of a better life, are phenomena as familiar in East Europe as in China. Marxism has failed to prove that it can both grow more cabbages and give people freer, richer lives – or, indeed, that it can do either.

Less than a decade ago, China was seen as the great 'alternative' form of Marxism. Not a few highly intelligent people from Western countries believed that the Marxist vision – distorted and brutalized in the Soviet Union – had at last found form and meaning in the Chinese system. Radicals, conservatives and middle-of-the-road people who could afford the trip converged on China to see for themselves the 'new-born things of the Cultural Revolution' – barefoot doctors, cadre re-education schools, worker education schemes, rustication of surplus urban youth. To radicals, it looked like a possible future for an increasingly disorganized, violent and resource-starved world. Conservatives, sensing with capitalist acumen that such high-minded reforms would never generate enough wealth to turn China into a threat to their own system, smiled quietly and praised it as 'just what China needs'.

In addition, the Chinese had a neat and seemingly watertight argument about how and why the Russians had gone wrong. The means of production – so this argument ran – were no longer effectively under public control in the Soviet Union. A new class of 'revisionist' bureaucrats had arisen who monopolized control of the economy for their own benefit. This showed itself in manifestations of social decline, such as class privilege, huge disparities in income, and the exploitation of workers and peasants. With these undesirable developments in Soviet socialism, the Chinese held, went the symptoms of national decay: mass alcoholism, juvenile delinquency, a high rate of divorce, and so on. Just as capitalism, in Lenin's theory, spawned an imperialist set of foreign policies involving aggression and colonization of other countries, so current-day 'revisionism' had led the Soviet Union into a new form of imperialism – 'hegemonism', or the domination of one country over others – which the Chinese also dubbed 'social imperialism'.

This Chinese theory of Soviet imperialism conveniently ignored the fact that the Soviet Union's modern empire was acquired during the rule of Stalin, whose policies the Peking ideologues still profess to be by-and-large correct. It was also silent on the growing dissident movement in the Soviet Union – one of the biggest propaganda sticks which the Western world has to beat Moscow with, following the Helsinki agreement on human rights. Though the Chinese might view dissent in Russia as a result of 'revisionism', that did not necessarily make China a friend of dissidents; the crackdown on them in 1980 in Peking showed that the Chinese Politburo was still less happy about permitting such a movement to thrive than the Kremlin was, whereas in the Soviet Union the movement had gained enough momentum to be self-sustaining even in the face of quite severe persecution.

Despite these paradoxes, the Chinese image of socialism attracted great attention and respect, especially as a system geared to solve the worldwide problem of rural poverty and the failure of other Asian revolutions to create equitable social structures and promote steady economic progress.

It was with dismay, then, that the strongest supporters of the Chinese system – mainly radical intellectuals in Western countries – saw mounting evidence after Mao's death that the country was veering back to a social system which until then its leaders had castigated as 'revisionist'. The return to power of Deng Xiaoping in 1977, and his gradual but sure elimination of all real or possible challenges to his authority, cleared the way for the dismantling of almost everything Maoism and the Cultural Revolution had stood for. The Dazhai experiment in agriculture, the 'revolutionary' stage works, politicized art, rustication of urban youth, levelling of incomes between workers and intellectuals, emphasis on the political attitudes of cadres rather than on their technical expertise – just about all the 'newborn things' of the Eleven Years were swept away.

In their place came such unmistakably revisionist innovations as advertising, hair-styling, colourful clothing, imported consumer goods, foreign investments and credits, and vastly stepped-up cultural exchanges with the outside world. Workers were encouraged to go after cash bonuses, industrial managers were told to make profits and plenty of them, and the peasants had restored to them old freedoms which were anathema to the Maoists. The very word 'revisionism' was banned from the official vocabulary, and China declared a hands-off policy with regard to the internal state of affairs in the Soviet Union, while continuing to oppose Soviet expansion abroad.

Though much of what has happened in China since 1976 seems quite familiar from Soviet experience, there are important aspects of Chinese life which will never be bent into any kind of Soviet mould, old or new. For one thing, China is a genuinely ancient polity which has set up social cohesion and stability as the most important goal of human life. This cannot be said of the Russians, in whose much younger nation deep-seated insecurities govern many aspects of national behaviour and are reflected in rampant alcoholism – the nation's scourge.

The near absence of alcoholism in China is a significant pointer to that deep-down self-confidence which has marked that civilization from ancient times, and not just a function of the scarcity of grain from which to make hard liquor. The shelves of the liquor counters in department stores positively groan under the weight of multicoloured brews flavoured with everything from cassia flowers to rat embryos. But in my first four years in China, I saw only three people drunk in public. Nor is this because of any moralistic prejudice against alcohol; the Chinese, like the Japanese, are most tolerant of drinking when the occasion calls for it and view tipsiness merely as the sign that a guest has enjoyed the dinner. Many of their most celebrated poets and sages were heavy drinkers, and the Chinese seem to believe that in their exalted frame of mind they were able to draw on spiritual and intellectual resources denied them in sobriety. The vast majority of ordinary Chinese people are quite happy to go through life with only occasional enjoyment of alcohol.

Chinese life is geared to make everyone feel wanted – the surest defence against personal insecurity. What insecurity they have sometimes collectively shown has been the result of misgovernment, which from the earliest times has resulted in sudden explosions of popular rage against the rulers – from the 'Yellow Turban' rebels of the second century A.D. to the spontaneous rioting and arson on Tiananmen Square in April 1976. Like plastic explosive, the Chinese can be bent and moulded in different directions, but it is unwise to jolt them or neglect proper safety precautions.

All in all, this should be good news for the world: the biggest mass of humanity in history is of a fundamentally stable temperament – industrious when properly motivated, unambitious of conquest or expansion, good-humoured in the main, appreciative of all the pleasures of life, and inventive in coping with its problems.

Yet the homely, almost cosy image which the Chinese project today is not always their national model of behaviour. Embitterment, violence and hysteria have characterized their history as much as that of any other country. The invasion of Vietnam in February 1979 was infused with a spirit of vengefulness and hate which barely sought to cover itself with a political apologia. Vietnam, the Chinese felt, had harmed China and been ungrateful, mistreated people of Chinese race, created incidents on the border, burdened China with a refugee problem, and embraced the arch-enemy, Russia. That was seen as good enough cause to strike across the border much farther than any Vietnamese patrols had strayed into China, at a cost of some 50,000 dead or seriously wounded on both sides. It was an action in the grand manner of the nineteenth century, when nations went to war almost for the fun of it, and it bore echoes of the erstwhile punitive expeditions of the Chinese empire into borderlands to strike at marauding tribes who had gone altogether too far.

Challenged to defend the invasion of a neighbouring state, the Chinese would point to Vietnamese occupation of Kampuchea and Soviet occupation of Afghanistan. While two wrongs cannot make a right, the Chinese evidently feel justified in breaking the rules of international coexistence if their enemies are doing the same thing and getting away with it. (Conversely, there was a clear understanding between China and the United States in the 1960s that if American planes did not bomb China, China would not send troops to help North Vietnam. The understanding was honoured with only minor breaches.)

Aspects of Chinese foreign policy are still highly self-assertive, especially where sovereignty or exploitation rights in adjacent seas are concerned. Peking claims nearly all significant islands in the South China Sea, in a loop reaching southward almost to the coast of Malaysian Borneo. It has challenged Japanese claims to sovereignty over the Diaoyu (Senkaku) islands and blocked South Korean and Japanese exploration for oil in the Yellow Sea.

Not only oil is at stake in China's extensive claims to rights over the seas which wash her shores. In the South China Sea, the shipping routes which handle any amount of China's exports and imports could be interdicted in the event of another war between China and Vietnam, this time perhaps involving Soviet naval support for the latter.

China is a fundamentally peaceable country, but she exists in a world environment which promises security only to those who look out for themselves. Living in sole occupation of our planet, the Chinese could well have continued indefinitely with Mao's policy of developing the economy only in so far as it did not conflict with his almost Calvinist-ically austere views of human nature. But no country is granted the right nowadays to look after its own affairs in peace and quiet, without worrying what the neighbours are up to. Peking must either be prepared to face subjugation to Russia or go all out to strengthen its economy, technology and armed forces. This is the meaning of the 'Four Modernizations'.

Many Americans worry that in extending technical and financial aid to China, the West may be breeding a new monster which, once strong, will be no less aggressive than the Soviet Union. Others believe that strengthening China is the cheapest and safest way to keep the Russians on the hop. The Soviet Union is sorely displeased at the prospect of Western arms sales to China, and the governments of Western Europe wonder whether it is really sensible to antagonize a country which could drive tanks into all their capital cities in less than three weeks, and thus risk destruction of half the planet.

China's biggest safeguard in recent years has been the very paucity of her resources, which has meant that with the exception of the war against Vietnam she has undertaken hardly any effective action anywhere in the world to back up her policy of support for all countries menaced with Soviet domination. This leads other governments to take her foreign policy lightly, as a kind of entertaining theatrical programme in which nobody really gets hurt. Yet that policy, short though it may be on forms of implementation, is long on schemes and strategies to hold the Soviet Union off until a near-global alliance of China, the United States, Japan, Western Europe and as many Third World countries as possible can deprive the Russians of any hope of real victory in a world war.

What American statesmen have to ponder is whether China is an asset or a liability in the confrontation with the Soviet Union. Obviously, it is better if she is anti-Soviet, even fiercely so; but to side with her too obviously or sell her arms is likely to stall efforts for détente with the Soviet Union. The Afghanistan crisis has made this question academic for the time being, however, and if the entire détente/SALT process should founder on it, 'playing the China card' will be an obvious policy for the United States.

Looking further into the future, the Russians discern danger areas in China's global relations if she succeeds in modernizing and industrializing herself. The long-term dangers of growing ties between China, the United States, Japan and the rest of the developed world are all too evident to the men in the Kremlin. With massive injections of capital and expertise, China could become a formidable economic power, not as soon as A.D. 2000 but perhaps by about 2030 – a mere fifty years from now. With her ingrained habit of parsimony in the use of resources, she can come through the recession of the 1980s with less social disruption than is likely to be felt in the Western world – indeed, with hardly any. This will lead the Soviet Union to eye her more and more speculatively – either as a threat, to be dealt with militarily, or once more as an important trading partner and eventually, perhaps, a friend.

So far the Chinese have shown a masterly command of the tactics needed to deter the Soviet Union from outright invasion and installation of a pro–Moscow regime, through the dropping of tantalizing hints that a better government-to-government relationship is indeed possible. At the same time, China has been adamant that a settlement of contested border areas must be achieved, and this the Russians are unwilling to do since their principle is never to give up any territory anywhere, not even as part of a negotiated package of mutual concessions. (When Moscow claimed in 1969 that China's northern frontier since the fourth century B.C. has been defined by the Great Wall and that areas north of the wall were not historically subject to Chinese sovereignty, a Chinese historian acidly commented, 'Where, one may ask, were the frontiers of the *Russian* state in the fourth century B.C.?')

The biggest contributor to the insecurity which governs much of Russian behaviour today is the fact that their country lacks natural barriers against invasion, a fact from which numerous aggressors, including the Mongol Tartars, have profited. In Europe, the Russians have no longer any need to fear invasion; their frontier is guarded by the most formidable land armies in history, straddled across the satellite buffer states of the Warsaw Pact. It is to China that the Russians look with true apprehension – and at the same time a blustering bravado which proclaims, 'We will wipe the Chinese out if we have to!' There are countless wry jokes in Russia and East Europe about the near-inexhaustible manpower resources of China. In the imagination of the ordinary Russian citizen, China is 'over there' – where the Mongol Tartars came from in the Middle Ages, to subjugate Russia.

Soviet propaganda since the late 1960s has encouraged this latent anxiety, which amounts almost to neurosis, with regard to China. During the last decade of Mao's life, the Soviet media portrayed him as a madman and hinted that he was more fearsome than Stalin. They made America's reconciliation with Peking out to be just a cynical manoeuvre to threaten the Soviet Union's rear. And doubtless this was not far from the thoughts of many statesmen and strategists in the West, for whom China's daily outpourings of anti-Soviet invective were a real gift.

In their triangular waltz, the great powers have an unfortunate way of stepping on the toes of smaller dancers. The course of history since the Second World War has been a depressing chronicle of wars and armed upheavals on almost everybody else's territory but that of the great powers themselves, who have nevertheless sought to profit from disorder. This tendency shows no sign of abating; indeed, if anything it is becoming more marked. The principles of peaceful coexistence and non-interference in other countries' internal affairs – which China likes to take as the banner of her foreign policy – are becoming meaningless except among the rich, developed countries, who have too much at stake to be warring with each other.

Understanding China, and the reasons why she is what she is, can never be just a simple exercise in foreign policy analysis. The social and economic background from which policies arise is equally important, both as a guide to Chinese behaviour in the international arena and as an object lesson in how (and how not) to organize a large, poor country in the modern world. Since most of our planet's nations are getting bigger all the time, and a good few of them are simultaneously getting poorer, the Chinese experience deserves study.

China is in a transitional phase – a poor country in terms of incomes and resources, but potentially a great power and even, though she disclaims any such ambition, a superpower. The other two super-powers have made gross miscalculations in their past dealings with China. To do so in the future will be dangerous for all.

Index

MORE ABOUT PENGUINS, PELICANS AND PUFFINS

For further information about books available from Penguins please write to Dept EP, Penguin Books Ltd, Harmondsworth, Middlesex UB7 0DA.

In the U.S.A.: For a complete list of books available from Penguins in the United States write to Dept DG, Penguin Books, 299 Murray Hill Parkway, East Rutherford, New Jersey 07073.

In Canada: For a complete list of books available from Penguins in Canada write to Penguin Books Canada Limited, 2801 John Street, Markham, Ontario L3R 1B4.

In Australia: For a complete list of books available from Penguins in Australia write to the Marketing Department, Penguin Books Australia Ltd, P.O. Box 257, Ringwood, Victoria 3134.

In New Zealand: For a complete list of books available from Penguins in New Zealand write to the Marketing Department, Penguin Books (N.Z.) Ltd, Private Bag, Takapuna, Auckland 9.

In India: For a complete list of books available from Penguins in India write to Penguin Overseas Ltd, 706 Eros Apartments, 56 Nehru Place, New Delhi 110019.

check. JF US & China

Liu

China Q.

Mod. Asian Studies.

Harry & Judith Shapiro, <u>Son of the Rev?</u>